KARL MARX
Theory of Social Change

KARL MARX
Theory of Social Change

Amitabh Bhatt

CENTRUM PRESS
NEW DELHI-110002 (INDIA)

CENTRUM PRESS

H.O.: 4360/4, Ansari Road, Daryaganj,
New Delhi-110002 (India)
Tel: 23278000, 23261597, 23255577, 23286875

B.O.: No. 1015, Ist Main Road, BSK IIIrd Stage,
IIIrd Phase, IIIrd Block, Bengaluru-560085 (INDIA)
Tel: 080-41723429

Email: centrumpress@gmail.com
Visit us at: www.centrumpress.com

Karl Marx: Theory of Social Change

First Edition, 2011

ISBN 978-93-81293-50-8

PRINTED IN INDIA

Printed at Suman Printers, Jagatpuri Extn., Delhi

Contents

Preface

In Marxist theory, socialism, or the socialist mode of production, refers to a specific historical phase of economic development and its corresponding set of social relations that eventually supersede capitalism. Socialism is a mode of production where economic activity is based on directly maximizing use-value through conscious economic planning, where monetary relations in the form of exchange-value and wage labour cease to exist out. Socialism is characterized by the working-class effectively controlling the means of production and the means of their livelihood either through cooperative enterprises or public ownership and self management.

As a set of social relationships, socialism is defined by the degree to which economic activity in society is planned by the associated producers, so that the surplus product of the population is controlled by a majority of the population through democratic processes. The sale of labour power is abolished so that every individual participates in running their institution and no one controls anyone else. The incentive structure changes in a socialist society given the change in the social environment, so that an individual laborers' work becomes increasingly autonomous and creative, creating a sense of responsibility for his or her institution as a stakeholder. The individual is no longer alienated from his or her work; work now becomes a means by which the individual fulfils his or her humanity (pursues his or her interests). Inequality and incentive-based systems would still exist under socialism, but to a diminishing extent as all members of society are de facto workers. This eliminates the severity of previous tendencies towards inequality and conflicts arising from these. The method of compensation and reward in a socialist society would be based on an authentic meritocracy, along the principle of "from each according to his ability, to each according to his contribution".

In Marxist theory, the state is a mechanism dominated by and utilized in the interests of the ruling class to subjugate other classes, to legitimize the existing socio-economic system and to promote the interests of the dominant class. After a workers revolution, the state initially becomes the instrument of the working-class. Conquest of the state apparatus by the working class must take place to establish a socialist system. As socialism is built, the role and scope of the state changes as class distinctions (based on ownership of the means of production) gradually deteriorate due to the concentration of means of production in state hands. From the point where all means of production become state property, the nature and primary function of the state would change from one of political rule (via coercion) over men by the creation and enforcement of laws into a scientific administration of things and a direction of processes of production; that is the state would become a coordinating economic entity rather than a mechanism of class or political control, and would no longer be a state in the Marxian sense.

This book provides deep insight to various dimensions of issues relating to the subject.

—Editor

1

Introduction

Karl Marx's (1818-1883) thought was strongly influenced by:

- The dialectical method and historical orientation of Georg Wilhelm Friedrich Hegel;
- The classical political economy of Adam Smith and David Ricardo;
- French socialist and sociological thought, in particular the thought of Jean-Jacques Rousseau.

THE MOST IMPORTANT CONCEPTS OF KARL MARX

The following concepts of Marx have aided sociological thought significantly;

- Dialectical Materialism
- Materialistic Interpretation of History i.e Historical Materialism
- Class and Class conflict
- Alienation.

Marx believed that he could study history and society scientifically and discern tendencies of history and the resulting outcome of social conflicts. Some followers of Marx concluded, therefore, that a communist revolution is inevitable. However, Marx famously asserted in the eleventh of his Theses on Feuerbach that "philosophers have only interpreted the world, in various ways; the point however is to change it", and he clearly dedicated himself to trying to alter the world. Consequently, most followers of Marx are not fatalists, but activists who believe that revolutionaries must organize social change.

Marx's view of history, which came to be called the materialist conception of history (and which was developed further as the philosophy of dialectical materialism) is certainly influenced by Hegel's claim that reality (and history) should be viewed dialectically. Hegel believed that the direction of human history is characterized in the movement from the fragmentary toward the complete and the real (which was also a movement towards greater and greater rationality). Sometimes, Hegel explained, this progressive unfolding of the Absolute involves gradual, evolutionary accretion but at other times requires discontinuous, revolutionary leaps-episodal upheavals against the existing status quo. For example, Hegel strongly opposed the ancient institution of legal slavery that was practiced in the United States during his lifetime, and he envisioned a time when Christian nations would radically eliminate it from their civilization. While Marx accepted this broad conception of history, Hegel was an idealist, and Marx sought to rewrite dialectics in materialist terms. He wrote that Hegelianism stood the movement of reality on its head, and that it was necessary to set it upon its feet. (Hegel's philosophy remained and remains in direct opposition to Marxism on this key point.)

Marx's acceptance of this notion of materialist dialectics which rejected Hegel's idealism was greatly influenced by Ludwig Feuerbach. In The Essence of Christianity, Feuerbach argued that God is really a creation of man and that the qualities people attribute to God are really qualities of humanity. Accordingly, Marx argued that it is the material world that is real and that our ideas of it are consequences, not causes, of the world. Thus, like Hegel and other philosophers, Marx distinguished between appearances and reality. But he did not believe that the material world hides from us the "real" world of the ideal; on the contrary, he thought that historically and socially specific ideologies prevented people from seeing the material conditions of their lives clearly.

The other important contribution to Marx's revision of Hegelianism was Engels' book, The Condition of the Working Class in England in 1844, which led Marx to conceive of the historical dialectic in terms of class conflict and to see the modern working class as the most progressive force for revolution. The notion of labour is fundamental in Marx's thought. Basically, Marx argued that it is human nature to transform nature, and he calls this process of transformation "labour" and the capacity to transform nature labour power. For Marx, this is a natural capacity for a physical activity, but it is intimately tied to the human mind and human imagination: A spider conducts operations that resemble those of a weaver, and a bee puts to shame many an architect in the construction of her cells.

But what distinguishes the worst architect from the best of bees is this, that the architect raises his structure in imagination before he erects it in reality. Karl Marx inherits that Hegelian dialectic and, with it, a disdain for the notion of an underlying invariant human nature. Sometimes Marxists express their views by contrasting "nature" with "history". Sometimes they use the phrase "existence precedes consciousness".

The point, in either case, is that who a person is, is determined by where and when he is-social context takes precedence over innate behaviour; or, in other words, one of the main features of human nature is adaptability. Marx did not believe that all people worked the same way, or that how one works is entirely personal and individual. Instead, he argued that work is a social activity and that the conditions and forms under and through which people work are socially determined and change over time.

Marx's analysis of history is based on his distinction between the means/forces of production, literally those things, such as land, natural resources, and technology, that are necessary for the production of material goods, and the relations of production, in other words, the social and technical relationships people enter into as they acquire and use the means of production. Together these comprise the mode of production; Marx observed that within any given society the mode of production changes, and that European societies had progressed from a feudal mode of production to a capitalist mode of production. In general, Marx believed that the means of production change more rapidly than the relations of production. For Marx this mismatch between (economic) base and (social) superstructure is a major source of social disruption and conflict. Marx understood the "social relations of production" to comprise not only relations among individuals, but between or among groups of people, or classes. As a scientist and materialist, Marx did not understand classes as purely subjective. He sought to define classes in terms of objective criteria, such as their access to resources. For Marx, different classes have divergent interests, which is another source of social disruption and conflict. Conflict between social classes being something which is inherent in all human history: The history of all hitherto existing society is the history of class struggles.

Marx was especially concerned with how people relate to that most fundamental resource of all, their own labour-power. Marx wrote extensively about this in terms of the problem of alienation. As with the dialectic, Marx began with a Hegelian notion of alienation but developed a more materialist conception. For Marx, the possibility that one may give up ownership of one's own labour-one's capacity to transform the world-is tantamount to being alienated from one's own nature; it is a spiritual loss. Marx described this loss in terms of commodity fetishism, in which the things that people produce, commodities, appear to have a life and movement of their own to which humans and their behaviour merely adapt. This disguises the fact that the exchange and circulation of commodities really are the product and reflection of social relationships among people. Under capitalism, social relationships of production, such as among workers or between workers and capitalists, are mediated through commodities, including labour, that are bought and sold on the market.

Commodity fetishism is an example of what Engels called false consciousness, which is closely related to the understanding of ideology. By ideology they meant ideas that reflect the interests of a particular class at a particular time in history, but which are presented as universal and eternal. Marx and Engels' point was not only that such beliefs are at best half-truths; they serve an important political function. Put another way, the control that one class exercises over the means of production includes not only the production of food or manufactured goods; it includes the production of ideas as well.

Thus, while such ideas may be false, they also reveal in coded form some truth about political relations. For example, although the belief that the things people produce are actually more productive than the people who produce them is literally absurd, it does reflect the fact that people under capitalism are alienated from their own labour-power. Another example of this sort of analysis is Marx's understanding of religion, summed up in a passage from the preface to his 1843 Contribution to the Critique of Hegel's Philosophy of Right: Religious suffering is, at one and the same time, the expression of real suffering and a protest against real suffering. Religion is the sigh of the oppressed creature, the heart of a heartless world, and the soul of soulless conditions. It is the opium of the people. Whereas his Gymnasium senior thesis argued that the primary social function of religion was to promote solidarity, here Marx sees the social function as a way of expressing and coping with social inequality, thereby maintaining the status quo. Marx argued that this alienation of human work is precisely the defining feature of capitalism. Prior to capitalism, markets existed in Europe where producers and merchants bought and sold commodities. According to Marx, a capitalist mode of production developed in Europe when labour itself became a commodity-when peasants became free to sell their own labour-power, and needed to do so because they no longer possessed their own land or tools necessary to produce. People sell their labour-power when they accept compensation in return for whatever work they do in a given period of time. In return for selling their labour power they receive money, which allows them to survive. Those who must sell their labour power to live are "proletarians." The person who buys the labour power, generally someone who does own the land and technology to produce, is a "capitalist" or "bourgeois.". The proletarians inevitably outnumber the capitalists.

Marx distinguished industrial capitalists from merchant capitalists. Merchants buy goods in one place and sell them in another; more precisely, they buy things in one market and sell them in another. Since the laws of supply and demand operate within given markets, there is often a difference between the price of a commodity in one market and another. Merchants, then, practice arbitrage, and hope to capture the difference between these two markets. According to Marx, capitalists, on the other hand, take advantage of the difference between the labour market and the market for whatever commodity is produced by the capitalist. Marx observed that in practically every successful industry input unit-costs are lower than output unit-prices. Marx called the difference "surplus value" and argued that this surplus value had its source in surplus labour.

The capitalist mode of production is capable of tremendous growth because the capitalist can, and has an incentive to, reinvest profits in new technologies. Marx considered the capitalist class to be the most revolutionary in history, because it constantly revolutionized the means of production. But Marx argued that capitalism was prone to periodic crises.

He suggested that over time, capitalists would invest more and more in new technologies, and less and less in labour. Since Marx believed that surplus value appropriated from labour is the source of profits, he concluded that the rate of profit would fall even as the economy grew. When the rate of profit falls below a certain point, the result would be a recession or depression in which certain sectors of the economy would collapse. Marx understood that during such a crisis the price of labour would also fall, and eventually make possible the investment in new technologies and the growth of new sectors of the economy.

Marx believed that this cycle of growth, collapse, and growth would be punctuated by increasingly severe crises. Moreover, he believed that the long-term consequence of this process was necessarily the enrichment and empowerment of the capitalist class and the impoverishment of the proletariat. He believed that were the proletariat to seize the means of production, they would encourage social relations that would benefit everyone equally, and a system of production less vulnerable to periodic crises. In general, Marx thought that peaceful negotiation of this problem was impracticable, and that a massive, well-organized and violent revolution would in general be required, because the ruling class would not give up power without violence.

He theorized that to establish the socialist system, a dictatorship of the proletariat-a period where the needs of the working-class, not of capital, will be the common deciding factor-must be created on a temporary basis. As he wrote in his "Critique of the Gotha Program", "between capitalist and communist society there lies the period of the revolutionary transformation of the one into the other. Corresponding to this is also a political transition period in which the state can be nothing but the revolutionary dictatorship of the proletariat."

In the 1920s and '30s, a group of dissident Marxists founded the Institute for Social Research in Germany, among them Max Horkheimer, Theodor Adorno, Erich Fromm, and Herbert Marcuse. As a group, these authors are often called the Frankfurt School. Their work is known as Critical Theory, a type of Marxist philosophy and cultural criticism heavily influenced by Hegel, Freud, Nietzsche, and Max Weber. The Frankfurt School broke with earlier Marxists, including Lenin and Bolshevism in several key ways.

First, writing at the time of the ascendance of Stalinism and Fascism, they had grave doubts as to the traditional Marxist concept of proletarian class consciousness. Second, unlike earlier Marxists, especially Lenin, they rejected economic determinism. While highly influential, their work has been criticized by both orthodox Marxists and some Marxists involved in political practice for divorcing Marxist theory from practical struggle and turning Marxism into a purely academic enterprise. Other influential non-Bolshevik Marxists at that time include Georg Lukacs, Walter Benjamin and Antonio Gramsci, who along with the Frankfurt School are often known by the term Western Marxism. Henryk Grossman, who elaborated the mathematical basis of Marx's 'law of capitalist breakdown', was another affiliate of the Frankfurt School. Also prominent during this period was the Polish revolutionary Rosa Luxemburg.

In 1949 Paul Sweezy and Leo Huberman founded Monthly Review, a journal and press, to provide an outlet for Marxist thought in the United States independent of the Communist Party.In 1978, G. A. Cohen attempted to defend Marx's thought as a coherent and scientific theory of history by reconstructing it through the lens of analytic philosophy. This gave birth to Analytical Marxism, an academic movement which also included Jon Elster, Adam Przeworski and John Roemer. Bertell Ollman is another Anglophone champion of Marx within the academy.

SOCIALISM AND MARXISM

In Marxist theory, socialism, or the socialist mode of production, refers to a specific historical phase of economic development and its corresponding set of social relations that eventually supersede capitalism. Socialism is a mode of production where economic activity is based on directly maximizing use-value through conscious economic planning, where monetary relations in the form of exchange-value and wage labour cease to exist out. Socialism is characterized by the working-class effectively controlling the means of production and the means of their livelihood either through cooperative enterprises or public ownership and self management.

Mode of Production

Socialism is a post-commodity economic system, meaning production is carried out to maximize use-value (to directly satisfy human needs, or demand) rather than to exchange on the market to generate a profit (to maximize exchange-value). The stage in which the accumulation of capital was viable and effective is rendered insufficient at the socialist stage of social and economic development, leading to a situation where production is carried out independently of capital accumulation in a planned fashion.

Planning can refer to democratic participatory planning, industrial democracy or administrative economic planning. Instead of relying on the coercive forces of the market to compel capitalists to produce use-values as a byproduct in the pursuit of exchange-value, socialist production is based on the rational planning of use-values and coordinated investment decisions to attain economic goals. As a result, the cyclical fluctuations that occur in a capitalist market economy will not be present in a socialist economy. The value of a good in socialism is its physical utility rather than its embodied labour, cost of production and exchange value as in a capitalist system.

The advanced stage of socialism, referred to as "upper-stage communism" in Marxist theory, is based on the socialist mode of production but is differentiated from socialism in a few fundamental ways. While socialism implies public ownership (by a state apparatus) or cooperative ownership (by a worker cooperative enterprise), communism would be based on common ownership of the means of production. Class distinctions based on ownership of capital cease to exist, along with the need for a state. A superabundance of goods and services are made possible by automated production that allow for goods to be distributed based on need rather than merit.

Intermediate Phases

The period in which capitalism becomes increasingly insufficient as an economic system and immediately after the proletarian conquest of the state, an economic system that features elements of both socialism and capitalism will probably exist until both the productive forces of the economy and the cultural and social attitudes develop to a point where they satisfy the requirements for a full socialist society (one that has lost the need for monetary value, wage labour and capital accumulation). Specifically, market relations will still exist but economic units are either nationalized or re-organized into cooperatives. This transitional phase is sometimes described as "state capitalism" or "market socialism".

Social Relations

As a set of social relationships, socialism is defined by the degree to which economic activity in society is planned by the associated producers, so that the surplus product of the population is controlled by a majority of the population through democratic processes. The sale of labour power is abolished so that every individual participates in running their institution and no one controls anyone else. The incentive structure changes in a socialist society given the change in the social environment, so that an individual laborers' work becomes increasingly autonomous and creative, creating a sense of responsibility for his or her institution as a stakeholder. The individual is no longer alienated from his or her work; work now becomes a means by which the individual fulfils his or her humanity (pursues his or her interests).

Inequality and incentive-based systems would still exist under socialism, but to a diminishing extent as all members of society are de facto workers. This eliminates the severity of previous tendencies towards inequality and conflicts arising from these. The method of compensation and reward in a socialist society would be based on an authentic meritocracy, along the principle of "from each according to his ability, to each according to his contribution".

Role of the State

In Marxist theory, the state is a mechanism dominated by and utilized in the interests of the ruling class to subjugate other classes, to legitimize the existing socio-economic system and to promote the interests of the dominant class. After a workers revolution, the state initially becomes the instrument of the working-class. Conquest of the state apparatus by the working class must take place to establish a socialist system. As socialism is built, the role and scope of the state changes as class distinctions (based on ownership of the means of production) gradually deteriorate due to the concentration of means of production in state hands. From the point where all means of production become state property, the nature and primary function of the state would change from one of political rule (via coercion) over men by the creation and enforcement of laws into a scientific administration of things and a direction of processes of production; that is the state would become a coordinating economic entity rather than a mechanism of class or political control, and would no longer be a state in the Marxian sense.

MARX'S THOUGHT

The American Marx scholar Hal Draper once remarked, "there are few thinkers in modern history whose thought has been so badly misrepresented, by Marxists and anti-Marxists alike." The legacy of Marx's thought has become bitterly contested between numerous tendencies which each see themselves as Marx's most accurate interpreters, including (but not limited to) Leninism, Trotskyism, Maoism, Luxemburgism, and libertarian Marxism.

Philosophy

Fundamentally, Marx assumed that human nature involves transforming material nature. To this process of transformation he applies the term "labour", and to the capacity to transform nature the term "labour power". Marx stated: "A spider conducts operations that resemble those of a weaver, and a bee puts to shame many an architect in the construction of her cells. But what distinguishes the worst architect from the best of bees is this, that the architect raises his structure in imagination before he erects it in reality."— (*Capital*, Vol. I, Chap. 7, Pt. 1)

Unlike insects and arachnids, humans recognise that they possess both actual and potential selves. For both Marx and Hegel, self-development begins with an experience of internal alienation stemming from this recognition, followed by a realisation that the actual self, as a subjective agent, renders its potential counterpart an object to be apprehended. Marx further argues that, by molding nature in desired ways, the subject takes the object as its own, and thus permits the individual to be actualised as fully human. For Marx, then, human nature—*Gattungswesen*, or species-being—exists as a function of human labour. Fundamental to Marx's idea of meaningful labour is the proposition that, in order for a subject to come to terms with its alienated object, it must first exert influence upon literal, material objects in the subject's world. Marx acknowledges that Hegel "grasps the nature of *work* and comprehends objective man, authentic because actual, as the result of his *own work*", but characterises Hegelian self-development as unduly "spiritual" and abstract. Marx thus departs from Hegel by insisting that "the fact that man is a *corporeal*, actual, sentient, objective being with natural capacities means that he has *actual, sensuous objects* for his nature as objects of his life-expression, or that he can only *express* his life in actual sensuous objects." Consequently, Marx revises Hegelian "work" into material labour.

Marx's analysis of history focuses on the organisation of labour and depends on his distinction between:

1. the means/forces of production, literally those things (like land, natural resources, and technology) necessary for the production of material goods; and
2. the relations of production, in other words, the social relationships people enter into as they acquire and use the means of production.

Together these compose the mode of production, and Marx distinguished historical eras in terms of distinct modes of production. For example, he observed that European societies had progressed from a feudal mode of production to a capitalist mode of production. Marx believed that under capitalism, the means of production change more rapidly than the relations of production. Marx regarded this mismatch between (economic) base and (social) superstructure as a major source of social disruption and conflict.

As a scientist and materialist, Marx did not understand classes as purely subjective (in other words, groups of people who consciously identified with one another). He sought to define classes in terms of objective criteria, such as their access to resources—that is, whether or not a group owns the means of production. For Marx:

> *"The history of all hitherto existing society is the history of class struggles."* — (The Communist Manifesto, *Chapter 1)*

Marx had a special concern with how people relate to that most fundamental resource of all, their own labour power. He wrote extensively about this in terms of the problem of alienation. As with the dialectic, Marx began with a Hegelian notion of alienation but developed a more materialist conception. Capitalism mediates social relationships of production (such as among workers or between workers and capitalists) through commodities, including labour, that are bought and sold on the market. For Marx, the possibility that one may give up ownership of one's own labour—one's capacity to transform the world—is tantamount to being alienated from one's own nature; it is a spiritual loss. Marx described this loss as commodity fetishism, in which the things that people produce, commodities, appear to have a life and movement of their own to which humans and their behaviour merely adapt.

Commodity fetishism provides an example of what Engels called "false consciousness", which relates closely to the understanding of ideology. By "ideology", Marx and Engels meant ideas that reflect the interests of a particular class at a particular time in history, but which contemporaries see as universal and eternal. Marx and Engels' point was not only that such beliefs are at best half-truths; they serve an important political function. Put another way, the control that one class exercises over the means of production includes not only the production of food or manufactured goods; it includes the production of ideas as well (this provides one possible explanation for why members of a subordinate class may hold ideas contrary to their own interests).

Thus, while such ideas may be false, they also reveal in coded form some truth about political relations. For example, although the belief that the things people produce are actually more productive than the people who produce them is literally absurd, it does reflect (according to Marx and Engels) that people under capitalism are alienated from their own labour-power. Another example of this sort of analysis is Marx's understanding of religion, summed up in a passage from the preface to his 1843 *Contribution to the Critique of Hegel's Philosophy of Right*:

> "Religious *suffering is, at one and the same time, the* expression *of real suffering and a* protest *against real suffering. Religion is the sigh of the oppressed creature, the heart of a heartless world, and the soul of soulless conditions. It is the* opium *of the people.*" — (Contribution to the Critique of Hegel's Philosophy of Right)

Whereas his Gymnasium senior thesis argued that religion had as its primary social aim the promotion of solidarity, here Marx sees the social function of religion in terms of highlighting/ preserving political and economic inequality. Moreover, he provides an analysis of the ideological functions of religion: to reveal "an *inverted consciousness of the world.*" He continues: "It is the immediate *task of philosophy*, which is in the service of history, to unmask self-estrangement in its *unholy forms*, once religion, the *holy form* of human self-estrangement has been unmasked". For Marx, this unholy self-estrangement, the "loss of man", is complete once the proletariat realizes its potential to unite in revolutionary solidarity. His final conclusion is that for Germany, general human emancipation is only possible as a suspension of private property by the proletariat.

Political Economy

Marx argued that this alienation of human work (and resulting commodity fetishism) functions precisely as the defining feature of capitalism. Prior to capitalism, markets existed in Europe where producers and merchants bought and sold commodities. According to Marx, a capitalist mode of production developed in Europe when labour itself became a commodity—when peasants became free to sell their own labour-power, and needed to do so because they no longer possessed their own land. People sell their labour-power when they accept compensation in return for whatever work they do in a given period of time. In return for selling their labour-power they receive money, which allows them to survive. Those who must sell their labour-power are "proletarians". The person who buys the labour power, generally someone who does own the land and technology to produce, is a "capitalist" or "bourgeois". The proletarians inevitably outnumber the capitalists.

Marx distinguished industrial capitalists from merchant capitalists. Merchants buy goods in one market and sell them in another. Since the laws of supply and demand operate within given markets, a difference often exists between the price of a commodity in one market and another. Merchants, then, practise arbitrage, and hope to capture the difference between these two markets. According to Marx, capitalists, on the other hand, take advantage of the difference between the labour market and the market for whatever commodity the capitalist can produce. Marx observed that in practically every successful industry input unit-costs are lower than output unit-prices. Marx called the difference "surplus value" and argued that this surplus value had its source in surplus labour, the difference between what it costs to keep workers alive and what they can produce.

Capitalism can stimulate considerable growth because the capitalist can, and has an incentive to, reinvest profits in new technologies and capital equipment. Marx considered the capitalist class to be one of the most revolutionary in history, because it constantly improved the means of production. But Marx argued that capitalism was prone to periodic crises. He suggested that over time, capitalists would invest more and more in new technologies, and less and less in labour. Since Marx believed that surplus value appropriated from labour is the source of profits, he concluded that the rate of profit would fall even as the economy grew. When the rate of profit falls below a certain point, the result would be a recession or depression in which certain sectors of the economy would collapse. Marx thought that during such an economic crisis the price of labour would also fall, and eventually make possible the investment in new technologies and the growth of new sectors of the economy.

Marx believed that increasingly severe crises would punctuate this cycle of growth, collapse, and more growth. Moreover, he believed that in the long-term this process would necessarily enrich and empower the capitalist class and impoverish the proletariat. He believed that if the proletariat were to seize the means of production, they would encourage social relations that would benefit everyone equally, and a system of production less vulnerable to periodic crises. He theorized that between capitalism and the establishment of a socialist system, a dictatorship of the proletariat—a period where the working class holds political power and forcibly socializes the means of production—would exist. As he wrote in his "Critique of the Gotha Program", "between capitalist and communist society there lies the period of the revolutionary transformation of the one into the other. Corresponding to this is also a political transition period in which the state can be nothing but the revolutionary dictatorship of the proletariat." While he allowed for the possibility of peaceful transition in some countries with strong democratic institutional structures , he suggested that in other countries with strong centralized state-oriented traditions, like France and Germany, the "lever of our revolution must be force." As a Founder of Social Science

Marx is typically cited, along with Emile Durkheim and Max Weber, as one of the three principal architects of modern social science. Both Marx and Auguste Comte set out to develop scientifically justified ideologies in the wake of European secularisation and new developments in the philosophies of history and science. Whilst Marx, working in the Hegelian tradition, rejected Comtean sociological positivism, in attempting to develop a *science of society* he nevertheless came to be recognized as a founder of sociology as the word gained wider meaning. For Isaiah Berlin, Marx may be regarded as the "true father" of modern sociology, "in so far as anyone can claim the title."

> *To have given clear and unified answers in familiar empirical terms to those theoretical questions which most occupied men's minds at the time, and to have deduced from them clear practical directives without creating obviously artificial links between the two, was the principle achievement of Marx's theory ... The sociological treatment of historical and moral problems, which Comte and after him, Spencer and Taine, had discussed and mapped, became a precise and concrete study only when the attack of militant Marxism made its conclusions a burning issue, and so made the search for evidence more zealous and the attention to method more intense.* – Isaiah Berlin Karl Marx: His Life and Environment 1937,

Marx's Influence

> *"The merit of Marx is that he suddenly produces a qualitative change in the history of social thought. He interprets history, understands its dynamic, predicts the future, but in addition to predicting it, he expresses a revolutionary concept: the world must not only be interpreted, it must be transformed." — Che Guevara, Marxist revolutionary*

The work of Marx and Engels covers a wide range of topics and presents a complex analysis of history and society in terms of class relations. Followers of Marx and Engels have drawn on this work to propose grand, cohesive theoretical outlooks dubbed "Marxism". Nevertheless, Marxists have frequently debated amongst themselves over how to interpret Marx's writings and how to apply his concepts to their contemporary events and conditions. Moreover, one should distinguish between "Marxism" and "what Marx believed"; for example, shortly before he died in 1883, Marx wrote a letter to the French workers' leader Jules Guesde, and to his own son-in-law Paul Lafargue, accusing them of "revolutionary phrase-mongering" and of lack of faith in the working class. After the French party split into a reformist and revolutionary party, some accused Guesde..

Essentially, people use the word "Marxist" in one of two ways:

1. to describe those who rely on Marx's conceptual language to understand capitalist and other societies; or:
2. to describe those who regard a workers' revolution as the only means to a communist society.

Some, particularly in academic circles, who accept much of Marx's theory, but not all its implications, call themselves "Marxian" instead.

Six years after Marx's death, Engels and others founded the "Second International" as a base for continued political activism. This organization proved far more successful than the First International: it included mass workers' parties, particularly the large and successful Social Democratic Party of Germany, which predominantly expressed a Marxist outlook. The Second International collapsed in 1914, however, in part because some members turned to Edward Bernstein's "evolutionary socialism", and in part because of divisions precipitated by World War I.

World War I also led to the Russian Revolution of 1917, in the later stages of which a left-wing splinter-group of the Second International, the Bolsheviks, led by Vladimir Lenin, took power. The Russian Revolution dynamized workers around the world into setting up their own section of the Bolsheviks' "Third International". Lenin presented himself as both the philosophical and the political heir to Marx, and developed a political program, called "Leninism" or "Bolshevism", which called for revolution organized and led by a centrally organized vanguard "Communist Party".

Marx believed that communist revolution would take place in advanced industrial societies such as France, Germany and England, but Lenin argued that in the age of imperialism, and due to the "law of uneven development", where Russia had on the one hand, an antiquated agricultural society, but on the other hand, some of the most up-to-date industrial concerns, the "chain" might break at its weakest points, that is, in the so-called "backward" countries, and then ignite revolution in the advanced industrial societies of Europe, where society is ready for socialism, and which could then in turn come to the aid of the workers' state in Russia.

Marx and Engels make a very significant comment in the preface to the Russian edition of the *Communist Manifesto*:

> *"Now the question is: can the Russian obshchina, though greatly undermined, yet a form of primeval common ownership of land, pass directly to the higher form of Communist common ownership? Or, on the contrary, must it first pass through the same process of dissolution such as constitutes the historical evolution of the West?*
>
> *The only answer to that possible today is this: If the Russian Revolution becomes the signal for a proletarian revolution in the West, so that both complement each other, the present Russian common ownership of land may serve as the starting point for a communist development." — (Marx and Engels,* Preface to the Russian edition of the Communist Manifesto*)*

Marx's words served as a starting point for Lenin, who, together with Trotsky, always believed that the Russian revolution must become a "signal for a proletarian revolution in the West". Supporters of Trotsky argue that the failure of revolution in the West to come to the aid of the Russian revolution after 1917 led to the rise of Stalinism and set the cast of human history for seventy years.

In China Mao Zedong also portrayed himself as an heir to Marx, but argued that peasants—not just workers—could play leading roles in a Communist revolution, even in third-world countries marked by peasant feudalism in the absence of industrial workers. Mao termed this the New Democratic Revolution. Marxism-Leninism as espoused by Mao became known internationally as "Maoism". Under Lenin, and particularly under Joseph Stalin, Bolshevik oppression came to characterise Marxism abroad. Capitalism-oriented western states encouraged this impression, as did the politics of the Cold War. There were, nonetheless, always dissenting Marxist voices—Marxists of the old school of the Second International, the left communists who split off from the Third International shortly after its formation, and later Leon Trotsky and his followers, who set up a "Fourth International" in 1938 to compete with the Stalinist conception of Marxism.

Coming from the Second International milieu in the 1920s and 1930s, a group of dissident Marxists founded the Institute for Social Research in Germany, among them Max Horkheimer, Theodor Adorno, Erich Fromm, and Herbert Marcuse. As a group, these authors became known as the Frankfurt School. Their school of thought, known as Critical Theory, represents a type of Marxist philosophy and cultural criticism heavily influenced by Hegel, Freud, Nietzsche, and Max Weber.

The Frankfurt School broke with earlier Marxists, including Lenin and the Bolshevists in several key ways. First, writing at the time of the ascendancy of Stalinism, they had grave doubts as to the traditional Marxist concept of proletarian class consciousness. Second, unlike earlier Marxists, especially Lenin, they rejected economic determinism. Though the Frankfurt School became highly influential, both orthodox Marxists and some Marxists involved in political practice have criticized their work for divorcing Marxist theory from practical struggle and turning Marxism into a purely academic enterprise. Influential Marxists of the same period include the Third International's Georg Lukacs and Antonio Gramsci, both often grouped along with the Frankfurt School under the term "Western Marxism". Marx was also an important influence on the German philosopher and literary critic Walter Benjamin, an occasional associate of Adorno and the Frankfurt School.

In 1949 Paul Sweezy and Leo Huberman founded *Monthly Review*, a journal and press, to provide an outlet for Marxist thought in the United States independent of the American Communist Party.In 1978, G. A. Cohen attempted to defend Marx's thought as a coherent and scientific theory of history by restating its central tenets in the language of analytic philosophy. This gave birth to Analytical Marxism, an academic movement which also included Jon Elster, Adam Przeworski and John Roemer. Bertell Ollman became another Anglophone champion of Marx within the academy, as did the Israeli Shlomo Avineri.

In *Marx's 'Das Kapital'* (2006), biographer Francis Wheen reiterates David McLellan's observation that since Marxism had not triumphed in the West, "it had not been turned into an official ideology and is thus the object of serious study unimpeded by government controls". The following countries at some point had governments with leadership which at least nominally adhered to Marxism (those in bold still did as of 2009): Albania, Afghanistan, Angola, Bulgaria, China, Cuba, Cyprus, Czechoslovakia, East Germany, Ethiopia, Hungary, Laos, Moldova, Mongolia, Nepal, Mozambique, Nicaragua, North Korea, Poland, Romania, Soviet Union, Yugoslavia, Vietnam. In addition, the Indian states of Kerala, Tripura and West Bengal have had Marxist governments.

Marxist political parties and movements have significantly declined in influence since the fall of the Soviet Union, with some exceptions, perhaps most notably Nepal. In July 2005, 27.9% of listeners in a BBC *Radio 4* series *In Our Time* poll selected Marx as their favorite thinker. Accusations of Antisemitism Some authors like Bernard Lewis, Edward H. Flannery and Hyam Maccoby, view Marx's *On The Jewish Question* as an antisemitic work, and identify what they contend are antisemitic epithets in his published and private writings. According to them, Marx regarded Jews as the embodiment of capitalism and thus the creators of its evils.

The above authors often quote the following excerpt from *On The Jewish Question* to support their arguments:

> *"What is the secular basis of Judaism? Practical need, selfishness. What is the secular cult of the Jew? Haggling. What is his secular god? Money. Well then, an emancipation from haggling and money, from practical, real Judaism would be the self emancipation of our age...*
>
> *...The social emancipation of the Jew is the emancipation of society from Judaism. "*

On the other hand, the political-scientist Professor Iain Hamphsher-Monk wrote in his textbook: "This work [On The Jewish Question] has been cited as evidence for Marx's supposed anti-semitism, but only the most superficial reading of it could sustain such an interpretation." Also, McLellan and Francis Wheen argue readers should interpret *On the Jewish Question* in the context of Marx's debates with Bruno Bauer, author of *The Jewish Question*, about Jewish emancipation in Germany. Francis Wheen says: "Those critics, who see this as a foretaste of 'Mein Kampf', overlook one, essential point: in spite of the clumsy phraseology and crude stereotyping, the essay was actually written as a defence of the Jews. It was a retort to Bruno Bauer, who had argued that Jews should not be granted full civic rights and freedoms unless they were baptised as Christians", although Wheen also says that Marx "sprayed anti-Semitic insults at his enemies with savage glee". According to McLellan, Marx used the word *Judentum* colloquially, as meaning *commerce*, arguing that Germans suffer, and must be emancipated from, capitalism. McLellan concludes that readers should interpret the essay's second half as *an extended pun at Bauer's expense.* Jonathan Sacks, Chief Rabbi of the United Kingdom, regards application of the term "antisemitism" to Marx as an anachronism—because when Marx wrote *On the Jewish Question*, virtually all major philosophers expressed antisemitic tendencies, but the word "antisemitism" had not yet been coined, let alone developed a racial component, and little awareness existed of the depths of European prejudice against Jews. Marx thus simply expressed the commonplace thinking of his era, according to Sacks.

2

Basic Theories of Karl Marx

HISTORICAL MATERIALISM

Outside his specific economic theories, Marx's main contribution to the social sciences has been his theory of historical materialism. Its starting point is anthropological. Human beings cannot survive without social organisation. Social organisation is based upon social labour and social communication. Social labour always occurs within a given framework of specific, historically determined, social relations of production. These social relations of production determine in the last analysis all other social relations, including those of social communication. It is social existence which determines social consciousness and not the other way around.

Historical materialism posits that relations of production which become stabilised and reproduce themselves are structures which can no longer be changed gradually, piecemeal. They are modes of production. To use Hegel's dialectical language, which was largely adopted (and adapted) by Marx: they can only change qualitatively through a complete social upheaval, a social revolution or counter-revolution. Quantitative changes can occur within modes of production, but they do not modify the basic structure. In each mode of production, a given set of relations of production constitutes the basis (infrastructure) on which is erected a complex superstructure, encompassing the state and the law (except in a classless society), ideology, religion, philosophy, the arts, morality, etc. Relations of production are the sum total of social relations which human beings establish among themselves in the production of their material lives. They are therefore not limited to what actually happens at the point of production. Humankind could not survive, i.e. produce, if there did not exist specific forms of circulation of goods, e.g. between producing units and between production units and consumers. A priori allocation of goods determines other relations of production than does allocation of goods through the market. Partial commodity production also implies other relations of production than does generalised commodity production.

Except in the case of classless societies, modes of production, centred around prevailing relations of production, are embodied in specific class relations which, in the last analysis, over-determine relations between individuals. Historical materialism does not deny the individual's free will, his attempts to make choices concerning his existence according to his individual passions, his interests as he understands them, his convictions, his moral options etc. What historical materialism does state is: (1) that these choices are strongly predetermined by the social framework (education, prevailing ideology and moral 'values', variants of behaviour limited by material conditions etc.); (2) that the outcome of the collision of millions of different passions, interests and options is essentially a phenomenon of social logic and not of individual psychology. Here, class interests are predominant.

There is no example in history of a ruling class not trying to defend its class rule, or of an exploited class not trying to limit the exploitation it suffers. So outside classless society, the class struggle is a permanent feature of human society. In fact, one of the key theses of historical materialism is that 'the history of humankind is the history of class struggles' (Marx, *Communist Manifesto*, 1848).

The immediate object of class struggle is economic and material. It is a struggle for the division of the social product between the direct producers and those who appropriate what Marx calls the social surplus product, the residuum of the social product once the producers and their offspring are fed (in the large sense of the word; i.e. the sum total of the consumer goods consumed by that class) and the initial stock of tools and raw materials is reproduced. The ruling class functions as a ruling class essentially through the appropriation of the social surplus product. By getting possession of the social surplus product, it acquires the means to foster and maintain most of the superstructural activities mentioned above; and by doing so, it can largely determine their function-to maintain and reproduce the given social structure, the given mode of production-and their contents.

We say 'largely determine' and not 'completely determine'. First, there is an 'immanent dialectical', i.e. an autonomous movement, of each specific superstructural sphere of activity. Each generation of scientists, artists, philosophers, theologists, lawyers and politicians finds a given corpus of ideas, forms, rules, techniques, ways of thinking, to which it is initiated through education and current practice, etc. It is not forced to simply continue and reproduce these elements. It can transform them, modify them, change their interconnections, even negate them. Again: historical materialism does not deny that there is a specific history of science, a history of art, a history of philosophy, a history of political and moral ideas, a history of religion etc., which all follow their own logic. It tries to explain why a certain number of scientific, artistic, philosophical, ideological, juridical changes or even revolutions occur at a given time and in given countries, quite different from other ones which occurred some centuries earlier elsewhere. The nexus of these 'revolutions' with given historical periods is a nexus of class interests.

Second, each social formation while being characterised by predominant relations of production includes different relations of production which are largely remnants of the past, but also sometimes nuclei of future modes of production. Thus there exists not only the ruling class and the exploited class characteristic of that prevailing mode of production (capitalists and wage earners under capitalism). There also exist remnants of social classes which were predominant when other relations of production prevailed and which, while having lost their hegemony, still manage to survive in the interstices of the new society. This is, for example, the case with petty commodity producers (peasants, handicraftsmen, small merchants), semi-feudal landowners, and even slave-owners, in many already predominantly capitalist social formations throughout the 19th and part of the 20th centuries. Each of these social classes has its own ideology, its own religious and moral values, which are intertwined with the ideology of the hegemonic ruling class, without becoming completely absorbed by that ideology.

Third, even after a given ruling class (e.g. the feudal or semi-feudal nobility) has disappeared as a ruling class, its ideology can survive through sheer force of social inertia and routine (custom). The survival of traditional ancien régime catholic ideology in France during a large part of the 19th century, in spite of the sweeping social, political and ideological changes ushered in by the French revolution, is an illustration of that rule.

Finally, Marx's statement that the ruling ideology of each epoch is the ideology of the ruling class-another basic tenet of historical materialism-does not express more than it actually says. It implies that other ideologies can exist side by side with that ruling ideology without being hegemonic. To cite the most important of these occurrences: exploited and (or) oppressed social classes can develop their own ideology, which will start to challenge the prevailing hegemonic one. In fact, an ideological class struggle accompanies and sometimes even precedes the political class struggle properly speaking. Religious and philosophical struggles preceding the classical bourgeois revolutions; the first socialist critiques of bourgeois society preceding the constitution of the first working-class parties and revolutions, are examples of that type.

The class struggle has been up to now the great motor of history. Human beings make their own history. No mode of production can be replaced by another one without deliberate actions by large social forces, i.e. without social revolution (or counter-revolution). Whether these revolutions or counter-revolutions actually lead to the long-term implementation of deliberate projects of social reorganization is another matter altogether. Very often, their outcome is to a large extent different from the intention of the main actors.

Human beings act consciously, but they can act with false consciousness. They do not necessarily understand why they want to realise certain social and (or) political plans, why they want to maintain or to change economic or juridical institutions; and especially, they rarely understand in a scientific sense the laws of social change, the material and social preconditions for successfully conserving or changing such institutions. Indeed, Marx claims that only with the discovery of the main tenets of historical materialism have we made a significant step forward towards understanding these laws, without claiming to be able to predict 'all' future developments of society.

Social change, social revolutions and counter-revolutions are furthermore occurring within determined material constraints. The level of development of the productive forces-essentially tools and human skills, including their effects upon the fertility of the soil-limits the possibilities of institutional change. Slave labour has shown itself to be largely incompatible with the factory system based upon contemporary machines. Socialism would not be durably built upon the basis of the wooden plough and the potter's wheel. A social revolution generally widens the scope for the development of the productive forces and leads to social progress in most fields of human activity in a momentous way. Likewise, an epoch of deep social crisis is ushered in when there is a growing conflict between the prevailing mode of production (i.e. the existing social order) on the one hand, and the further development of the productive forces on the other. Such a social crisis will then manifest itself on all major fields and social activity: politics, ideology, morals and law, as well as in the realm of the economic life properly speaking.

Historical materialism thereby provides a measuring stick for human progress: the growth of the productive forces, measurable through the growth of the average productivity of labour, and the number, longevity and skill of the human species. This measuring stick in no way abstracts from the natural preconditions for human survival and human growth (in the broadest sense of the concept). Nor does it abstract from the conditional and partial character of such progress, in terms of social organisation and individual alienation.

In the last analysis, the division of society into antagonistic social classes rejects, from the point of view of historical materialism, an inevitable limitation of human freedom. For Marx and Engels, the real measuring rod of human freedom, i.e. of human wealth, is not 'productive labour'; this only creates the material pre-condition for that freedom. The real measuring rod is leisure time, not in the sense of 'time for doing nothing' but in the sense of time freed from the iron necessity to produce and reproduce material livelihood, and therefore disposable for all-round and free development of the individual talents, wishes, capacities, potentialities, of each human being.

As long as society is too poor, as long as goods and services satisfying basic needs are too scarce, only part of society can be freed from the necessity to devote most of its life to 'work for a livelihood' (i.e. of forced labour, in the anthropological/ sociological sense of the word, that is in relation to desires, aspirations and talents, not to a juridical status of bonded labour). That is essentially what represents the freedom of the ruling classes and their hangers-on, who are 'being paid to think', to create, to invent, to administer, because they have become free from the obligation to bake their own bread, weave their own clothes and build their own houses.

Once the productive forces are developed far enough to guarantee all human beings satisfaction of their basic needs by 'productive labour' limited to a minor fraction of lifetime (the half work-day or less), then the material need of the division of society in classes disappears. Then, there remains no objective basis for part of society to monopolise administration, access to information, knowledge, intellectual labour. For that reason, historical materialism explains both the reasons why class societies and class struggles arose in history, and why they will disappear in the future in a classless society of democratically self-administering associated producers.

Historical materialism therefore contains an attempt at explaining the origin, the functions and the future withering away of the state as a specific institution, as well as an attempt to explain politics and political activity in general, as an expression of social conflicts centred around different social interests (mainly, but not only, those of different social classes; important fractions of classes, as well as non-class social groupings, also come into play). For Marx and Engels, the state is not existent with human society as such, or with 'organised society' or even with 'civilised society' in the abstract, neither is it the result of any voluntarily concluded 'social contract' between individuals. The state is the sum total of apparatuses, i.e. special groups of people separate and apart from the rest (majority) of society, that appropriate to themselves functions of a repressive or integrative nature which were initially exercised by all citizens. This process of alienation occurs in conjunction with the emergence of social classes. The state is an instrument for fostering, conserving and reproducing a given class structure, and not a neutral arbiter between antagonistic class interests.

The emergence of a classless society is therefore closely intertwined, for adherents to historical materialism, with the process of withering away of the state, i.e. of gradual devolution to the whole of society (self-management, self-administration) of all specific functions today exercised by special apparatuses, i.e. of the dissolution of these apparatuses. Marx and Engels visualised the dictatorship of the proletariat, the last form of the state and of political class rule, as an instrument for assuring the transition from class society to classless society. It should itself be a state of a special kind, organising its own gradual disappearance.

We said above that, from the point of view of historical materialism, the immediate object of class struggle is the division of the social product between different social classes. Even the political class struggle in the final analysis serves that main purpose; but it also covers a much broader field of social conflicts. As all state activities have some bearing upon the relative stability of a given social formation, and the class rule to which it is submitted, the class struggle can extend to all fields of politics from foreign policy to educational problems and religious conflicts. This has of course to be proven through painstaking analysis, and not proclaimed as an axiom or a revealed truth. When conducted successfully, such exercises in class analysis and class definition of political, social and even literary struggles becomes impressive works of historical explanation, as for example Marx's *Class Struggles in France 1848-50*, Engels' *The German Peasant War*, Franz Mehring's *Die Lesssing-Legende*, Trotsky's *History of the Russian Revolution*, etc.

THEORY OF KARL MARX

According to Karl Marx, private property is the necessary and inevitable result of alienated labour or the product of the worker who is estranged from himself. The basis for this idea is found in the notion that the working class labors to produce products that belong to someone else, and that the compensation the working class receives is always less than the value of the product they create. "Private property is thus the product, the result, the necessary consequence of alienated labour, of the external relation of the worker to nature and to himself. Private property thus results by analysis from the concept of alienated labour, of alienated man, of estranged labour, of estranged life, of estranged man."

Believing that the product of one's labour should belong solely to the laborer, Marx postulated that in a capitalist system the laborer is forced to accept the notion that his labour belongs to someone else and is therefore estranged and alienated from his own being, in an almost schizophrenic manner. Even though the laborer is compensated, this compensation is insufficient due to the fact that it is less that the actual value of the commodity being produced; this being the source of the capitalist's profit.

The capitalist who hires the laborers is depicted as an exploiter of the working class, and the ultimate beneficiary of the property which should rightfully belong to the ones who created it. Private property serves as the basis for which Marx divides people into two classes; the property owners and the property-less workers. In his view all private property is ill-gained and the end-product of the exploitation and abuse of the working class, who are helpless victims.

Marx also views the idea of private property as the foundation for which Political Economy exists. He criticizes the political economy for failing to educate the masses on the economic laws that surround private property, and that the political economy itself does not fully understanding them. He further criticizes the political economy: "Political economy conceals the estrangement inherent in the nature of labour by not considering the direct relationship between the worker (labour) and production."

Again, the basis for this idea is found in the idea that the end product of one's labour should rightfully belong to its producer. This goes back to the alienation of the laborer from his work, from nature, and ultimately from himself. The above ideas also necessitate the idea that wages no matter how great or small are merely a token of slavery. Since the laborer is not working for himself, but for another, it is not possible to view the laborer as anything but a slave. This idea forms Karl Marx's fundamental notion of the employer/employee relationship. He views the worker's relationship to his employer in terms of power and that the employer is the master and the employee is the servant or slave. According to Marx, the servant is more valuable because he is the one doing the actual work. This work requires a certain amount of creative energy and therefore the employee will become smarter than the employer. At this point, the servant develops an enormous amount of resentment towards his employer and this evolves into a classic struggle.

Marx goes on to state that he believes that this class warfare harms the greater good by impoverishing the general public while empowering and enriching a minority elite and ruling class. This class war is further exasperated by the idea that the more valuable the product produced by the worker, the less valuable the worker becomes and that the more the workers produce, the less they have to consume, and the more civilized the product is the more barbaric it becomes to the worker. Due to the growth of capitalist systems, the laborer becomes less humanized and more of a commodity as the worker is nothing more than a source of labour which serves the capitalist and not the worker himself. To Karl Marx, the reduction of a worker to a mere commodity accompanied by his complete dehumanization, estrangement and alienation to himself and nature, as well as his ultimate enslavement and loss of happiness, are the end results of the existence of private property.

Competition is viewed as an endless war of greedy capitalists that is destructive to society and also results in the enslavement of the working class. One of the major problems with Karl Marx's philosophy is what I see as a fundamental flaw in its foundation. The idea that there are two classes of people as the result of private property is overly simplistic at best. It is also quick to simply dismiss the importance of wages and the power that they give to the working class. Is not the worker free to use his wages for the acquisition of property or employees for himself?

There is also no mention of the value of intellectual property, which gives the inventor of a product credit for his creation. Why should the worker own a product that they had no part in designing or inventing? The worker's choice in profession is certainly a factor in determining whether or not he or she can be replaced by a machine. A worker who chooses to do the work of an automaton is merely acting as a machine, and should a more efficient and less costly-machine become available to the employer, it is his right if not his duty to replace the outdated, more expensive, and less-efficient process for the newer, more efficient version for the sake of the consumer (a class which the employer and employee are both members of). While he is quick to criticize the employer for replacing workers with machines, he fails to mention anything about the inventors, engineers, salesman, managers, production workers, and other staff that create, build, market, and sell those machines. Obviously, he would view this as simply an expansion of the market which further impoverishes the working class rather than doing anything for its benefit.

There is also another terrible mistake made by Karl Marx. He assumes that people cannot and do not feel fulfilment or happiness in the labouring for the benefit of others. The world is full of people who labour because they believe strongly in a cause, in a product, or a service that they love or respect. Marx believes strongly that greed and self-importance are the driving factors in all humans. While, on a certain animalistic level, this is instinctual, it is not so simple. Psychologists have shown that when people act in ways that are selfless and beneficial to others they become happier.

This fundamental misunderstanding of human nature coupled with his over-simplification of complex economic systems into two categories proves to be fatal to many of Karl Marx's ideas, assumptions, and conclusions. While his ideas may find popularity among lower/entry-level workers, and were at the heart of the Soviet Revolution, they do nothing to advance the cause of the workers who adopt them, in fact by breeding hostility in workers towards their employers, the workers often find themselves worse off and more unhappy than before.

True Marxists would probably argue that the Soviets did not adopt true Marxist ideas, and the reason for this is probably due to the fact that his ideas are too impractical to exist in the real world. Some Israeli kibbutzim (communal farms) attempted to adopt a more idealistic form of Marxism and found a bit more success although it was short-lived. Most kibbutzim are no-longer functional or have altered the way they function in order to continue to exist. Although Karl Marx has some novel ideas and makes some valid points, I find that overall his conclusions and underlying philosophy are terribly flawed and only bring harm to society and serve little or no positive purpose.

MARX'S THEORY OF ALIENATION

Marx's theory of alienation (*Entfremdung* in German, which literally means "estrangement"), as expressed in the writings of the young Karl Marx (in particular the Manuscripts of 1844), refers to the separation of things that naturally belong together, or to put antagonism between things that are properly in harmony. In the concept's most important use, it refers to the social alienation of people from aspects of their "human nature" (*Gattungswesen*, usually translated as 'species-essence' or 'species-being'). He believed that alienation is a systematic result of capitalism. Marx's theory relies on Feuerbach's *The Essence of Christianity* (1841), which argues that the idea of God has alienated the characteristics of the human being. Stirner would take the analysis further in *The Ego and Its Own* (1844), declaring that even 'humanity' is an alienating ideal for the individual, to which Marx and Engels responded in *The German Ideology* (1845).

Types of the Labour Process

According to Karl Marx, alienation is a systemic result of Capitalism. Marx's theory of alienation is founded upon his observation that, within the Capitalist Mode of Production, workers invariably lose determination of their lives and destinies by being deprived of the right to conceive of themselves as the director of their actions, to determine the character of their actions, to define their relationship to other actors, to use or own the value of what is produced by their actions. Workers never become autonomous, self-realized human beings, but are directed and diverted into goals and activities dictated by the bourgeoisie, who own the means of production in order to extract from workers the maximal amount of surplus value possible within the current state of competition between industrialists. By working, each contributes to the common wealth. Alienation in Capitalist societies occurs because the worker can only express this fundamentally social aspect of individuality through a production system that is not collectively, but privately owned, a privatized asset for which each individual functions not as a social being, but as an instrument:

'Let us suppose that we had carried out production as human beings. Each of us would have in two ways affirmed himself and the other person. 1) In my production I would have objectified my individuality, its specific character, and therefore enjoyed not only an individual manifestation of my life during the activity, but also when looking at the object I would have the individual pleasure of knowing my personality to be objective, visible to the senses and hence a power beyond all doubt. 2) In your enjoyment or use of my product I would have the direct enjoyment both of being conscious of having satisfied a human need by my work, that is, of having objectified man's essential nature, and of having thus created an object corresponding to the need of another man's essential nature.... Our products would be so many mirrors in which we saw reflected our essential nature."' (*Comment on James Mill*)

In the *Economic and Philosophical Manuscripts of 1844* Marx identifies four types of alienation in labour under capitalism. These include:

Alienation of the worker from the work he produces, from the *product* of his labour. The product's design and the manner in which it is produced are determined not by its actual producers, nor even by those who consume products, but rather by the Capitalist class, which appropriates labour-including that of designers and engineers-and seeks to shape consumers' taste in order to maximize profit. Aside from the lack of workers' control over the design and production protocol, however, this form of alienation refers more broadly to the conversion of the activity of work, which is conducted to generate a use value in the form of a product, into a commodity itself which-like products-can be assigned an exchange value. In other words, the Capitalist gains control of the worker-including intellectual and creative workers-and the beneficial effects of his work by setting up a system that converts the worker's efforts not only into a useful, concrete thing capable of benefiting consumers, but also into an illusory, reified concept-something called "work"- which is compensated in the form of wages at a rate as low as possible to maintain a maximum rate of return on the industrialist's investment capital (an aspect of Exploitation). Furthermore, within this illusory framework, the exchange value that could be generated by the sale of products and returned to workers in the form of profits is absconded with by the managerial and Capitalist classes.

Alienation of the worker from working, from the act of *producing* itself. This kind of alienation refers to the patterning of work in the Capitalist Mode of Production into an endless sequence of discrete, repetitive, trivial, and meaningless motions, offering little, if any, intrinsic satisfaction. The worker's labour power is commodified into exchange value itself in the form of wages. A worker is thus estranged from the unmediated relation to his activity via such wages. Aside from the limitation of the inherent plurality of one's species being that the Capitalist division of labour imposes upon workers, Marx was also identifying another feature of exploitation with this kind of alienation. According to Marx, one's species being is fulfilled when it maintains control over the subject of its labour by the ability to determine how it shall be used directly or exchanged for something else. Capitalism removes the right of the worker to exercise control over the value or effects of his labour, robbing him of the ability to either consume the product he makes directly or receive the full value of the product when it is sold: this is the first alienation of worker from product. However, the first alienation contributes to the second alienation of worker from the very act of working, as it removes the worker's feeling of control over the use and exchange of his labour power. This loss of control disrupts the ability of the worker to specialize, focus, direct or apply the inherently plural potency of his species being, thus separating or alienating any activity that he does engage in from the intentional core of that being.

Alienation of the worker from himself as a *producer*, from his or her "*species being*" or "essence as a species". To Marx, this human essence is separate from activity or work, nor static, but includes the innate potential to develop as a human organism. Species being is a concept that Marx deploys to refer to what he sees as the original or intrinsic essence of the species, which is characterized both by *plurality* and dynamism: all beings possess the tendency and desire to engage in multiple activities to promote their mutual survival, comfort and sense of inter-connection. A man's value consists in his ability to conceive of the ends of his action as purposeful ideas distinct from any given step of realizing them: man is able to objectify his intentional efforts in an idea of himself (the subject) and an idea of the thing which he produces (the object). Animals, according to Marx, do not objectify themselves or their products as ideas because they engage in self-sustaining actions directly, without sustained future projection or conscious intention. While human nature or essence does not exist *apart* from specific, historically conditioned activity, it becomes actualized as man's species being when man-within his historical circumstances-is free to subordinate his will to the demands imposed by his own imagination and not those mandated solely for the purpose of allowing others to do so.

Notwithstanding, the character of an individual's consciousness (his will and imagination) is conditioned by his relationship to that which facilitates survival; since any individual's survival and betterment is fundamentally dependent upon cooperation with others, a given person's personal consciousness is determined inter-subjectively or collectively rather than merely subjectively or individually. As far as has been heretofore observed, all societies have, according to Marx, organized groups with differing basic relationships to the means of material survival available to them-i.e. the means of production. One group has owned and controlled the means while another has operated them, the goal of the former being to benefit as much as possible through the latter's efforts. Every time there is a shift in the organization of the means of production-as with say, the displacement of agrarian feudalism and pre-industrial mercantilism with the technologies that gave rise to Industrial Capitalism-there is a rearrangement and rupture of the social class structure that relates to those means-a class structure Marx termed the relations of production. That is to say, a new class relationship emerges, subordinating one group and the species beings of its members to the activities and corresponding values that enable it to operate the means of production for the profit of the dominant group, whose consciousness and values are also conditioned to maintain this dominance.

While industrialization holds the promise of the masses' eventual liberation from an imagination conditioned chiefly by brute necessity, the division of labour within Industrial Capitalism blunts the worker's "species being" and renders him as a replaceable cog in an abstract machine instead of a human being capable of defining his own value through direct, purposeful activity. And yet, industrialization, in Marx's view, would eventually progress to a state of near-total mechanization and automation of productive processes. During this progression, the newly dominant Bourgeoisie Capitalist class would exploit the Industrial working class or Proletariat to the degree that the value they excised from their labour would begin to infringe upon the ability of the Proletariat to materially survive. When this begins to occur, and when the productive forces are sufficiently developed, there will be a final revolution whose end result will be the reorientation of the relations of production to the means of production in a Communist mode of production. In the Communist mode of production, because all members of the society will relate to the means of production on a fundamentally equal and non-conflictual manner, there will be no fundamental differentiation between groups or classes as previously, and the species being of every individual will assume a full actualization of its tendencies, as the application of his efforts will return to him in direct, unmediated proportion to what he is able to conceive. This is partly due to the fact that a Communist society would distribute the benefits and duties of production evenly, in accordance with the capacities its members, such that each member could direct his action more directly towards his interests and preferences rather than a narrowly designated function designed to generate maximal return of value to an owner.

In this classless, collectively managed society, the dialectical exchange of value between one worker's objectified labour power (via production) and another's benefit from that objectification (via consumption) will not be directed by the narrow interest of one group over the needs of another, and will thus directly enrich the consciousness and material state of all of producers and consumers to the maximal possible degree. Though production will still be differentiated to some degree, it will be directed by the collective demand and not the narrow demand of one class at the expense of those of another. Since ownership will be shared, the relation of individuals' consciousness to the mode of production will be identical, and will assume the character that corresponds, as in previous times, to the interest of its group: the universal, Communist class. The direct, un-siphoned return of the fruit of each worker's labour to that group's interest-and thus as directly as possible to his own interest, which assumes the character of his group's-will constitute an un-alienated state of labour, restoring the worker to the fullest exercise and determination of his species being as is possible at any given moment in the future development of Communist society.

Alienation of the worker from other workers or *producers*. Capitalism reduces labour to a commercial commodity to be traded on the market, rather than a social relationship between people involved in a common effort for survival or betterment. The competitive labour market is set up in Industrial Capitalist economies to extract as much value as possible in the form of capital from those who work to those who own enterprises and other assets that control the means of production. This causes the relations of production to become conflictual...i.e. it pits worker against worker, alienating members of the same class from their mutual interest, an effect Marx called *False Consciousness*.

Marx also placed emphasis on the role of religion in the alienation process, independently from his famous quotation on the *opiate of the masses*.

SIGNIFICANCE IN MARX'S THOUGHT

Alienation is a foundational claim in Marxist theory. Hegel described a succession of historic stages in the human *Geist* (Spirit), by which that Spirit progresses towards perfect self-understanding, and away from ignorance. In Marx's reaction to Hegel, these two, idealist poles are replaced with materialist categories: spiritual ignorance becomes alienation, and the transcendent end of history becomes man's *realisation of his species-being*; triumph over alienation and establishment of an objectively better society. This teleological (goal-oriented) reading of Marx, particularly supported by Alexandre Kojève before World War II, is criticized by Louis Althusser in his writings about "random materialism". Althusser claimed that said reading made the proletariat the subject of history , was tainted with Hegelian idealism, the "philosophy of the subject" that had been in force for five centuries, which was criticized as the "bourgeois ideology of philosophy".

Relation to Marx's Theory of History

In *The German Ideology* Marx writes that 'things have now come to such a pass that the individuals must appropriate the existing totality of productive forces, not only to achieve self-activity, but, also, merely to safeguard their very existence'. In other words, Marx seems to think that, while humans do have a need for self-activity , this will be of secondary historical relevance. This is because he thinks that capitalism will increase the economic impoverishment of the proletariat so rapidly that they will be forced to make the social revolution just to stay alive-they probably wouldn't even get to the point of worrying that much about self-activity. This doesn't mean, though, that tendencies against alienation *only* manifest themselves once other needs are amply met, only that they are of reduced importance. The work of Raya Dunayevskaya and others in the tradition of Marxist humanism drew attention to manifestations of the desire for self-activity even among workers struggling for more basic goals.

Class

In this passage, from *The Holy Family*, Marx says that capitalists and proletarians are equally alienated, but experience their alienation in different ways: The propertied class and the class of the proletariat present the same human self-estrangement. But the former class feels at ease and strengthened in this self-estrangement, it recognizes estrangement as its own power and has in it the semblance of a human existence. The class of the proletariat feels annihilated, this means that they cease to exist in estrangement; it sees in it its own powerlessness and the reality of an inhuman existence. It is, to use an expression of Hegel, in its abasement the indignation at that abasement, an indignation to which it is necessarily driven by the contradiction between its human nature and its condition of life, which is the outright, resolute and comprehensive negation of that nature. Within this antithesis the private property-owner is therefore the conservative side, the proletarian the destructive side. From the former arises the action of preserving the antithesis, from the latter the action of annihilating it.

MARXIAN CLASS THEORY

Marxian Class Theory is a broad range of social concepts related to the study of Marxism. It asserts that an individual's position within a class hierarchy is determined by his role in the production process, and argues that political and ideological consciousness is determined by class position (Parkin). Within Marxian Class Theory, the structure of the production process forms the basis of class construction. Marxian Class Theory has been open to a range of alternate positions, most notably from scholars such as E. P. Thompson and Mario Tronti. Both Thompson and Tronti suggest class consciousness within the production process precedes the formation of productive relationships. In this sense, Marxian Class Theory often relates to discussion over pre-existing class struggles.

Origins of Marx's Theory

Marx's class theory derives from a range of philosophical schools of thought including left Hegelianism, Scottish Empiricism and Anglo-French political-economics. Marx's view of class originated from a series of personal interests relating to social alienation and human struggle, whereby the formation of class structure relates to acute historical consciousness. Political-economics also contributed to Marx's theories, centering around the concept of "origin of income" where society is divided into three sub-groups: Rentier, Capitalist, and Worker. This construction is based on Ricardo's theory of capitalism. Marx strengthened this with a discussion over verifiable class relationships. Marx sought to define class as embedded in productive relations rather than social status. His political and economic thought developed towards an interest in production as opposed to distribution, and this henceforth became a central theme in his concept of class.

Class Structure

Marx distinguishes one class from another on the basis of two criteria: ownership of the means of production and control of the labour power of others. From this, he defines modern society as having three distinct classes:

i. Capitalists, or bourgeoisie, own the means of production and purchase the labour power of others
ii. Workers, or proletariat, do not own any means of production or the ability to purchase the labour power of others. Rather, they sell their own labour power.
iii. A small, transitional class known as the petite bourgeoisie own sufficient means of production but do not purchase labour power. Marx's Communist Manifesto fails to properly define the petite bourgeoisie beyond "smaller capitalists".

Class is thus determined by property relations not by income or status. These factors are determined by distribution and consumption, which mirror the production and power relations of classes.

THE NATURE OF CLASS RELATIONS: CONFLICT

"The history of all hitherto existing society is the history of class struggles... Freeman and slave, patrician and plebeian, lord and serf, guild-master and journeyman, in a word, oppressor and oppressed, stood in constant opposition to one another, carried on an uninterrupted, now hidden, now open fight, a fight that each time ended, either in a revolutionary reconstruction of society at large, or in the common ruin of the contending classes....

The modern bourgeois society that has sprouted from the ruins of feudal society has not done away with class antagonisms. It has but established new classes, new conditions of oppression, new forms of struggle in place of the old ones. Our epoch, the epoch of the bourgeoisie, possesses, however, this distinctive feature: it has simplified class antagonisms. Society as a whole is more and more splitting up into two great hostile camps, into two great classes directly facing each other: Bourgeoisie and Proletariat." – Communist Manifesto

Marx established conflict as the key driving force of history and the main determinant of social trajectories (Kingston). However in order to understand the nature of "class conflict," we must first understand that such conflict arises from a unified class interest, also known as class consciousness. Class consciousness is an aspect of Marxist theory, referring to the self-awareness of social classes, the capacity to act in its own rational interests, or measuring the extent to which an individual is conscious of the historical tasks their class (or class allegiance) sets for them.

Moreover, by definition, the objective interests of classes are fundamentally in opposition; consequently, these opposing interests and consciousnesses eventually lead to class conflict. Marx first saw the development of class conflict confined to individual factories and capitalists. However, given the maturation of capitalism, the life conditions of bourgeoisie and proletariat began to grow more disparate. This increased the homogenization within classes to foster the environment for individual struggles to become more generalized. When increasing class conflict is manifested at the societal level, class consciousness and common interests are also increased. Consequently when class consciousness is augmented, policies are organized to ensure the duration of such interest for the ruling class. Here begins the use of the struggle for political power and classes become political forces.

Since the distribution of political power is determined by power over production, or power over capital, it is no surprise that the bourgeois class uses their wealth to legitimatize and protect their property and consequent social relations. Thus the ruling class is those who hold the economic power and make the decisions (Dahrendorf).

Inevitability of Socialist Revolution

Marx assumes the inevitability of the revolution of capitalist society into socialist society because of eventual discontent. The socialization of labour, in the growth of large-scale production, capitalist interest groups and organizations, as well as in the enormous increase in the dimensions and power of finance capital provides the principal material foundation for the unavoidable arrival of socialism. The physical, intellectual and moral perpetrator of this transformation is the proletariat. The proletariat's struggle against the bourgeoisie inevitably becomes a political struggle with the goal of political conquest by the proletariat. With the domination of the proletariat, the socialization of production cannot help but lead to the means of production to become the property of society. The direct consequences of this transformation are a tremendous rise in labour productivity, a shorter working day, and the replacement of small-scale unified production by collective and improved labour. Capitalism breaks for all time the ties between producer and owner, once held by the bond of class conflict. Now a new union will be formed based on the conscious application of science and the concentration of collective labour.

He also extended this redistribution to the structure of power in families. Marx imagined that with socialism women's status would increase, leading to the break-up of the patriarchal family...

"Modern industry, by assigning as it does, an important part in the socially organized process of production, outside the domestic sphere, to women, to young persons, and to children of both sexes, creates a new economic foundation for a higher form of the family and of the relations between the sexes... Moreover, it is obvious that the fact of the collective working group being composed of individuals of both sexes and all ages, must necessarily, under suitable conditions, become a source of human development; although in its spontaneously developed, brutal, capitalistic form, where the laborer exists for the process of production, and not the process of production for the laborer, that fact is a pestiferous source of corruption and slavery."

3

Marx's Theory of Human Nature

Marx's theory of human nature occupies an important place in his critique of capitalism, his conception of communism, and his 'materialist conception of history'. Marx, however, does not refer to "human nature" as such, but to *Gattungswesen*, which is generally translated as 'species-being' or 'species-essence'. What Marx meant by this is that humans are capable of making or shaping their own nature to some extent. According to a note from the young Marx in the *Manuscripts of 1844*, the term is derived from Ludwig Feuerbach's philosophy, in which it refers both to the nature of each human and of humanity as a whole. However, in the sixth *Thesis on Feuerbach* (1845), Marx criticizes the traditional conception of "human nature" as "species" which incarnates itself in each individual, on behalf of a conception of human nature as formed by the totality of "social relations". Thus, the whole of human nature is not understood, as in classical idealist philosophy, as permanent and universal: the *species-being* is always determined in a specific social and historical formation, with some aspects being biological.

THE SIXTH THESIS ON FEUERBACH

Norman Geras claimed in *Marx's theory of human nature* (1983) that although many Marxists denied that there was a "human nature" to be found in Marx's words , there is in fact a Marxist conception of human nature which remains, to some degree, constant throughout history and across social boundaries. The sixth of the *Theses on Feuerbach* provided the basics for this interpretation of Marx according to which there was no eternal human nature to be found in his works. It states:

*Feuerbach resolves the essence of religion into the essence of man [*menschliche Wesen = *'human nature']. But the essence of man is no abstraction inherent in each single individual. In reality, it is the ensemble of the social relations. Feuerbach, who does not enter upon a criticism of this real essence is hence obliged:*

1. *To abstract from the historical process and to define the religious sentiment regarded by itself, and to presuppose an abstract — isolated-human individual.*
2. *The essence therefore can by him only be regarded as 'species', as an inner 'dumb' generality which unites many individuals only in a natural way.*

Thus, Marx appears to say that human nature is no more than what is made by the 'social relations'. Norman Geras's *Marx's Theory of Human Nature*, however, offers an extremely detailed argument against this position. In outline, Geras shows that, while the social relations are held to 'determine' the nature of people, they are not the only such determinant. In fact, Marx makes statements where he specifically refers to a human nature which is more than what is conditioned by the circumstances of one's life. In *Capital*, in a footnote critiquing utilitarianism, he says that utilitarians must reckon with 'human nature in general, and then with human nature as modified in each historical epoch'. Marx is arguing against an abstract conception of human nature, offering instead an account rooted in sensuous life. While he is quite explicit that '[a]s individuals express their life, so they are. Hence what individuals are depends on the material conditions of their production' , he also believes that human nature will condition (against the background of the productive forces and relations of production) the way in which individuals express their life. History involves 'a continuous transformation of human nature' , though this does not mean that every aspect of human nature is wholly variable; what is transformed need not be wholly transformed. Marx did criticise the tendency to 'transform into eternal laws of nature and of reason, the social forms springing from your present mode of production and form of property' , a process sometimes called "reification". For this reason, he would likely have wanted to criticise certain *aspects* of some accounts of human nature. Some people believe, for example, that humans are naturally selfish-Kant and Hobbes , for example. (Both Hobbes and Kant thought that it was necessary to constrain our human nature in order to achieve a good society-Kant thought we should use rationality, Hobbes thought we should use the force of the state-Marx, as we shall see, thought that the good society was one which allows our human nature its full expression.) Most Marxists will argue that this view is an ideological illusion and the effect of commodity fetishism: the fact that people act selfishly is held to be a product of scarcity and capitalism, not an immutable human characteristic. For confirmation of this view, we can see how, in *The Holy Family* Marx argues that capitalists are not motivated by any essential viciousness, but by the drive toward the bare 'semblance of a human existence'.

Needs and Drives

In the *1844 Manuscripts* the young Marx wrote: *Man is directly a natural being. As a natural being and as a living natural being he is on the one hand endowed with natural powers, vital powers – he is an active natural being. These forces exist in him as tendencies and abilities – as instincts. On the other hand, as a natural, corporeal, sensuous objective being he is a suffering, conditioned and limited creature, like animals and plants. That is to say, the objects of his instincts exist outside him, as objects independent of him; yet these objects are objects that he needs – essential objects, indispensable to the manifestation and confirmation of his essential powers.*

In the *Grundrisse* Marx says his nature is a 'totality of needs and drives, which exerts a force upon me'. In *The German Ideology* he uses the formulation: 'their *needs*, consequently their nature'. We can see then, that from Marx's early writing to his later work, he conceives of human nature as composed of 'tendencies', 'drives', 'essential powers', and 'instincts' to act in order to satisfy 'needs' for external objectives. For Marx then, an explanation of human nature is an explanation of the needs of humans, together with the assertion that they will act to fulfil those needs. Norman Geras gives a schedule of the some of the needs which Marx says are characteristic of humans:...*for other human beings, for sexual relations, for food, water, clothing, shelter, rest and, more generally, for circumstances that are conducive to health rather than disease. There is another one... the need of people for a breadth and diversity of pursuit and hence of personal development, as Marx himself expresses these, 'all-round activity', 'all-round development of individuals', 'free development of individuals', 'the means of cultivating [one's] gifts in all directions', and so on.*

Marx says 'It is true that eating, drinking, and procreating, etc., are... genuine human functions. However, when abstracted from other aspects of human activity, and turned into final and exclusive ends, they are animal.'

PRODUCTIVE ACTIVITY, THE OBJECTS OF HUMANS AND ACTUALISATION

In several passages throughout his work, Marx shows how he believes humans to be essentially different from other animals. 'Men can be distinguished from animals by consciousness, by religion or anything else you like. They themselves begin to distinguish themselves from animals as soon as they begin to produce their means of subsistence, a step which is conditioned by their physical organisation.' In this passage from *The German Ideology*, Marx alludes to one difference: that humans produce their physical environments. But do not a few other animals also produce aspects of their environment as well? The previous year, Marx had already acknowledged:

It is true that animals also produce. They build nests and dwellings, like the bee, the beaver, the ant, etc. But they produce only their own immediate needs or those of their young; they produce only when immediate physical need compels them to do so, while man produces even when he is free from physical need and truly produces only in freedom from such need; they produce only themselves, while man reproduces the whole of nature; their products belong immediately to their physical bodies, while man freely confronts his own product. Animals produce only according to the standards and needs of the species to which they belong, while man is capable of producing according to the standards of every species and of applying to each object its inherent standard; hence, man also produces in accordance with the laws of beauty.

In the same work, Marx writes: The animal is immediately one with its life activity. It is not distinct from that activity; it is that activity. Man makes his life activity itself an object of his will and consciousness. He has conscious life activity. It is not a determination with which he directly merges. Conscious life activity directly distinguishes man from animal life activity. Only because of that is he a species-being. Or, rather, he is a conscious being – i.e., his own life is an object for him, only because he is a species-being. Only because of that is his activity free activity. Estranged labour reverses the relationship so that man, just because he is a conscious being, makes his life activity, his essential being, a mere means for his existence.

Also in the segment on Estranged Labour: Man is a species-being, not only because he practically and theoretically makes the species – both his own and those of other things – his object, but also – and this is simply another way of saying the same thing – because he looks upon himself as the present, living species, because he looks upon himself as a universal and therefore free being.

More than twenty years later, in *Capital*, he came to muse on a similar subject: A spider conducts operations that resemble those of a weaver, and a bee puts to shame many an architect in the construction of her cells. But what distinguishes the worst architect from the best of bees is this, that the architect raises his structure in imagination before he erects it in reality. At the end of every labour-process, we get a result that already existed in the imagination of the labourer at its commencement. He not only effects a change of form in the material on which he works, but he also realises a purpose of his own that gives the law to his *modus operandi*, and to which he must subordinate his will. And this subordination is no mere momentary act.

From these passages we can observe something of Marx's beliefs about humans. That they characteristically produce their environments, and that they would do so, even were they not under the burden of 'physical need'-indeed, they will produce the 'whole of [their] nature', and may even create 'in accordance with the laws of beauty'. Perhaps most importantly, though, their creativity, their production is *purposive* and *planned.* Humans, then, make plans for their future activity, and attempt to exercise their production (even lives) according to them. Perhaps most importantly, and most cryptically, Marx says that humans make both their 'life activity' and 'species' the 'object' of their will. They relate to their life activity, and are not simply identical with it. Michel Foucault's definition of biopolitics as the moment when "man begins to take itself as a conscious object of elaboration" may be compared to Marx's definition hereby exposed.

Life and the Species as the Objects of Humans

To say that A is the object of some subject B, means that B (specified as an agent) acts upon A in some respect. Thus if 'the proletariat smashes the state' then 'the state' is the object of the proletariat (the subject), in respect of smashing. It is similar to saying that A is the *objective* of B, though A could be a whole sphere of concern and not a closely defined aim. In this context, what does it mean to say that humans make their 'species' and their 'lives' their 'object'? It's worth noting that Marx's use of the word 'object' can imply that these are things which humans produces, or makes, just as they might produce a material object. If this inference is correct, then those things that Marx says about human production above, also apply to the production of human life, by humans. And simultaneously, 'As individuals express their life, so they are. What they are, therefore, coincides with their production, both with what they produce and with how they produce. The nature of individuals thus depends on the material conditions determining their production.'

To make one's life one's object is therefore to treat one's life as something that is under one's control. To raise in imagination plans for one's future and present, and to have a stake in being able to fulfil those plans. To be able to live a life of this character is to achieve 'self-activity' (actualisation), which Marx believes will only become possible after communism has replaced capitalism. 'Only at this stage does self-activity coincide with material life, which corresponds to the development of individuals into complete individuals and the casting-off of all natural limitations. The transformation of labour into self-activity corresponds to the transformation of the earlier limited intercourse into the intercourse of individuals as such'. What is involved in making one's species one's object is more complicated. In one sense, it emphasises the essentially social character of humans, and their need to live in a community of the species. In others, it seems to emphasise that we attempt to make our lives expressions of our species-essence; further that we have goals concerning what becomes of the species in general. The idea covers much of the same territory as 'making one's life one's object': it concerns self-consciousness, purposive activity, and so forth.

Humans as *Homo* Faber?

It is often said that Marx conceived of humans as *homo faber*, referring to Benjamin Franklin's definition of 'man as the tool-making animal'-that is, as 'man, the maker' , though he never used the term himself. Above, we indicated that one of Marx's central contentions about humans was that they were differentiated by the manner in which they produce and that thus, somehow, production was one of humans' essential activities. In this context, it is worth noting that Marx does not always address 'labour' or 'work' in such glowing terms. He says that communism 'does away with labour'. Furthermore, 'If it is desired to strike a mortal blow at private property, one must attack it not only as a material state of affairs, but also as activity, as labour. It is one of the greatest misapprehensions to speak of free, human, social labour, of labour without private property. "Labour" by its very nature is unfree, unhuman, unsocial activity, determined by private property and creating private property.' Under Capitalism '[t]he capitalist functions only as capital personified, capital as a person, just as the worker only functions as the personification of labour, which belongs to him as torment, as exertion'.

It is generally held that Marx's view was that productive activity is an essential human activity, and can be rewarding when pursued freely. Marx's use of the words 'work' and 'labour' in the section above may be unequivocally negative; but this was not always the case, and is most strongly found in his early writing. However, Marx was always clear that under capitalism, labour was something inhuman, and dehumanising. 'labour is external to the worker – i.e., does not belong to his essential being; that he, therefore, does not confirm himself in his work, but denies himself, feels miserable and not happy, does not develop free mental and physical energy, but mortifies his flesh and ruins his mind'. While under communism, 'In the individual expression of my life I would have directly created your expression of your life, and therefore in my individual activity I would have directly confirmed and realised my true nature, my human nature, my communal nature'.

HUMAN NATURE AND HISTORICAL MATERIALISM

Marx's theory of history attempts to describe the way in which humans change their environments and (in dialectical relation) their environments change them as well. That is: Not only do the objective conditions change in the act of reproduction, e.g. the village becomes a town, the wilderness a cleared field etc., but the producers change, too, in that they bring out new qualities in themselves, develop themselves in production, transform themselves, develop new powers and ideas, new modes of intercourse, new needs and new language.

Further Marx set out his 'materialist conception of history' in opposition to 'idealist' conceptions of history; that of Hegel, for instance. 'The first premise of all human history is, of course, the existence of living human individuals. Thus the first fact to be established is the physical organisation of these individuals and their consequent relation to the rest of nature.' Thus 'History does nothing, it "possesses no immense wealth", it "wages no battles". It is man, real, living man who does all that, who possesses and fights; "history" is not, as it were, a person apart, using man as a means to achieve its own aims; history is nothing but the activity of man pursuing his aims'. So we can see that, even before we begin to consider the precise character of human nature, 'real, living' humans, 'the activity of man pursuing his aims' is the very building block of Marx's theory of history. Humans act upon the world, changing it and themselves; and in doing so they 'make history'. But even beyond this, human nature plays two key roles. In the first place, it is part of the explanation for the growth of the productive forces, which Marx conceives of as the driving force of history.

Secondly, the particular needs and drives of humans explain the class antagonism which is generated under capitalism.

The Productive Forces

It has been held by several writers that it is Marx's conception of human nature which explains the 'primacy thesis' (Cohen, 1978) concerning the expansion of the productive forces, which according to Marx, is itself the fundamental driving force of history. If true, this would make his account of human nature perhaps the most fundamental aspect of his work. Geras writes, '*historical materialism itself, this whole distinctive approach to society that originates with Marx, rests squarely upon the idea of a human nature.* It highlights that specific nexus of universal needs and capacities which explains the human productive process and man's organised transformation of the material environment; which process and transformation it treats in turn as the basis both of the social order and of historical change.' G.A. Cohen (1988): 'The tendency's autonomy is just its independence of social structure, its rootedness in fundamental material facts of human nature and the human situation.' Allen Wood (2004): 'Historical progress consists fundamentally in the growth of people's abilities to shape and control the world about them. This is the most basic way in which they develop and express their human essence'.

In his article *Reconsidering Historical Materialism*, however, Cohen gives an argument to the effect that human nature cannot be the premise on which the plausibility of the expansion of the productive forces is grounded. 'Production in the historical anthropology is not identical with production in the theory of history. According to the anthropology, people flourish in the cultivation and exercise of their manifold powers, and are especially productive-which in *this* instance means creative-in the condition of freedom conferred by material plenty. But, in the production of interest to the theory of history, people produce not freely but because they have to, since nature does not otherwise supply their wants; and the development in history of the productive power of *man* (that is, of man as such, of man as a species) occurs at the expense of the creative capacity of the *men* who are agents and victims of that development.' The implication of this is that hence 'one might... imagine two kinds of creature, one whose essence it was to create and the other not, undergoing similarly toilsome histories because of similarly adverse circumstances. In one case, but not the other, the toil would be a self-alienating exercise of essential powers'.

Hence, 'historical materialism and Marxist philosophical anthropology are independent of, though also consistent with, each other'. The problem is this: it seems as though the motivation most people have for the work they do isn't the exercise of their creative capacity; on the contrary, labour is alienated by definition in the capitalist system based on salary, and people only do it because they have to.

They go to work not to express their human nature but to find theirs means of subsistence So in that case, why do the productive forces grow-does human nature have anything to do with it? The answer to this question is a difficult one, and a closer consideration of the arguments in the literature is necessary for a full answer than can be given in this article. However, it is worth bearing in mind that Cohen had previously been committed to the strict view that human nature were *sufficient* for the development of the productive forces-it could be that they are only one *necessary* constituent. It is also worth considering that by 1988, he appears to consider that the problem is resolved.

Some needs are far more important than others. In *The German Ideology* Marx writes that 'life involves before everything else eating and drinking, a habitation, clothing and many other things'. All those other aspects of human nature which he discusses are therefore subordinate to the priority given to these. Marx makes explicit his view that humans develop new needs to replace old: 'the satisfaction of the first need (the action of satisfying, and the instrument of satisfaction which has been acquired) leads to new needs'.

ETHICAL THOUGHT AND ALIENATION

Geras says of Marx's work that: 'Whatever else it is, theory and socio-historical explanation, and scientific as it may be, that work is a moral indictment resting on the conception of essential human needs, an ethical standpoint, in other words, in which a view of human nature is involved' (1983).

Alienation

Alienation, for Marx, is the estrangement of humans from aspects of their human nature. Since-as we have seen-human nature consists in a particular set of vital drives and tendencies, whose exercise constitutes flourishing, alienation is a condition wherein these drives and tendencies are stunted. For essential powers, alienation substitutes disempowerment; for making one's own life one's object, one's life becoming an object of capital. Marx believes that alienation will be a feature of all society before communism. The opposite of, alienation is 'actualisation' or 'self-activity'-the activity of the self, controlled by and for the self.

Gerald Cohen's Criticism

One important criticism of Marx's 'philosophical anthropology' (i.e. his conception of humans) is offered by Gerald Cohen, the leader of "Analytical Marxism", in *Reconsidering Historical Materialism*. Cohen claims: 'Marxist philosophical anthropology is one sided. Its conception of human nature and human good overlooks the need for self identity than which nothing is more essentially human.' The consequence of this is held to be that 'Marx and his followers have underestimated the importance of phenomena, such as religion and nationalism, which satisfy the need for self identity.. Cohen describes what he sees as the origins of Marx's alleged neglect: 'In his anti-Hegelian, Feuerbachian affirmation of the radical objectivity of matter, Marx focused on the relationship of the subject to an object which is in no way subject, and, as time went on, he came to neglect the subject's relationship to itself, and that aspect of the subject's relationship to others which is a mediated (that is, indirect), form of relationship to itself'.

Consequently, Cohen believes, 'A person does need to develop and ENJOY his POWERS, he needs to gain and gain until he is the best and no one else can overpower him, people are BAD" He must, as Hegel saw, find something outside himself which he did not create, and to which something inside himself corresponds, because of the social process that created him'. Cohen believes that people are driven, typically, not to create identity, but to preserve that which they have in virtue, for example, of 'nationality, or race, or religion, or some slice or amalgam thereof'. Cohen does not claim that 'Marx denied that there is a need for self definition, but [instead claims that] he failed to give the truth due emphasis'. Nor does Cohen say that the sort of self understanding that can be found through religion etc. is accurate. Of nationalism, he says 'identifications [can] take benign, harmless, and catastrophically malignant forms' and does not believe 'that the state is a good medium for the embodiment of nationality'.

MARXIST HUMANISM

Marxist humanism is a branch of Marxism that primarily focuses on Marx's earlier writings, especially the *Economic and Philosophical Manuscripts of 1844* in which Marx espoused his theory of alienation, as opposed to his later works, which are considered to be concerned more with his structural conception of capitalist society. The Praxis School, which called for radical social change in Josip Broz Tito's Yugoslavia in the 1960s, was one such Marxist humanist movement.

Marxist humanism was opposed by the "antihumanism" of Marxist philosopher Louis Althusser, who described it as a revisionist movement.

The Theory of "Marxist Humanism"

The term "Marxist humanism" has as its foundation Marx's conception of the "alienation of the labourer" as he advanced it in his *Economic and Philosophic Manuscripts of 1844* — an alienation that is born of a capitalist system in which the worker no longer functions as (what Marx termed) a free being involved with free and associated labour. And although many scholars consider late Marx less of a humanist than the Marx who wrote pre-*Das Kapital* , as his later works are rather bereft of references to this alienation, others {for example David McLellan, Robert C. Tucker, George Brenkert } argue that the notion of alienation remains a part of Marx's philosophy. Theodor Shanin) and Raya Dunayevskaya go further, asserting that not only is alienation present in the late Marx, but that there is no split between the young Marx and mature Marx.

Criticism

The most potent criticism of Marxist Humanism has come from within the Marxist movement. Louis Althusser, the French

Structuralist Marxist, criticises Marxist Humanists for not recognising the dichotomy between 'Young Marx' and 'Mature Marx'. Althusser believes Marx's thought to be marked by a radical "epistemological break". For Althusser, the humanism of Marx's early writings-influenced by Hegel and Feuerbach-is fundamentally incongruous with the "scientific", structure-concerned theory found in Marx's mature works such as *Das Kapital*. Of the Marxist Humanist's reliance on the 1844 *Economic and Philosophic Manuscripts* Althusser writes, "We do not publish our own drafts, that is, our own mistakes, but we do sometimes publish other people's". The Humanists contend that 'Marxism' developed lopsidedly because Marx's early works were unknown until after the orthodox ideas were in vogue — the Manuscripts of 1844 were published only in 1932 — and to understand his latter works properly it is necessary to understand Marx's philosophical foundations. Althusser, however, does not defend orthodox Marxism's economic reductionism and determinism; instead, he develops his own theories regarding ideological hegemony and conditioning within class societies, through the concept of Ideological State Apparatuses (ISA) and interpellation which constitutes the subject.

MARXIST PHILOSOPHY OF NATURE

There is no specific "Marxist philosophy of nature", as Karl Marx didn't conceive of Nature as separate from Society. As the young Marx exposed in the *Economic and Philosophical Manuscripts of 1844*, labour transforms Nature which becomes the "inorganic body" of Man. In the same way, Marx's conception of "human nature" (*Gattungswesen*) is problematic, since he opposed himself to the traditional conception of an eternal human nature which remained the same in all places and times. Later, Friedrich Engels wrote the *Dialectics of Nature* (1883), in opposition to German *Naturphilosophie*. Marx and Engels' thought was then codified into "dialectical materialism", which is what is usually referred to when speaking of a "Marxist philosophy of nature". Such a doctrine was rejected by several Marxist philosophers, starting by Georg Lukács and Walter Benjamin. The basic Marxist idea is that everything can be explained by one thing — Matter. Matter is the total explanation for space, nature, man, psychic consciousness, human intelligence and every other aspect of existence. Marxism then assigns the task of knowing all truth to science. If science can get to know everything about matter, then it can get to know about everything. Conclusively, matter is accepted as the beginning and ending of all reality. Taking the concept of matter, Marxism then sets forth to answer three questions: What is the origin of energy or motion in nature? What causes galaxies, solar system, planets, animals and all kingdoms of nature to constantly increase their numerical quantity? What is the origin of life, the origin of species and the origin of consciousness and mind? Marx and Engels answer all of these questions with three laws. The law of opposites, the law of negation and the law of transformation.

Law of Opposites

Marx and Engels started with the observation that everything in existence is a combination or unity of opposites. For example, electricity is characterized by a positive and negative charge and atoms consist of protons and electrons which are unified but are ultimately contradictory forces. Even humans through introspection find that they are a unity of opposite qualities. Masculinity and femininity, selfishness and altruism, humbleness and pride, etc. The Marxist conclusion being that everything "contains two mutually incompatible and exclusive but nevertheless equally essential and indispensable parts or aspects."[1] The basic concept being that this unity of opposites in nature is the thing that makes each entity auto-dynamic and provides this constant motivation for movement and change. This idea was borrowed from Georg Wilhelm Hegel who said: "Contradiction in nature is the root of all motion and of all life."

Law of Negation

This law was created to account for the tendency in nature to constantly increase the numerical quantity of all things. Marx and Engels decided that each entity tends to negate itself in order to reproduce itself in higher quantity. Engels often cited the case of the barley seed which, in its natural state, germinates and out of its own death or negation produces a plant. The plant in turn grows to maturity and is itself negated after bearing many barley seeds. Thus, all nature is constantly expanding through dying. The elements of opposition which produce conflict in each thing and give it motion also tend to negate the thing itself; but out of this dynamic process of dying the energy is released to expand and produce many more entities of the same kind.[3]

Law of Transformation

This law states that a continuous quantitive development by a particular class often results in a "leap" in nature whereby a completely new form or entity is produced. This theory draws many parallels to the theory of Evolution. The Marxist philosophers concluded that matter is not only auto-dynamic and inclined to increase itself numerically, but through quantitative accumulations it is also inherently capable of "leaps" to new forms and levels of reality. Marx and Engels saw these laws as the discovery of the greatest mystery of all: What is life?

The Origin of Life

On the basis of these principles the Marxist Philosophers decided that the phenomenon of life was the product of one of these leaps. Engels stated that the complex chemical structure of matter evolved until albuminous substance was formed, and from this substance life emerged. He insisted that just as you cannot have matter without motion, so also you cannot have albumin without life. It is an inherent characteristic of albumin, a higher form of motion in nature. He also suggested that as soon as life emerged it would gradually grow in complexity. Consistent with evolutionary theories of punctuated equilibrium, Marxists believe that new forms in nature are not the result of gradual change but that quantitative multiplication gradually builds up momentum for a "leap" in nature which produces a change or a new species. They believe that incidental to one of these leaps, the phenomenon of consciousness emerged. The creature became aware of the forces which were playing on it. Then at an even higher level another form of life appeared with the capacity to work with these impressions and to arrange them in associations. Thus mind evolved as an intelligent, self-knowing, self-determining quality in matter. However, matter is primary and mind is secondary. Therefore there can be no soul and no God. They believe that everything in existence came as a result of objective tendencies (i.e. movement, negation, etc.) inherent in nature. There is no law, or design, or God. Only matter and force in nature. As for man, he is an accident like all other forms of life except he had the good fortune to possess the highest intelligence in existence. This is said to make man the real god of himself and the universe.

Opposition Views

Since the creation of the ideology of Marxism it has been scrutinized greatly. Opponents of dialectical materialism point out a number of fallacies. They point out that the Law of Opposites is intended to explain the origin of motion, but two contradictory elements would never come together in the first place unless they already had energy in themselves. Contradictory forces in nature are found to have energy independent of each other, bringing them together simply unifies motion or energy already in existence. Therefore, opponents point out that the Law of Opposites does not explain motion but presupposes it. The Law of Negation is critiqued as only describing a process of nature. Not only that, but the law doesn't take into account that its negation may be unrelated to its reproduction, and that it may reproduce many times or not at all before it negates. Opposition also point to the Law of Transformation as merely describing a process in nature without accounting for it. They claim that the possibility of a series of accidents leading to something as complex as the eye, circulatory system or other parts of the body and then making them work in perfect unison are extremely low. Such an argument bears similarities to irreducible complexity, a common argument against evolution.

4

Nature and Society

Marx comprised in his materialistic investigation of society all the phenomena of a comprehensive field of experience which until then had been dealt with by a number of altogether different, old and new, sciences. On the one hand he recognized no "higher" spheres of a so-called "spiritual" life which would be exempted from the crude material necessities of the historical and social spheres. All juridical, political, religious, philosophical and artistic conceptions, the whole of the so-called "consciousness" of man and all its philosophical disguises as, for example, the Hegelian terms of an "objektiver" and "absoluter Geist," the Kantian concepts of "Gattungsvernunft," and "Bewusstsein überhaupt," the philosophical "idea" generally, and all other, even the most "universal" categories of thought exist only as given forms of a "*social consciousness*," temporary products of a continuous development, attributes of a definite historical epoch and of a definite economic order of society.

To all "legal conditions and forms of the State" there applies the materialistic principle that they can neither be understood (as the exponents of dogmatic jurisprudence and political science believe) "out of themselves" nor (as the philosophers had believed) "out of the so-called general development of the human mind," but are rooted in the material conditions of the present-day bourgeois society. To all forms of social consciousness there applies the twofold antithesis formulated by Marx in contrast both to the philosophical idealism of Kant, Fichte and Hegel, and to the naturalistic materialism of Feuerbach: "It is not the consciousness of men that determines their existence but, on the contrary, their *social existence* which determines their consciousness."

On the other hand, Marx comprised in his materialistic formula also the natural foundation of all historical and social phenomena and, for this purpose, conceived and represented even nature itself in the terms of a strictly historical and social science as "Industry," "Economy," or "Material Production." In spite of a genuine recognition of the "priority of external nature" he does not derive the historical development of society from any kind of extra-historical and extra-social natural factors like climate, race, struggle for existence, man's physical and mental powers, etc., but from a "nature" which has itself been already "modified" by an historical and social process or, more distinctly, from the historically and socially conditioned developments of material production. The materialist philosopher Plechanov, in supporting his contrary opinion, reminds us, that "Hegel had already noted in his *Philosophy of History* the important part played by the geographical foundations of the world history." He did not see that the scientific advances made by Marx's historical and social materialism over the idealism of Hegel and the materialism of Feuerbach consists just in this difference that he conceived of "matter" itself in historical terms, while all his philosophical predecessors, both the idealistic and the materialistic brand had conceived of "matter" as a dumb, dead or, at the utmost, biologically animated nature only.

While according to Hegel "physical nature, indeed, exerts a direct effect upon world history," Marx started from an altogether different viewpoint from the outset. Physical nature according to him, does not directly enter into history. It does so by indirection, i.e., as a process of material production which goes on not only between man and nature, but at the same time between man and men. Or, to use a phraseology which will be clear even to the philosophers, in the strictly social research of Marxian materialism that "pure" nature which is presupposed to all human activity (the economic *natura naturans*) is replaced everywhere by a "nature" mediated and modified through human social activity, and thus at the same time capable of a further change and modification by our own present and future activity, i.e., by nature as *material production* (or the economic *natura naturata*).

Being "social," nature has a specifically historical character varying in the different epochs. As an historical and social nature it has above all, a distinct class character. For example, as emphasized by Marx in his controversy with Feuerbach, that cherry tree before the philosopher's window, whose ancestors were "artificially" transplanted to Europe a few hundred years ago, is thereby for the modern European no nature-given growth; just as, on the same grounds, the potato is no "nature-given" food for the modern European poor, or, at most, only in the same sense as the adulterated bread and the "sophisticated" wine sold in the back streets are "nature-given" products of the modern capitalist mode of production. The den of the modern poor is even less than the lair of the wild beast a "nature-given" shelter in which he can move at ease like the fish in the water. It is not a house where he can feel at home, but it is the house of his landlord who will evict him when he cannot afford to pay his rent. "My house is my castle" originating from the world of simple commodity production, holds good for the slum barracks of our big cities no more than it did for the cots of the English farm-labourers of 1860, as described in *Capital*. Modern "hunger," which satisfies itself with cooked meat, eaten with knife and fork, is quite another thing than that hunger which "swallowed raw meat with the aid of hand, nail and tooth." So do those "normal" periods of hunger natural to primitive hordes, that have been artificially reintroduced in modern capitalist society for those sections of the unemployed who, for some reason or another, have been taken off the dole, represent a vastly different thing from the hunger, be it ever so great, that may occasionally, by the accident of a temporary stoppage of their regular food supplies, cause a "thrilling" sensation to the idle rich.

None of those things, in the definite forms in which they appear in present bourgeois society or for that matter in any earlier or later epochs, comes from "nature" alone. They depend upon the existing historical conditions of material production and can be changed with the change of those conditions. This happens through an historical development, which may take a shorter or longer time, but which is nowhere stopped by any absolute barrier, through an objective process which is at the same time a struggle between social classes.

This viewpoint of a strictly *social*, that is of an *historical* and *practical* science dominated from the very beginning the whole novel system of concepts which Marx and Engels built up in their controversy with the then existing idealistic and materialistic currents of thought. The existence of physical man, the external world in which he moves, and the natural objective development of those natural conditions in large periods of "cosmological time," independent of that altogether different development of the social forms which is accomplished by man's action in "historical time," all these "real presuppositions" of history and society are, of course, real presuppositions also for the materialistic research of Marx. They do not, however, appear as theoretical premises within the system of the new social science which starts from its own materialistic principles defined in historical and social terms.

This is no way contradicted but, on the contrary, even more clearly demonstrated by the terms of so-called "*naturally grown forms of society*" and of so-called "*social laws of nature*" which are continually used by Marx in the presentation of his theory. The concept of "*natural growth*" as applied to historical forms, has with Marx an altogether different meaning than it had with the historians, poets, and philosophers of the "Romanticist School" who in a conscious opposition to the preceding period of Enlightenment and Revolution glorified everything "naturally grown." Marx, on the contrary, used the term in a negative sense for the description of such conditions, relations, connections which have not as yet been subjected to a conscious human action. In this sense Marx speaks in his Critique of the *German Ideology* and twenty years later, in *Capital*, of the "nature-grown" ("naturwüchsige") forms of division of labour, of a worldwide historical connection between individuals, of the State, of legal conditions, of language, and of such apparently immutable differences as the variations of race. In all these cases the "naturwüchsige" form of a social relation is in contrast to those other forms which this relation assumes in the course of social development when it is either consciously maintained and further worked out, or changed to a greater or lesser extent by a conscious human action. The "naturwüchsige" forms are thus described as social forms which have arisen historically just as all other, more or less consciously created forms and are therefore capable of a further change both in the present and the future. Thus they are not eternal forms of all social life but can be overthrown by the united individuals in a deliberate action, which will finally strip them of their present crude and oppressive "nature-grown" character. One sees at first glance the positive bearing of this thought not only on the theoretical extension of the realm of social knowledge but also on the practical socialistic and communistic tendencies which are necessarily bound up with this knowledge.

The same holds good for the other apparently nature-bound term of the new Marxian science, which we have already discussed when dealing with the economic law of value, i.e., the so-called "*social laws of nature*." Here again we have to deal with a term which is at first defined in a negative manner only. The economic laws prevailing in the capitalistic mode of production do not have within the new materialistic science of society that positive and final meaning which the real "laws of nature" have for the physicist and which, according to their first discoverers and inventors, pertained also to those "natural" laws which would in future govern the new "civil" mode of existence emerging from the artificial fetters of mediaeval feudalism. They are even less what Marx and Engels in their earlier, philosophical, period called a "law of the mind" as opposed to a "mere law of nature" and what recurs in their later writings when they speak of a "leap from the realm of necessity into the realm of freedom" and of the "true realm of freedom blossoming out of the realm of necessity in the fully developed Communist Society of the future."

However, just from the negative definition that the so-called "laws of nature" of the bourgeois economists are, in fact, not laws of nature at all, there derives the positive significance which the term of the "social" laws of nature assumes in the revolutionary science of Marx. The fact that the general conditions of bourgeois society which had been proclaimed as laws by the bourgeois economists, are restricted to a definite historical epoch, implies that in the further development of society all those apparent laws can be abrogated through the conscious social act of the class which is at present oppressed by them, to be replaced by another, a willed and planned form of the social activities of man.

Thus neither of the two Marxian terms conforms with the perpetuation of the so-called economic laws asserted by the classical economists; even less with that further extension of the realm of "natural growth in society" which had been the dream of the early counter-revolutionary theorists in France and of the German and English romanticists. Marx, on the contrary, applies both terms for the purpose of extending the realm of history and society, i.e., of a conscious social action as against the so-called eternal necessities of an altogether inaccessible "realm of nature."

Far behind the "immutable laws" invented and maintained by the bourgeois economists for the preservation of an order of production allegedly "natural" and "rational," but in fact ever more artificial, more arbitrary, and ever more dependent on force, and at the same time more hampering to the further development of society and more destructive of human life, stand those real necessities of nature which condition the whole life of man and which are also recognized by the Marxists as unchangeable facts and as natural presuppositions of all social development. Even this recognition applies to a given time only. There is, from the historical and social principle of Marxian science, no absolute and predetermined limit beyond which an apparently "naturwüchsige" foundation of all social life might not in future be discovered to be no more than an historical and historically changeable form, and thus a form which can be modified and overthrown by a conscious action. "Even the naturally-grown variations of the human species such as differences of race, etc., can and must be abolished in the historical process."

As with all other innovations embodied in the new materialistic theory, Marx's methodical extension of society at the expense of nature is proved mainly on the field of economic science. The Marxian critique of the fetish character of the commodity and of all other economic categories refutes once and for all those mystical ideas by which the earlier economists had attributed economic phenomena to an immediate physical cause, be it some external force of nature, or the physical constitution of man or, finally, his so-called "innate" psychological qualities. There is, above all, no such thing as an immediate "natural basis of the surplus value." The only significance which can be claimed for physical conditions in the genesis of the socio-historical phenomenon of the exploitation of propertyless wage-labourers by property-owning capitalists, is that of a natural limit or barrier fixing the points at which the labour-time necessary for the maintenance and reproduction of the labourer ceases and thus "labour for others can begin." "*In proportion as industry advances, those natural limits recede.*"

The same applies to the so-called "natural basis of the State" which is asserted by a whole school of modern bourgeois sociologists. The political phenomenon of the State results, in fact, as little from unchangeable physical conditions as the economic phenomenon of the surplus value upon which it depends as a secondary and derived form. Just as things useful for human needs and produced by human labour are "commodities," and gold and silver are "money," under definite social conditions only and not by any inherent physical qualities, so is the physically weaker individual or race the slave of the physically stronger not by any eternal necessity but through the accident of temporary circumstances. By a definite historical process the class which under the social conditions prevailing in the present epoch produces all social wealth, has been separated from the material means of production and is now ruled and exploited by the class which through the same historical process has monopolized for itself the means of social production as "capital." The apparently "naturalistic" theory which assigns such existing social and political facts to the Command of Nature is but a secularized form of those older theories which derived the same facts from the Command of God or, for that matter, from such intermediate agencies as the philosophical unfolding of an eternal Idea, Reason, or Humanity itself.

MARXISM AND SOCIOLOGY

What is the relationship between Marxism and modern sociological teaching? If we think of the Sociology begun by Comte and in fact first named by him, we shall not find any affinity or link between it and Marxism. Marx and Engels, with all their keen desire to extend and enhance the knowledge of society, paid no attention to either the name or contents of that ostensibly new approach to the social studies. Nor were they impressed by the gains the Comtist school made among the progressive intelligentsia of their time. It appears from their correspondence that Marx at one time in the sixties, with his main attention concentrated on the final manuscript of his principal work, picked up from the shelves of the British Museum and read through Comte's *Cours de philosophie positive* of 1830-42, "because the English and French make such a fuss about the fellow." Yet there is even more evidence in the text of *Capital* itself that this reading left no mark in his theoretical work. On still another occasion, in writing to an otherwise highly esteemed Comtist, Marx made it perfectly clear that he was "thoroughly opposed to Comtism as a politician" and had "a very poor opinion of it as a man of science."

Marx's attitude is theoretically and historically well founded. The science of socialism as formulated by Marx, owed nothing to this "sociology" of the 19th and 20th centuries which originated with Comte and was propagated by Mill and Spencer. It would be more correct to say that since the days when young Auguste Comte, hitherto the most enthusiastic disciple of the Utopian socialist Saint-Simon, suddenly broke with his "great master" to work out his own pedantic system of a "positivistic" sociology from a few of the formidable mass of ideas continuously poured forth by that excessively productive mind, bourgeois social thought has been a reaction against the theory and thus also against the practice of modern socialism. Up to the present day "sociologists" have endeavoured to submit another way of answering the embarrassing questions first raised by the rising proletarian movement. From this standpoint only is it possible to understand the essential unity of the manifold theoretical and practical tendencies which during the last hundred years have found their expression under the common denomination of Sociology.

Marxism, then, stands in a much more original and direct relationship to those new problems which modern historic development has put on the agenda of present-day society, than the whole of the so-called "sociology" of Comte, Spencer, and their followers. Bourgeois sociologists refer to the revolutionary socialist science of the proletariat as an "unscientific mixture of theory and politics." Socialists, on the other hand, dismiss the whole bourgeois sociology as mere "ideology." There is, however, quite a different relation between the Marxian theory and another body of social thought which descended from an earlier time when the name of "sociology" had not yet been invented, but "society" had already been discovered and recognized along with physical nature as an equally material and important realm of human knowledge and human action.

As Marx himself records in 1859, he embarked upon his new materialistic theory of society, sixteen years before, because of certain grave doubts which had recently assailed his belief in the idealistic philosophy of Hegel. He had at that time just gone through the new and stimulating experiences of his first short period of political activity. As an editor of the *Rheinische Zeitung* (1842-43) he had for the first time found himself called upon to take part in the discussion of "so-called material interests." He had thus been led to occupy himself with "economic questions." On the other hand, he had become aware of the decisive importance which a closer study of the ideas of "French socialism and communism" was bound to have for the furtherance of revolutionary developments in Germany. While the combined effect of all these new impulses had already considerably undermined his faith in the old Hegelian formulae, the real nature of that Prussian State which had been so sublimely exalted by Hegel was finally revealed to him by a most conclusive personal experience. He was compelled to resign from the staff of the *Rheinische Zeitung* which under his leadership within less than a year had become the most conspicuous organ of the progressive movement in pre-revolutionary Germany. Nor was his withdrawal sufficient, as had been hoped by the frightened managers, to arrest the judgment of suppression pronounced against the *Rheinische Zeitung* by an equally frightened government.

Thus confronted with an increasing number of striking discrepancies between his philosophical creed and his actual experiences, Marx turned once more to Hegel. A detailed "critical revision" of Hegel's *Philosophy of Law,* on which he concentrated for the next five months, led him to the conclusion that legal relations as well as forms of State cannot be understood out of themselves nor out of the so-called general development of the human mind but, on the contrary, are rooted in the material conditions of life, the aggregate of which Hegel, following the precedent of the English and French of the 18th century, grouped together under the name of "civil society," and that the anatomy of civil society is to be sought for in Political Economy.

We see here the decisive significance which the concept of "civil society" had gained for the young Marx who was then just passing from Hegelian idealism to his later materialistic theory. While still formally basing his criticism of Hegel's glorification of the State on the realistic statements concerning the nature of civil society embodied in the same Hegelian work, Marx now definitely abandoned Hegel and all his idealistic philosophy. Instead, he associated himself with those great enquirers into the social nature of man who, in the preceding centuries, had first set up the new idea of Civil Society as a revolutionary slogan, and had even unearthed, in the new science of Political Economy, the material foundations of that new and "civilized" form of society.

Hegel, indeed, had not derived the deep realistic knowledge which, under the heading of *Civil Society,* stands out in such sharp relief against the rest of his book from an independent study of the as yet extremely backward conditions of German society. He took both the name and contents of his "civil society" ready-made from the French and English social philosophers, politicians, and economists. Behind Hegel, as Marx said, stood the "English and French of the 18th century" with their new discoveries of the structure and movement of society who, in their turn, reflected the real historical development which culminated in the Industrial Revolution in England after the middle of the 18th century and in the great French Revolution of 1789-1815.

Marx, then, in developing his new socialist and proletarian science, took his cue from that early study of society which, although first communicated to him by Hegel, had really been born of the revolutionary epoch of the bourgeoisie. This appears most strikingly in his complete adoption of the scientific results of classical Political Economy as developed by Petty and Boisguillebert, Quesnay, Smith, and Ricardo, and taken from them by Marx's immediate predecessors, the German idealist philosophers Kant, Fichte, and Hegel. There is, so far, not much difference between Marx's reference to Political Economy as an "anatomy of civil society," and Hegel's philosophical attempt to base the State on Civil Society, and Civil Society on the "System of Needs" as explored by the new science of "Political Economy."

He had even more expressly, in an earlier study, described the "system of needs" as the "first form of government," underlying such higher developed forms as the State and the law. Yet there is this tremendous difference from the outset that Hegel had all along used the realistic knowledge borrowed from the classical economists only for the purpose of enhancing the importance of his ultimately idealistic system, while Marx made Political Economy the pivot of a wholly materialistic theory of society.

The very pungency with which Marx in his later writings repeatedly pointed out that post-classical bourgeois economy (the so-called "vulgar" economy) had not advanced beyond Ricardo in any important points, and scornfully dismissed the new socio-scientific synthesis of Comte's "Positivism" for the infinitely greater achievement of Hegel, shows once more the lasting importance of that early phase of economic and social thought for the theory of Marx.

This is true even though he far transcended those older theories in asserting the new development of society and the new needs and aims of the proletariat, now arising as an independent class. The proletariat guided by Marxian theory is therefore not only, as Friedrich Engels put it, "the inheritor of German classical philosophy." It is also the inheritor of classical bourgeois economics and social research. As such, it has transformed the traditional classical theory in accordance with the intervening changes in historical conditions.

Marx no longer regards bourgeois society from the standpoint of its first phase of development and its opposition to the feudal structure of mediaeval society. He is not interested only in the static laws of its existence. He treats bourgeois society in all its aspects as a transitory historical phenomenon. He explores the whole process of its genesis, and the tendencies contained therein which, in their further development, will lead to its revolutionary overthrow. He finds these tendencies twofold: *objective* in the economic basis of bourgeois society, *subjective* in the new division of social classes arising out of this same economic basis and not out of politics, law, ethics, etc. Thus "civil society," which until then had constituted a homogeneous whole, opposed only to feudalism, is now torn into two opposed "parties."

The assumed "civil society" is in reality "bourgeois society," namely, a society based on the cleavage of classes, in which the bourgeois class controls other classes economically and therefore politically and culturally. So at last "la classe la plus laborieuse et la plus misérable" enters the widened horizon of social science.

Marxian theory recognizes the class war of the oppressed and exploited wage labourers to be a war for the abolition of present-day society. As a materialistic science of the contemporary development of bourgeois society, Marxian theory is at the same time a practical guide for the proletariat in its struggle to realize proletarian society. The later artificial detachment of sociology as a special branch of learning, which dates its scientific origin from Comte, and at its best allows the great original thinkers who did the real productive work in this field to stand as its "forerunners," represents nothing more than an escape from the practical, and therefore also theoretical, tasks of the present historical epoch. Marx's new socialist and proletarian science which, in a changed historical situation, further developed the revolutionary theory of the classical founders of the doctrine of society, is the genuine social science of our time.

THE MATERIALISTIC SCHEME OF SOCIETY

As early as 1843 it had become clear to Marx that Political Economy was the keystone to all social science. In the following years as a political exile in Paris and Brussels and during a first visit to London and Manchester from July to August 1845, he completed the first important portion of that Herculean task to which after a short interruption in 1848-50, he was to devote his energies throughout his life. This was not merely an investigation of particular economic topics resulting in a solution of particular economic problems. It was the initiation of a hitherto mainly politically interested philosopher into the newly discovered field of a really "materialistic" science. In the retrospective account given in the *Preface* to his *Critique of Political Economy*, 1859, he sums up the general result:

In the social production of their means of existence human beings enter into definite and necessary relations which are independent of their will — production-relations which correspond to a definite stage in the development of their material forces of production.

The aggregate of these production-relations constitutes the economic structure of society, the real basis on which a juridical and political superstructure arises, and to which definite forms of social consciousness correspond. The mode of production of the material life conditions the whole process of the social, political, and intellectual life. It is not men's consciousness that determines their existence, but their social existence that determines their consciousness.

At a certain stage of their development the material productive forces of society come into contradiction with the existing production-relations, or what is only a legal expression for them with the property-relations within which they hitherto moved. From being forms of development, those relations turn into fetters upon the forces of production. Then a period of social revolution sets in. With the change in the economic foundation, the whole of the vast superstructure is more or less rapidly overturned.

In considering such revolutionary processes one must always distinguish between the economic conditions of production whose material changes can be determined with the precision of natural science, and the legal, political, religious, artistic, or philosophical, in short, ideological forms in which men become conscious of this conflict and fight it out. As one cannot judge an individual by what he thinks of himself, just as little can he judge such a revolutionary epoch by its own consciousness; he must, on the contrary, explain that consciousness by the contradictions of its material life, by the existing conflict between the social forces of production and the production-relations.

A formation of society never perishes until all the forces of production for which it is wide enough have been developed; new and higher production-relations never come into being until the material conditions for their existence have ripened within the womb of the old society itself. Therefore mankind always sets itself such tasks only as it can solve; for looking closer, we shall always find that the task itself arises only when the material conditions for its solution are already existent or, at least, in process of formation.

In broad outline the Asiatic, the Antique, the Feudal, and the modern Bourgeois modes of production can be designated as epochs in progress of the economic formation of society. The bourgeois production-relations are the final antagonistic form of the social production-process — antagonistic not in the sense of individual antagonism, but as growing out of the social conditions determining the life of the individuals. The forces of production developing within the womb of bourgeois society create at the same time the material conditions for the solution of that antagonism. That is why with that formation of society the prehistory of human society comes to an end.

The foregoing propositions which Marx, after fifteen years of labours presented as the carefully tested principles of his materialistic research of society, give a clear insight into the connection established by the materialistic conception of history between the social conditions of life, their historical development, and their practical overthrow.

The connection appears at first as a *static connection* linking together the different strata lying, as it were, above each other in a given socio-economico formation. That connection is alternately described as a similarity of "structure," a relation of "basis" and "superstructure," or a "correspondence" between those forms of social organization which directly spring from the process of material production and such other phenomena as arise from various other social, political and intellectual activities in any particular historical period.

This apparently static connection is, however, simply a particular case of the *dynamic connection* through which all sections and cross-sections of social life are bound together in their development. In the various phases of the origin, rise, and fall of a given socio-economic formation and its revolutionary replacement by the new and higher production-relations of a further developed social formation, that particular connection between all social conditions which, at first, from a static approach, appeared as a "consensus" undergoes a change of form. From a harmonious "consensus" it is at a certain point transformed into a "dissensus." (To use the Hegelian formula: the "correspondence" already contains within itself the "contradiction" through whose further development the production-relations and, even more, the legal relations, forms of State, and ideologies based upon them, in due course are turned from forms of development of the forces of production into fetters restraining the further development of such forces of production.)

But this dynamic connection is not yet the final and definite form of the materialistic connection which forms the subject matter of the Marxian research. With all its apparent comprehensiveness the Marxian formula hitherto discussed in this chapter does not aim at a complete description of the materialistic principle. It was inserted into the Preface of his main theoretical work for the definite purpose of disclosing to his readers the theoretical principles underlying his investigation of Political Economy as the "anatomy of bourgeois society." The historical development of society is, accordingly, represented here mainly as an objective process.

History is explained as an objective development of the material forces of production at first corresponding to and then contradicting the existing production-relations, which thus from being forms of development are turned into fetters. The historical "subject" of that development is not mentioned in the formula. The production-relations of all hitherto existing economic forms of society are shown to be "antagonistic" forms of the social process of production, but the closer definition of this social antagonism as a class opposition and a class war is not given.

The violent overthrow of the existing order of society by the oppressed class appears in the formula as an "epoch of social revolution" in which the superstructure of society is transformed with the change taking place in the economic foundation. And in striking contrast to the severe criticism previously raised by Marx and Engels against such a metaphysical language, we read here that "mankind" sets itself certain tasks, and even the "epoch of transformation" itself possesses a consciousness. The aim of the whole development is not concretely defined as a transition to socialist and communist society, but is only implied in the description of present bourgeois society as being the conclusion of the "prehistory of human society."

The full sense of the materialist investigation of society results from the statements by which Marx and Engels at other times and in other contexts opposed their materialistic principle to the various conflicting opinions with which they had to deal. The objective formula in the Preface to the *Critique of Political Economy:* The history of society is the history of the material production and of the contradictions between the material forces of production and the production-relations which arise and are solved in the course of development is supplemented by the subjective formula in the *Communist Manifesto:* The history of all hitherto existing society is a history of class struggles.

The subjective formula clarifies the objective formula. It calls by its proper name the class which brings about the objective development by a practical action. The same production-relations which fetter the forces of production (at the present stage, Capital and Wage Labour), are also the bonds of the labouring masses. The oppressed workers who in the revolutionary class struggle burst their own fetters, at the same time liberate production. The acting subject of history at the present stage is the proletariat.

Only by taking into account this *practical connection* can the theoretical statements of the materialistic investigation of society be put to their fullest use. The *theoretical fact* that according to the materialistic principle of Marx legal conditions and forms of State no longer form an independent subject matter which is to be understood by virtue of its inherent qualities or derived from a higher immaterial principle but, on the contrary, are rooted in the material conditions of existing bourgeois society, coincides with the *practical fact* that in modern bourgeois society, after the abolition of all the privileges of the superior orders of the feudal society, the inequalities destroyed in the political and legal sphere are preserved in the opposition of social classes arising from the material conditions of life.

By a radical elucidation of this state of affairs Marx breaks through the ideological confusion with which the panegyrists of the modern democratic State distract the attention of the proletariat from its real position, as an economically oppressed and exploited class, and from the measures to be taken for a practical change of that basic condition. Furthermore, the materialistic exposure of the illusions of the State and the law, and of all other high-pitched ideologies of modern bourgeois society, serves as a caution for the revolutionary proletarian class to keep itself free, as far as possible, from those new illusions, with which, in earlier epochs, revolutionary parties concealed from themselves the real content of the conflicts they were engaged in.

For this reason Marx instilled into the minds of the workers the materialistic lesson that their emancipation from the particular form of oppression and exploitation which they suffer in the present epoch cannot result from any change of the existing political, legal, and cultural conditions, but must be brought about by themselves through a social revolution penetrating to the economic basis of existing bourgeois society.

5

Social Class and Class Structure

For Marx, the analysis of social class, class structures and changes in those structures are key to understanding capitalism and other social systems or modes of production. In the *Communist Manifesto* Marx and Engels comment that the history of all hitherto existing society is the history of class struggles. Analysis of class divisions and struggles is especially important in developing an understanding of the nature of capitalism.

For Marx, classes are defined and structured by (i) who owns or possesses property and means of production and who performs t he work in the production process, (ii) the social relationships involved in work and labour, and (iii) who produces and who controls the surplus human social labour can produce. These economic factors more fully govern social relationships in capitalis m than they did in earlier societies. While earlier societies contained various strata or groupings which might be considered classes, these may have been strata or elites that were not based solely on economic factors – e.g. priesthood, knights, or mili tary elite.

Marx did not complete the manuscript that would have presented his overall view of social class. Many of his writings concern the class structures of capitalism, the relationship among classes the dynamics of class struggle, political power and classe s, and the development of a classless society, and from these a Marxian approach to class can be developed. Note that Hadden does not discuss class in any detail, although the class structure of capitalism is implicit in the labour theory of value and can be derived from this theory.

Classes in Capitalism

The main classes in capitalism are the bourgeoisie and the proletariat. However, other classes such as landlords, petty bourgeoisie, peasants, and lumpenproletariat also exist, but are not primary in terms of the dynamics of capitalism.

Bourgeoisie. The bourgeoisie or capitalists are the owners of capital, purchasing and exploiting labour power, using the surplus value from employment of this labour power to accumulate or expand their capital. It is the ownership of capita l and its use to exploit labour and expand capital are key here. Being wealthy is, in itself, not sufficient to make one a capitalist (e.g. managers in the state sector or landlords). To be a capitalist or member of the bourgeoisie, the owner of a sum o f money must be actively involved in capital accumulation, using this money to organize production, employ and exploit labour, and make the money self-expansive by using the surplus value to continue this cycle of capital accumulation.

Historically, the bourgeoisie began cities of medieval Europe, with the development of traders, merchants, craftspersons, industrialists, manufacturers and others whose economic survival and ability to increase wealth came from trade, commerce, or indu stry. In order for each of these to expand their operations, they needed greater freedom to market products and expand economic activities. In the struggle against the feudal authorities (church and secular political authorities) this class formed and t ook on a progressive role. That is, they helped undermine the old hierarchical and feudal order and create historical progress. For a segment of this class, wealth came by employing labour (industrial capital), for others it came through trade (merchan t capital), banking and finance (finance capital), or using land in a capitalist manner (landed capital). It was the industrial capitalists who employed labour to create capital that became the leading sector of the bourgeoisie, whose economic activities ultimately changed society. In Britain, this class became dominant politically and ideologically by the mid-nineteenth century. By employing workers, industrial capital created the surplus value that could take on the various forms such as profit, inte rest, and rent. This system has continued to expand, with capital accumulation by the bourgeoisie conducted on a global scale today.

Proletariat. The proletariat are owners of labour power (the ability to work), and mere owners of labour power, with no resources other than the ability to work with their hands, bodies, and minds. Since these workers have no property, in order to survive and obtain an income for themselves and their families, they must find employment and work for an employer. This means working for a capitalist-employer in an exploitative social relationship, that is, the worker works extra time for a capitalist.

This exploitative work relationship recreates or reproduces itself continually. If the capitalist-employer is to make profits and accumulate capital, wages must be kept low. This means that the proletariat is exploited, with the surplus time (above t hat required for providing subsistence) worked by the worker creating surplus products. While the worker produces, the products created by this labour are taken by the capitalist and sold – thus producing surplus value or profit for the capitalist but poverty for workers. This occurs each day of labour process, preventing workers from gaining ownership of property and recreating the conditions for further exploitation.

The antagonistic and contradictory nature of this system is evident as capitalists attempting to reduce wages and make workers work more intensively, while workers have exactly the opposite set of interests. Work and the labour process in the capitalist mode of production are organized so that workers remain propertyless members of the proletariat. The surplus products and value created by workers turns into capital, which is accumulated. There is a certain unity between the classes, in that capitalists and workers are in a social relationship with each other, but it is a unity of opposites, an antagonistic social relationship, with struggle between these two classes.

Historically, the proletariat emerged as the aristocracy began to suffer financial difficulties in the later middle ages. Many of those who were supported by working for the aristocracy lost their livelihood – the "disbanding of the feudal retainers and the dissolution of the monasteries." Using enclosures, changing the conditions of production in agriculture, and denying peasants access to common lands and resources, landowners transformed land into pasture land for raising sheep, or sold land to farmers who began to develop grain and livestock production. People who had subsisted on the land were denied the possibility of making a living on the land, and they become propertyless. Population growth was also considerable, and in some areas forced labour was used. While some people subsisted in rural industry and craft production, factory production, with its cheaper mass produced commodities, began to undermine this in the eighteenth and nineteenth centuries. Together these changes created a large class of landless and propertyless people who had no choice but to become members of the proletariat – many working in factories. These people became free wage labourers, free from feudal ties and free from a source of livelihood. Today we still talk of free labour markets and the dual meaning is much the same.

While the relationship between workers and capitalists, or between labour and capital may appear to be no more than an economic relationship of equals meeting equals in the labour market, Marx shows how it is an exploitative social relationship. Not only is it exploitative, it is contradictory, with the interests of the two partners in the relationship being directly opposed to each other. Although at the same time, the two opposed interests are also partners in the sense that both capital and labour are required in production and an exploitative relationship means an exploiter and someone being exploited.

This relationship is further contradictory in that it is not just two sets of interests, but there is no resolution of the capital-labour contradiction within the organization of capitalism as a system. The contradictory relationship has class conflict built into it, and leads to periodic bursts of strikes, crises, political struggles, and ultimately to the overthrow of bourgeois rule by the proletariat. Class conflict of this sort results in historical change and is the motive force in the history of capitalism.

Landlords. In addition to the bourgeoisie and the proletariat, Marx discussed a number of other classes. First, Marx mentions landowners or landlords as a class in Britain. While these were historically important, and many still retain their wealth even today (e.g. the Royal Family), they were considered by Marx to be a marginal class, once powerful and dominant but having lost their central role in production and the organization of society. In order to retain their wealth, some of these landowners were able to transform their wealth in land into landed capital. While this constituted a somewhat different form than industrial capital, this meant that the land was also used as capital, to accumulate. Labour may not be directly employed by landowners, but the land is used as a means by which capital can be expanded.

Petty Bourgeoisie and Middle Class. The lower middle class or the petty (petite) bourgeoisie (the bourgeoisie was sometimes called the middle class in this era), "are smallowners who still work their own means of production, or owner-workers". The characteristic of this class is that it does own some property, but not sufficient to have all work done by employees or workers. Members of this class must also work in order to survive, so they have a dual existence – as (small scale) property owners and as workers. Because of this dual role, members of this class have divided interests, usually wishing to preserve private property and property rights, but with interests often opposed to those of the capitalist class. This class is split internally as well, being geographically, industrially, and politically dispersed, so that it is difficult for it to act as a class. Marx expected that this class would disappear as capitalism developed, with members moving into the bourgeoisie or into the working class, depending on whether or not they were successful. Many in this class have done this, but at the same time, this class seems to keep recreating itself in different forms.

Marx considers the petite bourgeoisie to be politically conservative or reactionary, preferring to return to an older order. This class has been considered by some Marxists to have been the base of fascism in the 1920s and 1930s. At other times, when it is acting in opposition to the interests of large capital, it may have a more radical or reformist bent to it (anti-monopoly).

Note on the Middle Class. The issue of the middle class or classes appears to be a major issue within Marxian theory, one often addressed by later Marxists. Many Marxists attempt to show that the middle class is declining, and polarization of society into two classes is a strong tendency within capitalism.

Marx's view was that the successful members of the middle class would become members of the bourgeoisie, while the unsuccessful would be forced into the proletariat. In the last few years, many have argued that in North America, and perhaps on a world scale, there is an increasing gap between rich and poor and there is a declining middle.

While there have been tendencies in this direction, especially among the farmers and peasantry, there has been no clear long run trend toward decline of the middle class. At the same time as there has been polarization of classes, there have been new middle groupings created.

Some of these are small business people, shopkeepers, and small producers while others are professional and managerial personnel, and some intellectual personnel. Well paid working class members and independent trades people might consider themselves to be members of the middle class. Some segments of this grouping have expanded in number in recent years. While it is not clear that these groups hold together and constitute a class in any Marxian sense of being combined in opposition to other classes, they do form a middle grouping. Since Marx's prediction has not come true, sociologists and other writers have devoted much attention to explaining this middle grouping – what is its basis, what are the causes of its stability or growth, how it fits into the class structure, and what are the effects of its existence on proletariat and bourgeoisie.

Lumpenproletariat. Marx also mentions the "dangerous class" or the social scum. Among the members of this group are "ruined and adventurous offshoots of the bourgeoisie, vagabonds, discharged soldiers, discharged jailbirds.. pickpockets, brothel keepers, rag-pickers, beggars" etc. This is the lumpenproletariat. He does not consider this group to be of any importance in terms of potential for creating socialism, if anything they may be considered to have a conservative influence. Other writers and analysts have considered them to have some revolutionary potential. One of the main reasons for mentioning them is to emphasize how capitalism uses, misuses and discards people, not treating them as humans. Today's representative of this class of lumpenproletariat are the homeless and the underclass.

Peasantry and Farmers. Marx considered the peasantry to be disorganized, dispersed, and incapable of carrying out change. Marx also expected that this class would tend to disappear, with most becoming displaced from the land and joining the proletariat. The more successful might become landowners or capitalist farmers. With respect to family farmers as a group, much the same could be said. However, Marx was not really very familiar with these as a group, and had little to say about these. Canadian political and sociological analyses of the role of farmers in the Prairies constitute a more adequate view of what may be expected from this group. They could be considered to form a class when they act together as a group. In the early day s of Prairie settlement, farms were of similar size, farmers had generally similar interests, and the farm population acted together to create the cooperative movement and the Wheat Board. More recently, Prairie farmers have been split into different groups or strata, dependent on type of farming, size of farm, and whether or not they employ labour. Farmers have not been able to act together as a class in political and economic actions in recent years. Lobbying by some farm groups have been successful, but these do not usually represent farmers as a whole.

Features of Marx's Analysis

Group Basis. For Marx, classes cannot be defined by beginning observation and analysis from individuals, and building a definition of a social class as an aggregate of individuals with particular characteristics. For example, to say that t he upper class is all families with incomes of $500,000 or more is not an adequate manner of understanding social class. The latter is a stratification approach that begins by examining the characteristics of individuals, and from this amassing a view of social class structure as a whole. This stratification approach often combines income, education, and social prestige or status into an index of socioeconomic status, creating a gradation from upper class to lower class. The stratification approach i s essentially a classification, and for Marx classes have meaning only as they are real groups in the social structure. Groups mean interaction among members, common consciousness, and similar types of behaviour that are connected in some way with group behaviour. Categories such as upper class, middle class and lower class, where those in each category may be similar only in the view of the researcher are not fully Marxian in nature.

Classes are groups, and Marx discusses the bourgeoisie and the proletariat, not individual capitalists and individual workers. As individuals, these people may be considered members of a class, but class only acquires real meaning when it the class as a whole and the social relationships defining them that are considered. For example, "The bourgeoisie... has put an end to all feudal, patriarchal, idyllic relations.... ". Here the bourgeoisie is historically created and is an actor in politics, economics and history.

In terms of individuals as members of classes, they are members of a class as they act as members of that class. For example, Marx notes that burghers or members of the bourgeoisie in early capitalist Europe:

the class in its turn achieves an independent existence over against the individuals, so that the latter find their conditions of existence predestined, and hence have their position in life and their personal development assigned to them by their class, become subsumed under it..

To the extent that individuals are considered in the social system, they are defined by their class. For Marxists, class structures exist as objective facts, and a researcher could examine class and membership of a class, but would have to understand the nature of the whole social and economic structure in order to do so. To the extent that these members act in society, they act as representatives of their class, although Marx would leave some room for individual freedom of action.

Property and Class. Classes are formed by the forces that define the mode of production, and classes are an aspect of the relations of production. That is, classes do not result from distribution of products (income differences, lender an d borrower), social evaluation (status honour), or political or military power, but emerge right from relationship to the process of production. Classes are an essential aspect of production, the division of labour and the labour process. Giddens notes: Classes are constituted by the relationship of groupings of individuals to the ownership of private property in the means of production.

This yields a model of class relations which is basically dichotomous [since some own and others do not, some work and others live off the fruits of those who labour]: all class societies are built around a primary line of division between two antagonistic classes, one dominant and the other subordinate.

In describing various societies, Marx lists a number of classes and (antagonistic) social relationship such as "freeman and slave,... lord and serf,... oppressor and oppressed" that characterize different historical stages or modes of production. While Marx also mentions various ranks and orders of society, such as vassals and knights, the forms of struggle between classes are primarily viewed as occurring around control and use of property, the means of production, and production as a whole, and t he manner in which these are used. The basic struggle concerns who performs the labour, and who obtains the benefits from this labour.

An elite is not necessarily a class for Marx. Examples of elites are military elites, priests or religious leaders, and political elites – these may may very powerful and oppressive, and may exercise formal rule at a certain time or place. An elite could form a class, but a political or military elite is not necessarily a class – an elite may be based on recruitment (rather than ownership) and may not have much ultimate say in determining the direction of society. Or the elite may be based on religious, military, political or other structures. This would especially be the case in pre-capitalist or non-capitalist societies. For Marx, and especially in capitalism, domination came from control of the economy or material factors, although it was not confined to this. Thus, the dominant class was the class which was able to own, or at least control, the means of production or property which formed the basis for wealth. This class also had the capability of appropriating much of the social surplus created by workers or producers. An elite may have such power, but might only be able to administer or manage, with real control of the means of production in the hands of owners.

Class as Social Relationship – Conflict and Struggle. At several points, Marx notes how the class defines itself, or is a class only as it acts in opposition to other classes. Referring to the emergence of the burghers or bourgeoisie as a class in early capitalist Europe, Marx notes how The separate individuals form a class only insofar as they have to carry on a common battle against another class; otherwise they are on hostile terms with each other as competitors.

Both competition and unity can thus characterize a class; there can be very cut-throat competition among capitalists, but when the property relations and existence of the bourgeois class is threatened, the bourgeoisie acts together to protect itself.

This becomes apparent when rights of private property or the ability of capital to operate freely comes under attack. The reaction of the bourgeoisie may involve common political action and ideological unity, and it is when these come together that the bourgeoisie as a class exists in its fullest form. In commenting on France, Marx notes that the French peasantry may be dispersed and lacking in unity. In so far as millions of families live under economic conditions of existence that separate their mode of life, their interests and their culture from those of the other classes, and put them in hostile opposition to the latter, they form a class.

It is when the peasantry as a group is in opposition to other classes that the peasantry form a class. These quotes do not provide an example of the same with respect to the proletariat, but in his other writings Marx noted that the proletariat is a t rue class when organized in opposition to the bourgeoisie, and creating a new society.

Class, for Marx, is defined as a (social) relationship rather than a position or rank in society. In Marx's analysis, the capitalist class could not exist without the proletariat, or vice-versa. The relationship between classes is a contradictory or antagonistic relationship, one that has struggle, conflict, and contradictory interests associated with it. The structure and basis of a social class may be defined in objective terms, as groups with a common position with respect to property or the mean s of production. However, Marx may not be primarily interested in this definition of class. Rather, these classes have meaning in society and are historical actors only to the extent that they do act in their own interests, and in opposition to other c lasses. Unlike much other sociology, Marx's classes are defined by class conflict.

Class in and for Itself

Marx noted that there were many reasons why the proletariat would become a class that is conscious of its own position, power, responsibilities, and opportunities. The objective situation of a class exists because of its place in the productive process. Ownership or non-ownership of the means of production, position in the labour process, and the control over surplus determine this. But a class such as the bourgeoisie or proletariat, may not be aware of this position, or at least the implications of this position. A bourgeoisie may be in disarray and factions of the class may fight with each other. The peasantry rarely is aware of its common position, and situations such as the peasantry in the French Revolution are unusual. A class in itself is a class that exists in common conditions in a society. These are the classes such as the bourgeoisie, the proletariat, or the petty bourgeoisie. But members of such a class may not be aware of their common position or interests, and are not able to act on these. Adams and Sydie argue that the proletariat was initially such a class since "they do not recognize their common interests".

A class for itself is a class that develops consciousness of itself, knows its position and capabilities within society, and is able to take actions in its own interests using this knowledge. The working class may acquire a subjective awareness of its own position and situation, and thus develops a working class consciousness. This means that workers become aware of their common position, see the possibility of acting in their own interest, and believe it is possible to carry out action, and exercise change. If they take action, such as forming trade unions or using political measures to improve labour legislation, they become a class for itself, able to act in the interests of the working class. The bourgeoisie was able to do this in an earlier period, in the eighteenth and nineteenth centuries, and the capitalist class today seems very aware of its interests and power.

Some of the means by which the proletariat can become a class in itself is through forming trade unions and political parties. Trade unions may begin with narrow, sectional interests but move beyond this and act on behalf of the working class as a who le. Political parties, such as a labour party may also be necessary, because class struggle moves beyond the economic and into the political sphere. The experience of class conflict and class struggle is the school whereby the working class learns this. Farmers and farm movements in the early twentieth century on the Prairies exhibited a certain degree of class consciousness.

It may be that some workers, or the working class as a whole, is not able to develop into a class for itself because of false consciousness. Workers may believe the dominant ideology, or enough believe it to have a divisive effect on the working class. Other factors that may limit this are the development of a segmented working class (by income, strata, region, occupation, sex, ethnicity, etc.), the lack of struggle and experience, or open repression.

While Marx's views on these issues are incomplete, these are some of the ideas that followers have Marx have considered important. The necessity to link struggles, be involved in conflict experiences, and counter bourgeois ideology, all have become an important part of trade union and socialist movements.

MARXIAN ANALYSIS OF FAMILY AND GENDER

Marxism and Feminism

Some writers in the Marxian tradition analysed the family and sex and gender relations and inequalities. For Marxists, class inequalities and class struggles are the primary feature of the structure of any society, and play a key role in the development of these structures. At the same time, many Marxists recognize that women and men have not usually been equal in society, with women have a position inferior to that of men through much of history and in modern society. For some Marxists, this inequality is not just a byproduct of class inequality, but has its own separate explanation. Marx also argued that for women and men to be fully equal, private property would have to be abolished, and an egalitarian, socialist society created. Marxists have often considered class struggle, the working class, and a political program to attain socialism to be the primary goal of a socialist movement. The inequality of men and women may be considered secondary in importance to class inequality and oppression, and contradictions related to reproduction and gender relations play a secondary role in explaining social change. Women's struggles to attain equality with men have often had to take a secondary place to the struggles of the working cl ass. At the same time, work shapes consciousness, and women's work shapes her status and self-image.

Over the last thirty years, Marxist feminists have attempted to combine the classical Marxian view that class inequality is rooted in the control of material forces by a few, with an understanding of the roots of women's oppression and an examination of feminist social protest. Sydie notes that this may be an "unhappy marriage" of Marxism and feminism , but this approach has had an important influence on recent sociological theorizing. The Marxist feminist approach has also had an effect on the way women's struggles are viewed. Unlike a liberal feminist approach, Marxist feminists argue that inequality on the basis of sex cannot be solved within the capitalist system, but requires transformation to socialism and communism. Since sex inequalities and class oppression are intertwined, it is necessary to end capitalism to begin solving these problems. If this can be done, the promise of Marxism is to reconstitute human nature in ways that preclude all the pernicious dichotomies that have made slaves of some and masters of others.... there is something very liberating about the idea of women and men constructing together the social structures and social roles that will permit both genders to realize their full human potential..

In the Marxist feminist view, the promise of equality under socialism and communism is great, and women's struggles for equality should become part of the struggle for this. They argue that feminists might best attempt to work at causes such as unionizing women, attempting to get equal wages for women, and more generally integrate the struggles of women with the struggles of men for social change.

A further implication is that liberal feminism is bourgeois feminism. Liberal feminists argue for equal rights for women, but may concentrate on providing equal access to middle and upper middle class jobs, higher education, and professional careers. These are often areas that are not open to working class men or women, and providing equal access to upper level jobs for women will not help solve the basic problems of working class people. Further, welfare liberalism may make things look like they are improving. In fact, attempting to win concessions from the bourgeoisie can divert the attention of the working class from the fact that the basic position of workers is still opposed to that of the bourgeoisie.

Engels on the Family

Origin of the Family: The Marxian argument concerning male and female inequality is that male dominance began with the development of private property in agricultural societies. As capitalism developed, these inequalities were taken over and further developed as part of the class oppression that emerges from private property and the structure and development of capitalist oppression and exploitation.

The most important work, and basic reference point, in Marxist feminism is Friedrich Engels, *The Origin of the Family, Private Property and the State*. This was published in 1884 by Engels, a year after Marx died, but was based on Marx's notes, especially notes on the work of American anthropologist, Lewis Henry Morgan (1818-1881), in *Ancient Society* (1877). Morgan's work was an up to date anthropological work of that era, but would now appear quite dated and incorrect, with more recent anthropology yielding different evidence.

Partly as a result of this, partly due to the fact that Engels was attempting to explain the origin of the family in terms of the same material forces as he used for the economic system, and partly because Marx and Engels generally ignored cultural factors as playing an independent role, Engels's analysis appears inadequate today. But it was an attempt to explain the roots of the oppression of women, and the inequalities in the family, on a material basis. Adam s and Sydie note that "Marx and Engels saw relations between men and women as located primarily in the family" and Engels "tried to provide a materialist explanation of gender relations" Sociologists such as Weber and Durkheim paid less attention to these issues than did Marx or Engels. This work of Engels has been the reference point for later Marxists and socialists, so it is important to understand some of the main arguments in this book. Much of Engels' analysis concerns prehistoric periods, describing

Greek, Roman, German and Iroquois family structures. He begins his analysis by dividing history into three broad stages – (i) savagery, (ii) barbarism (prehistory – development of pottery), and (iii) civilization (development of agriculture) – each of which had several sub stages. These were characterized by different ways of organizing subsistence, producing food and other essential requirements (something like Marx's modes of product ion). The stages of development of the family parallel these stages of human history.

In the earlier stages, there were many different sorts of kinship, family and sexual relationship. Some of these were group marriage, polygamy, polyandry or promiscuous intercourse. In terms of family structures, Engels argues that group marriage was the earliest form of the family. As societies developed, there began to be "prohibitions regarding appropriate sexual partners.". There was gradually a development toward "the pairing family," a male-female form of relationship where one man lives with one women, but the relationship is such that polygamy and occasional infidelity remain the right of the men, even though for economic reasons polygamy is rare, while for the woman the strictest fidelity is generally demanded throughout the time she live with the man and adultery on her part is cruelly punished..

This is not necessarily monogamous marriage as we know it, but a weaker connection, one in which the male-female tie is easily broken, in which case the children remain with the mother.

For Engels, the history of the family involves the "progressive narrowing of the circle, originally embracing the whole tribe, within which the two sexes have a common conjugal relation.". In the period of barbarism, (a) men lived in the woman's household and (b) the sexual division of labour already existed. Women were responsible for subsistence in terms of reproduction and production and preparation of food and other goods – in general the household responsibilities. Such societies were most likely matrilineal and matriarchal, with "female rule". That is, lines of descent passed from mother to children, and women had more social and political power than did men. "The social order was constructed in terms of the biological link of mother and child, and this link comprised the family.". That is "fatherhood was impossible to determine with any certainty" , and this may have led to the supremacy of women.

Two key aspects of this early stage are important for dealing with this argument. First, the sexual division of labour already existed in savagery and barbarism, and Engels does not explain why it emerged. Sydie argues that Engels considers this biological in origin – since only women could have children, this explains the pre-eminence of women. He may also have viewed this as being naturally related to the responsibility of women for household labour. Sydie notes that Marx and Engels assumed that the greater strength of males meant that they hunt, fish and fight, whereas the weakness of women, compounded by their reproductive role, confined them to the home. Second, since production and human labour is important for how society is organized, the role that women had in providing subsistence in early societies gave them great power. These were not societies that had much surplus yet, and women's labour was necessary to ensure survival, with the result that this labour was the source of livelihood and also of power. Engels notes that "Peoples whose women have to work much harder than we would consider proper often have far more real respect for women than our Europeans have for theirs.".

Engels notes that "with the patriarchal family, we enter the field of written history." Males gained power within the family and in society with the development of agriculture. As societies moved from being hunter-gatherer societies to developing animal production, the animals (cattle, goats, etc.) became instruments of labour which the male could control and take with him. The domestication of animals, along with the development of farming, meant that more surplus products could be produced. Property soon developed as a result of this. That is, so long as societies were very close to subsistence, survival depended on cooperation of all. But with a social surplus, it became possible for some to control more of the products of society than did others. Factors such as the pre-existing division of labour, the mobility and strength of men, along with their control of tools and animals, may have allowed this. Men became property owners, and also wished to have a means of passing this property to their children. Given these conditions, the matrilineal form of descent had to end, since men did not have clear heirs. The result of this was that "the matriarchal law of inheritance was thereby overthrown, and the male line of descent and the paternal law of inheritance were substituted for them."

For Engels, the result was "the *world historical defeat of the female sex*. The man took command in the home also; the woman was degraded and reduced to servitude; she became the slave of his lust and a mere instrument for the production of children." Engels notes that "within the family he is the bourgeois, and the wife represents the proletariat." The husband, father and patriarch became the master with slaves, and with wife-servant (s) and children-servants. There were many different forms that this took in different societies, "but in all cases the general relationship is seen to hold that women are subject to men in and out of marriage."

With the development of private property and patrilineage, the monogamous family developed, at least monogamy for women. This ensured that the mother of child is known, and that the father is sure which children are his. The sole purpose of compulsory monogamy is thus to "serve as a vehicle for the orderly transfer of a father's private property to his children." Engels notes that right up through the middle ages, marriage was not decided by the two partners on the basis of "individual sex love" , but by parents and kin on economic grounds, paying attention to private property rights and inheritance. Dependence of marriage on economic considerations became the norm, with property being key to under standing family and marriage.

When capitalism emerged, this form of family structure existed, and "this manner of marriage exactly suited it." At the same time, the ideals of freedom and especially freedom of contract had to be met. These rights were formally extended to marriage and the family, but in practice marriage among the propertied class remained dominated by economic considerations. For the bourgeoisie, considerations of maintaining and extending property dominate over considerations related to freedom and love. In that sense, the family is a more important structure for the bourgeoisie than for the proletariat. Inheritance, female chastity, non-employed wives and the reproduction of legitimate heirs, all became important for the bourgeoisie.

For the proletariat, there is no property to pass on, and relationships between husbands and wives could be more equal. Engels also noted that proletarian women are often employed outside the home, and proletarian husbands had relatively few legal rights. As a result, there was no material basis for husbands oppressing their wives. In addition, by moving production outside the home, capitalism tends to destroy the need for families among ordinary producers. "Capital accumulation 'breaks up the family'" is a common Marxist view of what happens to families under capitalism.

Given that male oppression of females depends on property rights and inheritance, the solution to ending oppression is to eliminate property rights. This will create the possibility of true monogamy , although the exact form of sexual and family relations is uncertain. There will be much greater freedom in terms of choices that individuals can make and the family might be abolished. Some of the statements by Engels are:... the peculiar character of the supremacy of the husband over the wife in the modern family, the necessity of creating real social equality between them and the way to do it, will only be seen in the clear light of day when both possess legally complete equality of rights. Then it will be plain that the first condition for the liberation of the wife is to bring the whole family back into public industry, and that this in turn demands that the characteristic of the monogamous family as the economic unit of society will be abolished.

With the transfer of all means of ownership into common ownership, the single family ceases to be the economic unit of society. Private housekeeping is transformed into a social industry. The care and education of the children becomes a public affair; society looks after all children alike, whether they are legitimate or not. Since the basis on which the oppression of women rests is private property and rights of inheritance, abolishing these would lead to ending oppression of women. Engels argues that this may take a generation or two, but he seems to be optimistic that t his will happen.

Another implication of Engels' analysis is that women should enter public industry, and that those people interested in change should concentrate on organizing women in the workplace and dealing with issues in "the intersection between women's experience as workers and their position in the family." Sydie notes that if women entered into the paid labour force, this would also provide for her entry into class relationships. Women remain subordinate within the family so long as they have no property and have no basis for relating directly to the material productive forces.

In addition, the socialization of housework and child care are important social programs to help achieve this, although issues related to women's sexual and reproductive concerns are secondary. Certainly these efforts should not just be restricted to getting women into management or powerful political positions, as liberal feminists might argue, but should concentrate on working to develop the class consciousness and power of working class women, and the working class as a whole.

Critique and Summary of Origin of the Family

Production. The emphasis on production would appear to be both the strong and weak point of Engels's analysis. By emphasizing human labour and production, Marx and Engels point to a feature that has been very important in structuring and changing human societies. Private ownership of property and private property in the means of production are important bases for social organization, and also for the oppression of women. Marjorie Cohen's analysis of farm labour in nineteenth century Ontario shows the importance of inheritance and property rights among agricultural families. Early liberal writers argued for property rights among men, but argued that these rights should not be extended to women.

In terms of these relationships being the root cause of oppression of women though, several questions are not adequately answered by Engels. First, how did men obtain possession of the instruments of production that formed the basis for private property and inheritance? Second, Engels does not show how matrilineal and matriarchal systems changed into patrilineal and patriarchal ones, except to note that such a change could easily have occurred, given the development of private property and inheritance. Third, Engels all oppression of women is a result of private property in the means of production, and no other factors are considered. If there are cultural or other factors that originally played a role in this, or continue to exist, then removing private ownership may not eliminate women's oppression.

Division of Labour. Engels argues that there was a sexual division of labour before systems of agriculture developed. This sexual division was to make men responsible for obtaining food and doing "productive work" and women were responsible for the household. Whether this is correct, or why this developed is not clear. Engels may have viewed this as a natural division of labour, because he considers the origin of this division to have originated with the different functions of male and female in the sex act. Sydie notes that "physical strength has never been a major determinant of the division of labour" but nineteenth century writers may have considered this to be an important factor.

One problem with the approach of Marx and Engels is that it tends to devalue work and labour that are not productive economically or socially. In our society, this means all labour that is not performed for a wage – household work, volunteer work, car e for the elderly, child care, etc. The Marxian system is built on the analysis of productive labour, with the assumption that the rest of work or labour that is performed has little or nothing to do with exploitation or class structure. In this approach, work and labour become work for a wage, being exploited by an employer, with work performed outside the regular economy not forming part of the analysis.

Further, if the division of labour by sex preceded the development of private property, this division must proceed from something other than property. If that is the case, the abolition of private property may not end this form of inequality, and there may be not such a straightforward solution to this inequality.

Reproduction. Engels begins the Preface the 1884 edition of *Origin of the Family* by noting "According to the materialistic conception, the determining factor in history is, in the last resort, the production and reproduction of immediate life." Here Engels would seem to be according equality to production and reproduction. By the end of the same paragraph though, Engels notes that the development of the productivity of labour, exchange and private property lead to "a society in which the family system is entirely dominated by the property system, and in which the class antagonisms and class struggles, which make up the content of all hitherto *written* history, now freely develop."

One major problem with the Marxian analysis of production is that reproduction is taken for granted, it is not analysed. The development of the productive forces is certainly important, but Marx and Engels did not spend much time analysing reproductive forces. Even *Origin of the Family* contains little analysis of this in capitalist society.

This neglect of reproduction creates a number of problems for the Marxian analysis. First, if an argument is made that women are confined to the domestic sphere and are subordinated because of physiologically determined sex roles, then this is natural. Socialism and communism would not necessarily change this and women would consigned permanently to a secondary role. Second, reproduction takes place in very different ways in different societies. Other than the biological birth process, all other aspects surrounding reproduction can be organized very differently than they are – e.g. family structures, roles of children, amount and types of household work, care of the elderly, etc. Each of these is an aspect of the material forces, involving human labour, yet there is little analysis of these forces in Marxian analysis.

This is at the minimum an omission of important material forces, and to the extent that the relations of reproduction interact with the productive forces analysed within Marxian ana lysis, the latter analysis may be incorrect. Third, creation of surplus value in the Marxian model of capitalism emerges from a distinction between labour and labour power, and the value of labour power. Yet the theory of how the value of labour power i s determined is either nonexistent or incomplete. The same can be said concerning the theory of population. Fourth, what are the real roots of the inequality between men and women? Engels seems to say it is private property. But many feminists argue it is related more to reproductive than productive factors. Some of the radical approaches to feminism argue that sexual inequalities are related to male attempts to control reproduction and women's sexuality, and have little to do with private property and production.

Contributions. In spite of these problems, Marx and Engels certainly recognized oppression of women and patriarchy as major problems, both historically and in contemporary society. Many other theorists were unwilling to consider the differences a source of inequality and oppression of women. Marx and Engels continually emphasized the exploitative nature of property relationships, and used this to show various ways in which these hurt women. While they were overly optimistic about the ability to end sexual inequalities, their analysis focuses on a major source of social inequality. Followers of the Marxist approach have often been key in organizing women into trade unions, pushing for equal pay, etc.

Both liberalism and Marxism claim to be theoretical approaches with universal application, aiming to change society for the benefit of all. Both are concerned with universal human emancipation and the improvement of conditions of everyone, and these approaches do not emphasize sectional interests. It might be noted that the approach of Engels was almost exactly opposite to the liberal view that private property rights should be extended to all. Instead of extending them, it argues that they should b e abolished and that property should become common property – belonging to all. The working class was the key to this, the class that would be able to overcome "particular differences and realize a common identity: the human being as maker, realizing his 'species being' in the course of transforming nature."

CONTEMPORARY MARXIST FEMINISM

Out of the Marxian and the feminist tradition, there are a number of approaches to the analysis of women and of sex and gender inequalities. These are represented by various social and political movements, organizations, and theorists.

Inequality

Class structures are primary in determining the main social classes, the main forms of struggle within societies, and the life experiences of people in these classes. But secondary forms of inequality and oppression occur within each class, and these may take the form of racial and ethnic inequalities, or gender inequalities. Marxist feminists argue that "*within* any class, women are less advantaged than men in their access to material goods, power, status, and possibilities for self-actualization. The causes of this inequality lie in the organization of capitalism itself." Bourgeois women may be wealthy, but usually are secondary to their husbands in terms of power. These women "provide emotional, social, and sexual services for the men in their class. They are well rewarded for this, often are not able to develop an independent source of livelihood or power. Middle class women may be well off, but often lack property or labour force experience, and if divorced, could find themselves in poverty.

The position of working class women is likely to be mixed, depending on whether or not she participates in the labour force, and depending on her wage. If the latter is adequate to support her and her children, she may be able to have some independence. More likely though, the working class woman has little income, responsibility for household tasks, and is inferior socially and in terms of power and independence to her husband. This may allow a male wage earner to exercise "personal power, compensation for his actual powerlessness in society. She is in other words, 'the slave of a slave.'"

For women within the labour force, this work is often as alienating as that of men, or perhaps more alienating. Women are often paid less, and tend to be in subordinate positions. There are relatively few cases where women within the work force are managers or are in dominant positions within a hierarchy. For women who are not in the work force, alienation occurs in a different form, that of powerlessness, with women being required to serve others.

Household and Family

Some Marxists view the household as an institution that functions to support capitalism and it permits or even encourages exploitation. That is, by creating and recreating sexual inequalities, and keeping women in the home with responsibility for family subsistence, emotional support and reproduction, the family helps capitalism continue to exploit labour and helps maintains stability within a system of class oppression and inequality. There are various ways in which the family and sex roles do this.

i. First are the strictly economic features. So long as women have primary responsibility for reproduction (physical and socialization) and household and family maintenance, women constitute a cheap form of labour, a reserve army of labour. T hey have been a latent reserve over the last forty years, some are a short term reserve over the economic cycle, and women are a labour reserve in a generational sense. That is, the expectation that women will not be as committed to many jobs as men, wit h time taken off for childbearing, child care, care of elderly parents, etc., allows employers to pay women less than men. The lower status of women within society also allows women to be paid less, since some wages and salaries are structured on status considerations.

ii. A second feature is that these household and family responsibilities of women allow the extraction of surplus value, although in an indirect form. That is, much of the necessary labour of maintaining and reproducing workers is carried out as unpaid labour by women. Workers come to the labour force at no cost to employers, and if employers had to pay for reproducing workers, the cost would be considerably greater than what wages currently are. Where wages are family wages, so that the mal e wage is large enough to support the whole family, there is still much unpaid work in the home, and paying for this would result in a considerable redistribution of income from males to females.

iii. Third, households and families are good consuming units within modern capitalism. Each household is a separate consuming units, with separate needs. While these consuming units need not be organized on a family basis, or with sexual inequalities, in order to perform this role in society, in fact they are very well adapted to maintaining and expanding purchases.

In social and political terms, this role can also play a conservatizing force with respect to class struggles. Women's lower wages and the difficulty of supporting a family, can be used by employers as a means of undermining trade union struggles. Since the responsibility of women is to maintain the household, this can have a conservatizing effect. Where there is a need for change, women are often isolated by separation into private households, and organizing to create change can be difficult.

iv. Fourth, the unpaid labour performed by women for men can really be regarded as unpaid labour performed for capitalists. In the classical Marxian framework, such labour is unproductive. Marxist feminists argue that reproductive and household labour is productive of surplus value, and should be compensated in some manner. This has led some Marxists to argue that women should be paid wages for housework.

Others have argued that men exploit women in an economic sense, and men extract surplus value from women. Marxists like Zaretsky argue that the family must be abolished, that paying wages for housework will just preserve the traditional inequalities. What is necessary is more socialization of household work, with women being fully able to participate in the public sphere. Potentially, under communism, the division between public and private would disappear, and this could form the basis for sex and gender equalities.

Women as Class

Another line of argument that some feminists have adopted is that women are a class, or a sexual class as opposed to the common Marxist view of a social or economic class. Eisenstein considers women as a sexual class because they "constitute the basic and necessary activities of society: reproduction, child rearing, nurturing, consuming, domestic labouring, *and* wage-earning. Women are a sexual class because *what they do as women* — the activities they are responsible for in society, the labour that they perform — is essential and necessary to the operation of society as it presently exists." This consideration of women as a sexual class is based on a common position within the mode of production and reproduction, and a common position with respect to another sexual class, that is, males. This means a different set of interests, and also at least some opposed interests to those of males. Eisenstein argues that patriarchy is somewhat different than capitalism as a system, where the bourgeoisie is organized and must be opposed. Rather than struggling against men, the struggle of women is against patriarchy, and its expressions. The latter may be found in the market, in the state, in the family, etc. For Eisenste in, sexual class consciousness must be formed through social movements like the suffrage movement or feminist movements. The manner in which feminist struggles over the last thirty years have proceeded has develop this sexual class consciousness.

Solutions

Marxist and socialist feminist solutions embody a wide range of changes. Some would argue that the end of capitalism is sufficient, but the record of the socialist countries was not encouraging in this respect. More likely this approach would argue for an end of the nuclear family, at least as it is currently structured. But really ending patriarchy and inequality may require changes at all levels, in the economy, in attitudes, in institutions, etc.

CONCLUSIONS CONCERNING MARX

1. Predictions. Marx's predictions have often not come true. At the same time, the predictions concerning concentration and centralization, periodic crises, etc. all were accurate forecasts.
2. Concepts. Alienation, value and surplus value, exploitation (as rooted in economics, production and the labour process), labour power, class consciousness, etc. are all useful concepts, many of which have been incorporated into mainstream sociology.
3. Analysis of Capitalism. Marx's analysis of capitalism, and his basic critique of it remain as one of his great contributions. While missing some aspects of the system, the forces noted by Marx have continued to be important. Just as many of the forces noted by Smith and Ricardo still operate, so do the forces noted by Marx.
4. Methodology. Marx's method sets an example of how to do social research. Empirical work within an historical setting, whereby a philosophic approach is taken to construct a sound theoretical system. This system has wide scope and raises many hypotheses.

6

Karl Marx and Religion

It is vital to understand the meaning of Marx to grasp his ideas in relation to his development. In this connection, his conception of religion is one of the most important aspects of his notions.

As early as 1842, he wrote: I desired there to be less trifling with the label 'atheism' (which reminds one of children, assuring everyone who is ready to listen to them that they are not afraid of the bogy man), and that instead the content of philosophy should be brought to the people.

It was quite easy to deal with religion by just being against it, but that was not good enough. 'Everybody knows' that Marx wrote about religion being the opium of the people, so we shall look at the entire passage from which this comes.

The foundation of irreligious criticism is: *Man makes religion*, *religion* does not make man. Religion is indeed the self-consciousness and self-esteem of man who has either not yet won through to himself or has already lost himself again. But man is no abstract being squatting outside the world. Man is the world of man, state, society. This state and this society produce religion, which is an *inverted consciousness of the world*, because they are an *inverted world*. Religion is the general theory of this world, its encyclopaedic compendium, its logic in popular form, its spiritual *point d'honneur*, its enthusiasm, its moral sanction, its solemn complement and its universal basis of consolation and justification. It is the *fantastic realization* of the human essence since the human essence has not acquired any true reality. The struggle against religion is therefore indirectly the struggle against *that world* whose spiritual *aroma* is religion.

Religious suffering is at one and the same time the *expression* of real suffering and a protest against real suffering. Religion is the *sigh* of the oppressed creature, the heart of a heartless world and the soul of soulless conditions. It is the *opium* of the people.

'Everybody' thinks that Marx was saying that religion was dope manufactured by the ruling class to keep the masses happy. The real Marx, however, was concerned with much more weighty problems. Among other things, he was thinking about how an abstract human being could exist. He concludes that one could not. 'Man is the world of man, state, society', and the conception of God was a necessary conception in an 'inverted world'. Once the world was right side up, the idea would not be needed. Meanwhile we should pay attention to it.

The *Critique of Hegel's Philosophy of Right*: Introduction contains Marx's first mention of the proletariat. His views now took on more critical political-economic ideas, following Engels' brilliant essay, *Outlines of a Critique of Political Economy*, which Marx was pleased to publish in the *Deutsch-Franzosiche Jahrbuecher*.

Reading a French translation of James Mill's *Elements of Political Economy*, Marx takes up Mill's banal definition of money as the medium of exchange. Man becomes the poorer as man, i.e., separated from this mediator, the richer this mediator becomes. Christ *represents* originally: 1) men before God; 2) God for men; 3) men to men. Similarly, *money* represents originally, in accordance the idea of money: 1) private property for private property; 2) society for private property; 3) private property for society. But Christ is alienated God and alienated man. God has value only insofar as he represents Christ, and man has value only insofar as he represents Christ.

Marx is certain that his view of money as the mediator is necessary to comprehend the situation of the proletariat. Any easy rejection of this view would be as useless as atheism. The Paris Manuscripts, penned in 1844, returns to this theme. Since the *real existence* of man and nature has become evident in practice, through sense experience, because man has thus become evident for man as the being of nature, and nature for man as the being of man, the question about an *alien* being, about a being above nature and man — a question which implies admission of the unreality of nature and of man — has become impossible in practice. *Atheism*, as a *negation of God*, has no longer any meaning, and postulates the *existence of man* through this negation; but socialism as socialism no longer stands in any need of such a mediation. At this time, in 1843-4, Marx thought of himself as a follower of Feuerbach. But even this thinker, beloved of atheists, was not one of them. His target was not so much *religion* but *theology*, the formal study of God, 'the worst enemy of the awakened spirit'.

But, as Marx was to realise, Feuerbach was concerned to awaken man, but as an isolated individual. Some time in 1845, Marx scribbled eleven Theses on Feuerbach, and Theses 3, 4 and 6 particularly turn on the questions of religion.

Thesis 4.

Feuerbach starts off from the fact of religious estrangement [*Selbstentfremdung*], of the duplication of the world into a religious, imaginary world, and a secular [*wetliche*] one. His work consists in resolving the religious world into its secular basis. He overlooks the fact that after completing this work, the chief thing still remains to be done. For the fact that the secular basis lifts off from itself and establishes itself in the clouds as an independent realm can only be explained by the inner strife and intrinsic contradictoriness of this secular basis. The latter must itself be understood in its contradiction and then, by the removal of the contradiction, revolutionised. Thus, for instance, once the earthly family is discovered to be the secret of the holy family, former must itself be annihilated [*vernichtet*] theoretically and practically.

Thesis 6.

Feuerbach resolves the essence of religion into the essence of man [*menschliche Wesen* = "human nature"]. But the essence of man is no abstraction inherent in each single individual. In reality, it is the ensemble of the social relations. Feuerbach, who does not enter upon a criticism of this real essence is hence obliged:

1. To abstract from the historical process and to define the religious sentiment regarded by itself, and to presuppose an abstract — isolated — human individual.
2. The essence therefore can by him only be regarded as "species," as an inner "dumb" generality which unites many individuals only in a *natural* way.

Thesis 7.

Feuerbach consequently does not see that the "religious sentiment" is itself a *social product*, and that the abstract individual that he analyses belongs in reality to a particular social form. Marx, in these brief summaries, has thus cleared out of the way Feuerbach's treatment of the human individual. His 'awakening' of man is seen to be as a social atom, and not what Marx is striving for.

Let us jump now to Marx's chief work, which took much more than his lifetime to complete. We begin with a quote from the *Grundrisse*, the first attempt at a critique of political economy as a whole. "An example in the religious sphere is Christ the mediator between God and man-mere instrument of circulation between them-becomes their unity, God-man, and as such becomes more important than God; the saints more important than Christ; the priests more important than the saints.

This return to our familiar theme, is part of the exposition of Marx's of his explanation of the central importance of money. But his treatment of this notion in *Capital* is not the same as that we have seen in the other extracts.

The religious reflections of the real world can, in any case, vanish only when the practical relations of everyday life between man and man, and man and nature, generally present themselves to him in a transparent and rational form. The veil is not removed from the countenance of the social life-process, i.e. the process of material production, until it becomes production by freely associated men, and stands under their conscious and planned control. This, however, requires that society possess a material foundation, or a series of material conditions of existence, which in their turn are the natural and spontaneous product of a long and tormented historical development.

Here, Marx brings together his views on religion and his historical view of the communist revolution and the growth of production generally. He relates religion to the effort to unite human beings without really understanding the sweeping historical forces which have separated them. One more quotation, from a piece of *Capital*, the so-called 'Sixth Chapter', omitted from Volume 1, maintains this historical outlook.

This antagonistic stage cannot be avoided, any more than it is possible for man to avoid the stage in which his spiritual energies are given a religious definition as powers independent of himself. What we are confronted by here is the *alienation* [*Entfremdung*] of man from his own labour.

Here, Marx has set out his conception of religion in the light of his notion of the stages of history as a whole. First, humans see themselves as a local community, with their local gods. Then, in the era of money and exploitation, God Almighty rules over all. Finally, there is no use for Him, as humans freely govern their own lives.

KARL MARX ON RELIGION

This quote is reproduced a great deal and is probably the only Marx quote that most people are familiar with. Unfortunately, if someone is familiar with it they are likely only familiar with a small portion that, taken by itself, tends to give a distorted impression of what Marx had to say about religion.

Religious distress is at the same time the expression of real distress and the protest against real distress. Religion is the sigh of the oppressed creature, the heart of a heartless world, just as it is the spirit of a spiritless situation. It is the opium of the people. The abolition of religion as the illusory happiness of the people is required for their real happiness. The demand to give up the illusion about its condition is the demand to give up a condition which needs illusions.

Karl Marx, Critique of Hegel's Philosophy of Right

Usually all one gets from the above is "Religion is the opium of the people" (with no ellipses to indicate that something has been removed). Sometimes "Religion is the sigh of the oppressed creature" is included. If you compare these with the full quotation, it's clear that a great deal more is being said than what most people are aware of. In the above quotation Marx is saying that religion's purpose is to create illusory fantasies for the poor. Economic realities prevent them from finding true happiness in this life, so religion tells them that this is OK because they will find true happiness in the next life. Although this is a criticism of religion, Marx is not without sympathy: people are in distress and religion provides solace, just as people who are physically injured receive relief from opiate-based drugs.

The quote is not, then, as negative as most portray (at least about religion). In some ways, even the slightly extended quote which people might see is a bit dishonest because saying "Religion is the sigh of the oppressed creature..." deliberately leaves out the additional statement that it is also the "heart of a heartless world." What we have is a critique of society that has become heartless rather than of religion which tries to provide a bit of solace. One can argue that Marx offers a partial validation of religion in that it tries to become the heart of a heartless world. For all its problems, religion doesn't matter so much — it is not the <i>real</i> problem. Religion is a set of ideas, and ideas are expressions of material realities. Religion is a symptom of a disease, not the disease itself.

Still, it would be a mistake to think that Marx is uncritical towards religion — it may try to provide heart, but it fails. For Marx, the problem lies in the obvious fact that an opiate drug fails to fix a physical injury — it merely helps you forget pain and suffering. This may be fine up to a point, but only as long as you are also trying to solve the underlying problems causing the pain. Similarly, religion does not fix the underlying causes of people's pain and suffering — instead, it helps them forget why they are suffering and gets them to look forward to an imaginary future when the pain will cease.

Even worse, this "drug" is administered by the same oppressors who are responsible for the pain and suffering in the first place. Religion is an expression of more fundamental unhappiness and symptom of more fundamental and oppressive economic realities. Hopefully, humans will create a society in which the economic conditions causing so much pain and suffering would be eradicated and, therefore, the need for soothing drugs like religion will cease. Of course, for Marx such a turn of events isn't to be "hoped for" because human history was leading inevitably towards it.

So, in spite of his obvious dislike of and anger towards religion, Marx did not make religion the primary enemy of workers and communists, regardless of what might have been done by 20th century communists. Had Marx regarded religion as a more serious enemy, he would have devoted more time to it in his writings. Instead, he focused on economic and political structures that in his mind served to oppress people. For this reason, some Marxists could be sympathetic to religion. Karl Kautsky, in his *Foundations of Christianity*, wrote that early Christianity was, in some respects, a proletarian revolution against privileged Roman oppressors. In Latin America, some Catholic theologians have used Marxist categories to frame their critique of economic injustice, resulting in "liberation theology."

Marx's relationship with and ideas about religion are more complex than most realize. Marx's analysis of religion has flaws, but despite them his perspective is worth taking seriously. Specifically, he argues that religion is not so much an independent "thing" in society but, rather, a reflection or creation of other, more fundamental "things" like economic relationships. That's not the only way of looking at religion, but it can provide some interesting illumination on the social roles that religion plays.

7

Marxism and Class

THE CONCEPT OF SOCIAL CLASS

The concept of social class as "a division or order of society according to status is a very ancient one, the English word 'class' being derived from the Latin 'classis', meaning each of the "... ancient divisions of the Roman people". Servius Tullius, king of Rome in the 6th century BC, organised a classification system which divided citizens into five classes according to wealth".

The Marxist Definition of Class

Marxist-Leninists accept the *concept* of social class put forward above, but hold that a person's social class is determined not by the *amount* of his wealth, but by the *source* of his income *as determined by his relation to labour and to the means of production.*

"Classes are large groups of people differing from each other by the place they occupy in a historically determined system of social production, by their relation to the means of production, by their role in the social organisation of labour, and, consequently, by the dimensions of the share of social wealth of which they dispose and their mode of acquiring it".

To Marxist-Leninists, therefore, the class to which a person belongs is determined by *objective reality*, not by someone's opinion. On the basis of the above definition, Marxist-Leninists distinguish *three basic classes* in 19th century Britain: "There are three great social groups, whose members... live on wages, profit and ground rent respectively".

These three basis classes are 1) the proletariat or working class, 2) the bourgeoisie or capitalist class and 3) the landlord class, respectively.

The Landlord Class

Marxist-Leninists define the *landlord class* as *that class which owns land and derives its income from ground rent on that land:* "Land becomes... personified and... gets on its hind legs to demand... its share of the product created with its help...: rent

With the development of capitalist society, however, the landlord class progressively loses its importance and a new class emerges — the petty bourgeoisie. Thus, in a developed capitalist society, there are still three basic classes, but these are now: 1) the capitalist class or bourgeoisie; 2) the petty bourgeoisie; and 3) the working class or proletariat: "Every capitalist country... is basically divided into three main forces: the bourgeoisie, the petty bourgeoisie and the proletariat".

The Bourgeoisie

The English word '*bourgeoisie*' is derived from the French word 'bourgeoisie' meaning "... the trading middle class" as distinct from the landlord class.

Marxist-Leninists define the bourgeoisie or capitalist class as, "...the class of modern capitalists, owners of the means of social production and employers of wage labour".

The capitalist class includes persons whose remuneration may come nominally in the form of a salary, but which is in fact due to their position in the capitalist class (e.g., the directors of large companies). It also includes persons who are not employers, but who serve the capitalist class in *high* administrative positions:

"The latter group contains sections of the population who belong to the big bourgeoisie: all the rentiers (living on the income from capital and real estate...), then part of the intelligentsia, the high military and civil officials, etc. It also includes the dependents of these persons.

The Proletariat

The English word '*proletariat*' is derived from the Latin

'proles', meaning 'offspring', since according to Roman law a proletarian served the state "... not with his property, but only with his offspring.

Marxist-Leninists define the proletariat or working class as, "...that class of modern wage labourers who, having no means of production of their own, are reduced to selling their labour power in order to live.

In modern society, "... the proletariat alone is a really revolutionary class". so that, in producing the proletariat, the bourgeoisie produces "... its own gravediggers".

The 'Middle Class'

The term 'middle class' is used by Marxists — including Marx and Engels themselves — in two different ways:

Firstly, in the historical sense, "... in the sense of... the French word '*bourgeoisie* that possessing class which is differentiated from the so-called aristocracy. *secondly*, when speaking of modern capitalist society, with the meaning of petty bourgeoisie', discussed in the next section.

The Petty Bourgeoisie

Between the bourgeoisie and the proletariat, stands the *petty bourgeoisie*: "In countries where modern civilisation has become fully developed, a new class of petty bourgeois has been formed".

The English term 'petty bourgeoisie' is an anglicisation of the French term 'petite bourgeoisie', meaning 'little bourgeoisie'. Marxist-Leninists define the petty bourgeoisie as *a class which owns or rents small means of production which it operates largely without employing wage labour*, but often with the assistance of members of their families: "A petty bourgeois is the owner of small property",.

As a worker, the petty bourgeois has interests in common with the proletariat; as owner of means of production, however, he has interests in common with the bourgeoisie. In other words, the petty bourgeoisie has a divided allegiance towards the two decisive classes in capitalist society.

Thus, the 'independent' petty bourgeois producer, "... is cut up into two persons. As owner of the means of production he is a capitalist; as a labourer he is his own wage-labourer". and consequently petty bourgeois "...are for ever vacillating between the proletariat and the bourgeoisie".

This divided allegiance between the two decisive classes in modern capitalist society applies also to a section of *employed* persons — those who are involved in *superintendence and the lower levels of management* — e.g., foremen, charge-hands, departmental managers, etc. These employees have a supervisory function, a function is to ensure that the workers produce a maximum of surplus value for the employer. On the one hand, such persons are exploited workers, with interests in common with the proletariat (from which they largely spring); on the other hand, their position as agents of the management in supervising the efficient exploitation of their fellow employees gives them interests in common with the bourgeoisie:

"An industrial army of workmen, under the command of a capitalist, requires, like a real army, officers (managers) and sergeants (foremen, overlookers) who, while the work is being done, command in the name of the capitalist",.

"The labour of supervision and management... has a double nature. On the one hand, all labour in which many individuals cooperate necessarily requires a commanding will to coordinate and unify the process.... This is a productive job.... On the other hand, this supervision work necessarily arises in all modes of production based on the antithesis between the labourer, as the direct producer, and the owner of the means of production. The greater this antagonism, the greater the role played by supervision".

Because of this divided allegiance, which corresponds to that of the petty bourgeoisie proper, *Marxist-Leninists place such employees (and their dependents) in the petty bourgeoisie.* For the same reason, Marxist-Leninists also place persons in the *middle and lower ranks of the coercive forces of the capitalist state* — the army and police — (and their dependents) in the petty bourgeoisie.

THE POLARISATION OF CAPITALIST SOCIETY

Because of the small size of their means of production, petty-bourgeois are in constant danger of sinking into the proletariat: "The lower strata of the middle class... sink gradually into the proletariat, partly because their diminutive capital... is swamped in the competition with the large capitalists, partly their specialised skill is rendered worthless by new methods of production".

"The working class gains recruits from the *higher strata of society*... A mass of petty industrialists and small rentiers are hurled down into its ranks", and even the old, once highly respected petty bourgeois professions become proletarianised:

"The bourgeoisie has stripped of its halo every occupation hitherto honoured and looked up to with reverent awe. It has converted the physician, the lawyer, the priest, the poet, the man of science, into its paid wage-labourers". Thus, as capitalist society develops, it becomes *increasingly polarised into two basic classes* — wealthy bourgeois and poor proletarians:

"Society as a whole is more and more splitting up... into two great classes facing each other — bourgeoisie and proletariat".

"Accumulation of wealth at one pole is, therefore, at the same time accumulation of misery, agony of toil, slavery, ignorance, brutality, moral degradation, at the opposite pole".

The Peasantry

The English word 'peasant is derived from the Latin 'pagus', meaning a "... country district". and is defined as "... one who lives in the country and works on the land". The above definition excludes the landlord class from the peasantry since, even if a landlord 'lives in the country' he does not work on the land', but derives his income from ground rent. The peasantry do not form a class of society, but consist of *a number of different classes which live in the country and work on the land*: "It is best to distinguish the rich, the middle and the poor peasants".

The peasantry is composed of: *Firstly, rich peasants*, or *rural capitalists*, who *employ labour*, that is, who exploit poorer peasants: "One of the main features of the rich peasants is that they *hire farmhands and day labourers*. Like the landlords, the rich peasants also live by the labour of others.... They try to squeeze as much work as they can out of their farmhands, and pay them as little as possible". Sometimes rich peasants are called 'kulaks', a word derived from the Russian 'kulak', originally meaning a "... tight-fisted person".

Secondly, the *middle peasants* or the *rural petty bourgeoisie*, who own or rent land but who do not employ labour. Speaking of the middle peasantry, Lenin says: "Only in good years and under particularly favourable conditions is the independent husbandry of this type of peasant sufficient to maintain him and for that reason his position is a very unstable one. In the majority of cases the middle peasant cannot make ends meet without resorting to loans to be repaid by labour, etc., without seeking subsidiary' earnings on the side".

Thirdly, the *poor peasants* or *rural proletariat*. The poor peasant lives "... not by the land, not by his farm, but *by working for wages*.... He... has ceased to be an independent farmer and has become a hireling, a proletarian".

Sometimes Marxist-Leninists describe poor peasants as "... *semi-proletarians*", to distinguish them from urban proletarians, regarded as 'full' proletarians.

'Neo-Marxism'

'Revisionism' is "... a trend hostile to Marxism. within Marxism itself". In other words, a revisionist *poses as a Marxist* but in fact puts forward a programme which objectively serves the interests of a bourgeoisie: "The revisionists spearheaded their struggle mainly *against Marxism-Leninism*... and replaced this theory with an opportunist, counterrevolutionary theory in the service of the bourgeoisie and imperialism.

Despite all the torrents of propaganda levelled against it, Marxism-Leninism still retains enormous prestige among working people all over the world. It is for this reason that many modern revisionists call themselves 'Neo-Marxists' or 'Western Marxists' — claiming that they are not revising Marxism, but merely bringing it up to date, bringing into the age of the electronic computer which Marx and Engels never knew.

In general, 'neo-Marxists' pay their loudest tributes to Marx 's early writings, before he became a Marxist. 'Neo-Marxism' is essentially a product not merely of universities, but of the worst kind of university lecturer who equates obscurantism with intellectualism. One sees admiring students staggering from his lectures muttering 'What a brilliant man! I couldn't understand a word!'.

Even sociologists sympathetic to 'neo-Marxism' speak of "... the extreme difficulty of language characteristic of much of Western Marxism in the twentieth century". But, of course, this obscure language has a great advantage for those who use it, making it easy to claim, when challenged, that the challenger has misunderstood what one was saying.

Much 'Neo-Marxism' is an eclectic hotchpotch of Marxism with idealist philosophy — giving it, it is claimed, a 'spiritual aspect' lacking in the original. A typical example is the French philosopher Jean-Paul Sartre who writes: "I believe in the general schema provided by Marx", *but* — and it is a big 'but' — it must be a 'Marxism' liberated from "... the old guard of mummified Stalinists". And how, according to Sartre, is this 'liberation' to be effected? By merging it with the existentialism of the Danish idealist philosopher Soren Kierkegaard! "Kierkegaard and Marx... institute themselves... as our future".

However, this paper is concerned only with *revisionist theories which are based on distortions of the Marxist-Leninist definition of class.*

In particular, it will be concerned with 'neo-Marxist' definitions of the proletariat which narrow and restrict it as a class. While to these 'neo-Marxists' the proletariat may still be, in words, 'the gravedigger of capitalism', they portray it as *a gravedigger equipped with a teaspoon instead of a spade.*

The Unemployed

Some 'neo-Marxists' exclude the unemployed from the proletariat on the grounds that someone who is not working cannot be regarded as a member of the working class! But Marx explicitly characterises the unemployed, the "... industrial reserve army", as *part of the working class*, as "... a relative surplus population among the working class", and speaks of "... the working class (now actively reinforced by its entire reserve army)".. Clearly, therefore, the founders of Marxism did not exclude the unemployed from the working class.

Non-Productive Labour

Other 'neo-Marxists' exclude all workers engaged in *non-productive labour* from the working class. Certainly, for the purpose of analysing the complexities of capitalist society, Marx differentiated labour into *productive* and *unproductive* labour. According to Marx, "... only that labour is *productive* which creates a *surplus value*". It is on this basis that the Greek revisionist Nicos Poulantzas excludes non-productive workers from the working class: "I have a rather limited and restricted definition of the working class. The criterion of productive and unproductive labour is sufficient to exclude unproductive workers from the working class". Poulantzas therefore assigns non-productive workers to the "... new petty bourgeoisie" asserting that "... the new petty bourgeoisie constitutes a separate class".

But, "... the distinction between productive and unproductive labour has nothing to do... with the particular speciality of the labour. The same kind of labour may be productive or unproductive: "The same labour can be productive when I buy it as a capitalist, and unproductive when I buy it as a consumer"..

For example, a teacher in a private school is engaged in productive labour (in the Marxist sense of the term), because his labour produces surplus value for the proprietors of the school. But a teacher in a state school, working under identical conditions, is engaged in unproductive labour, because his labour does not create surplus value.

Furthermore, many kinds of unproductive labour, such as the labour of clerical workers in a capitalist production firm, "... while it does not create surplus value, enables him (the employer — Ed.) to appropriate surplus value which, in effect, amounts to the same thing with respect to his capital. It is, therefore, a source of profit for him". Thus the question of whether an employee is engaged in productive or unproductive labour has *no relevance* to the question of whether he belongs to the proletariat.

The 'Labour Aristocracy'

In developed capitalist states, "... the bourgeoisie, by plundering the colonial and weak nations, has been able to bribe the upper stratum of the proletariat with crumbs from the superprofits".

Superprofits are profits, "... obtained over and above the profits which capitalists squeeze out of the workers of their 'own' country".

Marxist-Leninists call employees in receipt of a share in such super profits "... the labour aristocracy". Some 'neo-Marxists' exclude employees who share in superprofits from the proletariat. Thus, according to the London-based 'Finsbury Communist Association', in Britain "... the proletariat consists of the workers on subsistence wages or below".

However, Lenin defines the labour aristocracy as *a part of the proletariat*, as a "... privileged upper stratum of the proletariat", as "... the upper stratum of the proletariat", as "... the top strata of the working class". Furthermore, while Lenin characterises the 'labour aristocracy' as "... an insignificant minority of the working class", the 'Finsbury Communist Association' presents it as "... the overwhelming majority of Britain's workers".

Thus, according to the 'Finsbury Communist Association', the British imperialists pay the overwhelming majority of Britain's workers' above the value of their labour power. Since there is not even a Marxist-Leninist party, much less a revolutionary situation, in Britain at present, this can only be out of the sheer goodness of their hearts! Clearly the 'neo-Marxist' picture of imperialism bears no relation to reality. It merely lends spurious support to the false thesis that, since the workers in developed capitalist countries are 'exploiters', the future for socialism lies only in the less developed countries in the East!

CLASS CONSCIOUSNESS

Class consciousness is consciousness of one's social class or economic rank in society. From the perspective of Marxist theory, it refers to the self-awareness, or lack thereof, of a particular class; its capacity to act in its own rational interests; or its awareness of the historical tasks implicit (given the precepts of Marxism) to it. Another Marxist approach is to consider the transition from a "class in itself", which is defined as a category of people having a common relation to the means of production, to a "class for itself", which is defined as a stratum organized in active pursuit of its own interests.

Members of "lower" classes are often more aware of their economic class than are members of the "upper" class. However, this may not necessarily be the case in societies where class hierarchy is a strict and deep tradition. In the United States, class consciousness is somewhat conflated with race consciousness. Because racial minority correlates with poverty in that country, members of racial minorities may focus more on racial identities than on identities arising from economic class.

Defining a person's social class can be a determinant for his awareness of it. Marxists define classes on the basis of their relation to the means of production – especially on whether they own capital. Non-Marxist social scientists distinguish various social strata on the basis of income, occupation, or status.

Early in the nineteenth century the labels "working classes" and "middle classes" were already coming into common usage. "The old hereditary aristocracy, reinforced by the new gentry who owed their success to commerce, industry, and the professions, evolved into an "upper class". Its consciousness was formed in part by public schools (in the British sense) and Universities. The upper class tenaciously maintained control over the political system, depriving not only the working classes but the middle classes of a voice in the political process."

Georg Lukács' *History and Class Consciousness* (1923)

Class consciousness, as described by Georg Lukács's famous *History and Class Consciousness* (1923), is opposed to any psychological conception of consciousness, which forms the basis of individual or mass psychology. According to Lukács, each social class has a determined class consciousness which it can achieve. In effect, as opposed to the liberal conception of consciousness as the basis of individual freedom and of the social contract, Marxist class consciousness is not an origin, but an achievement (i.e. it must be "earned" or won). Hence, it is never assured: the proletariat's class consciousness is the result of a permanent struggle to understand the "concrete totality" of the historical process.

According to Lukács, the proletariat was the first class in history that may achieve true class consciousness, because of its specific position highlighted in the *Communist Manifesto* as the "living negation" of capitalism. All others classes, including the bourgeoisie, are limited to a "false consciousness" which impedes them from understanding the totality of history: instead of understanding each specific moment as a portion of a supposedly-deterministic historical process, they universalize it and believe it is everlasting. Hence, capitalism is not thought as a specific phase of history, but is naturalized and thought of as an eternal solidified part of history. Says Lukács, this "false consciousness", which forms ideology itself, is not a simple error as in classical philosophy, but an illusion which can't be dispelled.

Marx described it in his theory of commodity fetishism, which Lukács completed with his concept of reification: alienation is what follows the worker's estrangement to the world following the new life acquired by the product of his work. The dominant bourgeois ideology thus leads the individual to see the achievement of his labour take a life of its own. Furthermore, specialization is also seen as a characteristic of the ideology of modern rationalism, which creates specific and independent domains (art, politics, science, etc.). Only a global perspective can point out how all these different domains interact, argues Lukács. He also points out how Kant brought to its limit the classical opposition between the abstract form and the concrete, historical content, which is abstractly conceived as irrational and contingent. Thus, with Kant's rational system, history becomes totally contingent and is thus ignored. Only with Hegel's dialectic can a mediation be found between the abstract form and the abstract notion of a concrete content.

Even if the bourgeois loses his individual point of view in an attempt to grasp the reality of the totality of society and of the historical process, he is condemned to a form of false consciousness. As an individual, he will always see the collective result of individual actions as a form of "objective law" to which he must submit himself (liberalism has gone so far as seeing an invisible hand in this collective results, making capitalism the best of all possible worlds). By contrast, the proletariat would be, according to Lukács, the first class in history with the possibility to achieve a true form of class consciousness, granting it knowledge of the totality of the historical process.

The proletariat takes the place of Hegel's *Weltgeist* ("World Spirit"), which achieves history through *Volkgeist* ("the spirit of the people"): the idealist conception of an abstract Spirit making history, which ends in the realm of Reason, is replaced by a materialist conception based not on mythical Spirits, but on a concrete "identical subject-object of history": the proletariat. The proletariat is both the "object" of history, created by the capitalist social formation; but it is also the "subject" of history, as it is its labour that shapes the world, and thus, knowledge of itself is also, necessarily, knowledge of the reality and of the totality of the historical process. The proletariat's class consciousness is not immediate; class consciousness musn't be mistaken either with the consciousness of one's future and collective interests, opposed to personal immediate interests.

The possibility of class consciousness is given by the objective process of history, which transforms the proletariat into a commodity, hence objectifying it. Class consciousness is thus not a simple subjective act: "as consciousness here is not the consciousness of an object opposed to itself, but the object's consciousness, the act of being conscious of oneself disrupts the objectivity form of its object" (in "Reification and the Proletariat's Consciousness" §3, III "The proletariat's point of view"). In other words, instead of the bourgeois subject and its corresponding ideological concept of individual free will, the proletariat has been transformed into an object (a commodity) which, when it takes consciousness of itself, transforms the very structure of objectivity, that is of reality.

This specific role of the proletariat is a consequence of its specific position; thus, for the first time, consciousness of itself (class consciousness) is also consciousness of the totality (knowledge of the entire social and historical process). Through dialectical materialism, the proletariat understands that what the individual bourgeois conceived as "laws" akin to the laws of nature, which may be only manipulated, as in Descartes's dream, but not changed, is in fact the result of a social and historical process, which can be controlled. Furthermore, only dialectical materialism links together all specialized domains, which modern rationalism can only think as separate instead of as forming a totality.

Only the proletariat can understand that the so-called "eternal laws of economics" are in fact nothing more than the historical form taken by the social and economical process in a capitalist society. Since these "laws" are the result of the collective actions of individuals, and are thus created by society, Marx and Lukács reasoned that this necessarily meant that they could be *changed*. Any attempt in transforming the so-called "laws" governing capitalism into universal principles, valid in all times and places, are criticized by Lukács as a form of false consciousness.

As the "expression of the revolutionary process itself", dialectical materialism, which is the only theory with an understanding of the totality of the historical process, is the theory which may help the proletariat in its "struggle for class consciousness". Although Lukács does not contest the Marxist primacy of the economic infrastructure on the ideological superstructure (not to be mistaken with vulgar economic determinism), he considers that there is a place for autonomous struggle for class consciousness.

In order to achieve a unity of theory and praxis, theory must not only tend toward reality in an attempt to change it; reality must also tend towards theory. Otherwise, the historical process leads a life of its own, while theorists make their own little theories, desperately waiting for some kind of possible influence over the historical process. Henceforth, reality itself must tend toward the theory, making it the "expression of the revolutionary process itself". In turn, a theory which has as its goal helping the proletariat achieve class consciousness must first be an "objective theory of class consciousness". However, theory in itself is insufficient, and ultimately relies on the struggle of humankind and of the proletariat for consciousness: the "objective theory of class consciousness is only the theory of its objective possibility".

Criticism

Ernest Van Den Haag has argued: "One way is to say that "objectively" people have common class interests and should act according to the class struggle pattern-but that they are not always "class conscious". They suffer from "false consciousness". But this is (a) not true; nor would it help (b) much if it were. a) There often are conflicts among objective economic interests within a Marxian class-e.g. among workers. Conflicts occur over migration, international trade, religion or race. And workers often have objective interests in common with capitalists and in conflict with the interests of other groups of workers. Class membership is no more and possibly less decisive than say race membership in determining one's political views. If you insist on the importance of race, you may persuade people to act according to their "racial interests" for a while-as the Nazis did. If you convince people that they should act according to what you tell them are your class interests, they might. The prophecy becomes self-fulfilling. But the action comes from race or class propaganda-not from race or class as objective facts. b) Further if we assume that classes are as important as Marx thought but that people do not act accordingly, because not having read Marx, they are not class conscious-if "class consciousness" becomes independent of class membership-and if class membership is neither sufficient nor necessary to bring the expected class behaviour, then social classes become one of many groups that influence man's action on some occasions. This would be a correct theory. But the distinctive point of Marxian theory is that class membership is decisive in determining most and particularly political actions. This is patently wrong.

KARL MARX: CLASS THEORY

Marx's class theory rests on the premise that "the history of all hitherto existing society is the history of class struggles." According to this view, ever since human society emerged from its primitive and relatively undifferentiated state it has remained fundamentally divided between classes who clash in the pursuit of class interests. In the world of capitalism, for example, the nuclear cell of the capitalist system, the factory, is the prime locus of antagonism between classes—between exploiters and exploited, between buyers and sellers of labour power—rather than of functional collaboration. Class interests and the confrontations of power that they bring in their wake are to Marx the central determinant of social and historical process.

Marx's analysis continually centers on how the relationships between men are shaped by their relative positions in regard to the means of production, that is, by their differential access to scarce resources and scarce power. He notes that unequal access need not at all times and under all conditions lead to active class struggle. But he considered it axiomatic that the potential for class conflict is inherent in every differentiated society, since such a society systematically generates conflicts of interest between persons and groups differentially located within the social structure, and, more particularly, in relation to the means of production. Marx was concerned with the ways in which specific positions in the social structure tended to shape the social experiences of their incumbents and to predispose them to actions oriented to improve their collective fate.

Yet class interests in Marxian sociology are not given ab initio. They develop through the exposure of people occupying particular social positions to particular social circumstances. Thus, in early industrial enterprises, competition divides the personal interests of "a crowd of people who are unknown to each other... But the maintenance of their wages, this common interest which they have against their employer, brings them together." "The separate individuals form a class only in so far as they have to carry on a common battle against another class; otherwise they are on hostile terms with each other as competitors."

Class interests are fundamentally different from, and cannot be derived from, the individual interests imputed by the utilitarian school and classical British political economy. Potential common interests of members of a particular stratum derive from the location of that stratum within particular social structures and productive relations. But potentiality is transformed into actuality, Klasse en sich (class in itself) into Klasse fuer sich (class for itself), only when individuals occupying similar positions become involved in common struggles; a network of communication develops, and they thereby become conscious of their common fate. It is then that individuals become part of a cohesive class that consciously articulates their common interests. As Carlyle once put it, "Great is the combined voice of men." Although an aggregate of people may occupy similar positions in the process of production and their lives may have objectively similar determinants, they become a class as a self-conscious and history-making body only if they become aware of the similarity of their interests through their conflicts with opposing classes. To Marx, the basis upon which stratification systems rest is the relation of aggregates of men to the means of production. The major modern classes are "the owners merely of labour-power, owners of capital, and landowners, whose respective sources of income are wages, profit and ground-rent." Classes are aggregates of persons who perform the same function in the organization of production. Yet self-conscious classes, as distinct from aggregates of people sharing a common fate, need for their emergence a number of conditions among which are a network of communication, the concentration of masses of people, a common enemy, and some form of organization. Self-conscious classes arise only if and when there exists a convergence of what Max Weber later called "ideal" and "material" interests, that is, the combination of economic and political demands with moral and ideological quests.

The same mode of reasoning that led Marx to assert that the working class was bound to develop class consciousness once the appropriate conditions were present also led him to contend that the bourgeoisie, because of the inherent competitive relations between capitalist producers, was incapable of developing an overall consciousness of its collective interests.

The classical economists picture the economic system of a market economy as one in which each man, working in his own interest and solely concerned with the maximization of his own gains, nevertheless contributes to the interests and the harmony of the whole. Differing sharply, Marx contended, as Raymond Aron has put it, that "each man, working in his own interest, contributes both to the necessary functioning and to the final destruction of the regime."

In contrast to the utilitarians who conceive of self-interest as a regulator of a harmonious society, Marx sees individual self-interest among capitalists as destructive of their class interest in general, and as leading to the ultimate self-destruction of capitalism. The very fact that each capitalist acts rationally in his own self-interest leads to ever deepening economic crises and hence to the destruction of the interests common to all.

The conditions of work and the roles of workers dispose them to solidarity and to overcoming their initial competitiveness in favor of combined action for their collective class interests. Capitalists, however, being constrained by competition on the market, are in a structural positions that does not allow them to arrive at a consistent assertion of common interests. The market and the competitive mode of production that is characteristic of capitalism tend to separate individual producers. Marx granted that capitalists also found it possible to transcend their immediate self-interests, but he thought this possible primarily in the political and ideological spheres rather than in the economic. Capitalists, divided by the economic competition among themselves, evolved a justifying ideology and a political system of domination that served their collective interests. "The State is the form in which the individuals of a ruling class assert their common interests." "The ideas of the ruling class are...the ruling ideas." Political power and ideology thus seem to serve the same functions for capitalists that class consciousness serves for the working class. But the symmetry is only apparent. To Marx, the economic sphere was always the finally decisive realm within which the bourgeoisie was always the victim of the competitiveness inherent in its mode of economic existence. It can evolve a consciousness, but it is always a "false consciousness," that is, a consciousness that does not transcend its being rooted in an economically competitive mode of production. Hence neither the bourgeoisie as a class, nor the bourgeois state, nor the bourgeois ideology can serve truly to transcend the self-interest enjoined by the bourgeoisie. The bourgeois reign is doomed when economic conditions are ripe and when a working class united by solidarity, aware of its common interests and energized by an appropriate system of ideas, confronts its disunited antagonists. Once workers became aware that they are alienated from the process of production, the dusk of the capitalist era has set in.

8

Karl Marx and the State

In April 1917, the Russian anarchist Voline met Leon Trotsky in a New York print works. Not surprisingly, both were producing revolutionary propaganda. Discussing the Russian situation, Voline told Trotsky that he considered it certain that the Bolsheviks would come to power. He went on to say he was equally certain that the Bolsheviks would persecute the anarchists once their power had been consolidated. Trotsky, taken aback by Voline's conviction, emphasized that the Marxists and the anarchists were both revolutionary socialists fighting the same battle. While it is true that they had their differences, these differences, according to Trotsky, were secondary, merely methodological differences-principally a disagreement regarding a revolutionary "transitional stage." Trotsky went on to dismiss Voline's prediction of persecution against the anarchists as nonsense, assuring him that the Bolsheviks were not enemies of the anarchists. Voline relates that in December 1919, less than three years later, he was arrested by Bolshevik military authorities in the Makhnovist region. Since he was a well-known militant, the authorities notified Trotsky of his arrest and asked how he should be handled. Trotsky's reply was terse: "Shoot out of hand.-Trotsky." Luckily, Voline lived to tell his tale.

It is on the basis of the Russian experience that anarchists generally affirm that their ideas have been vindicated. Bakunin's predictions about Marxist authoritarianism came true, or so it seems. Voline's story is the perfect snapshot of the anarchist's historical vindication. Years later, another prominent anarcho-syndicalist emphasized the main lesson of the Russian experience:

In Russia... where the so-called "proletarian dictatorship" has ripened into reality, the aspirations of a particular party for political power have prevented any truly socialistic reconstruction of economy and have forced the country into the slavery of a grinding state-capitalism. The "dictatorship of the proletariat," in which naïve souls wish to see merely a passing, but inevitable, transition stage to real Socialism, has today grown into a frightful despotism and a new imperialism, which lags behind the tyranny of the Fascist states in nothing. The assertion that the state must continue to exist until class conflicts, and classes with them, disappear, sounds, in the light of all historical experience, almost like a bad joke.

Here, in brief, is the historical verdict passed on Marxism by anarchism. But does this verdict discredit the theories of the supposed originator of Marxism, Karl Marx himself? This essay will begin with a look at Marx's basic understanding of the bourgeois state and move on to consider his conception of the transition to socialism in order to demystify Marx's political ideas.

THE BOURGEOIS STATE

Marx's critique of the bourgeois state, or his "critique of politics," first developed out of a critical confrontation with Hegel. The best place to start is thus his 1843 Critique of Hegel's Philosophy of Right, in which Marx challenges Hegel's dialectical justification for the status quo. There are two main lines of argument that we should pay close attention to: (1) Marx's conception of the political state as a separate sphere and (2) his radical conception of direct democracy as opposed to the democracy of the bourgeois state.

According to bourgeois theory, in "civil society" individual citizens pursue their own particular interests in competition with and at the expense of other citizens. In the state, on the other hand, only the general interest is pursued. The state stands above civil society both to act as a limiting force on competition (by declaring certain forms of competition to be illegal), and to provide the basic framework in which competition is to take place (through legal contract, property laws, and so forth). In this way, the state is supposed to guarantee the equal rights of all citizens.

Marx vehemently attacked this theory as it was found in Hegel. Far from seeing the state as a neutral arbiter that served to realize individual freedom, Marx considered the state to be a sphere of social life not only separate from, but also opposed to civil society. For Marx, this contradiction between the state and civil society is characteristic of a society divided against itself, in which the functions of government are administered against society. Marx writes, "The 'police', the 'judiciary', and the 'administration' are not the representatives of a civil society which administers its own universal interests in them and through them; they are the representatives of the state and their task is to administer the state against civil society." Furthermore, the idea of the general interest of all citizens being realized within the bourgeois state was a fiction to begin with. Firstly, the "bureaucrats," who perform state activities, use the general powers of the state to pursue their own particular interests within the state hierarchy. Marx writes, "As for the individual bureaucrat, the purpose of the state becomes his private purpose, *a hunt for promotion, careerism.*" Secondly, the participation of private individuals in state activities does not in fact shield those individuals from the class distinctions that constitute civil society. Instead, the individuals enter into political life with those class distinctions: "The *class distinctions* of civil society thus become established as political distinctions."

In elaborating the contradictory position of the state bureaucrats, Marx is simultaneously denouncing the competitive, hierarchical relations of the political sphere, which, while supposedly realizing the general interest of the citizenry, in fact disposes of the very social equality and transparency necessary for a democratic, general interest to emerge. Here, Marx's basic conception of democracy, a social form in which society "administers its *own* universal interests," is given in outline. This radical conception of democracy must be differentiated from a representative democracy in which it is the representatives who, although elected, hold the real power. The contradictions of modern, bourgeois government are briefly drawn out by Marx:

The separation of the political state from civil society takes the form of a separation of the deputies from their electors. Society simply deputes elements of itself to become its political existence. There is a twofold contradiction: (1) A *formal* contradiction. The deputies of civil society are a society which is not connected to its electors by any 'instruction' or commission. They have a formal authorization but as soon as this becomes *real* they *cease* to be *authorized*. They should be deputies but they are not. (2) A *material* contradiction. In respect to actual interests... Here we find the converse. They have authority as representatives of *public* affairs, whereas in reality they represent *particular* interests.

To reiterate Marx's point, there is a material contradiction in commissioning members of a divided and atomized civil society to somehow represent the general interest of that society. Even from a formal point of view, the deputies recognized as deriving their mandate solely from the popular masses, become, once elected, *independent* of their electors, and are free to make political decisions *on their behalf.* This is distinct from Marx's vision of a society that "administers its *own* universal interests." As Marx put it, "The efforts of *civil society* to transform itself into a political society, or to make the political society into the *real* one, manifest themselves in the attempt to achieve as general a participation as possible in the *legislature*.... The political state leads an existence *divorced* from civil society. For its part, civil society would cease to exist if everyone became a legislator." There is an important point here: the separation of the state from civil society *depends* on limiting popular participation in government.

Marx's analysis of the bourgeois state and civil society is presented even more clearly in his 1843 essay "On the Jewish Question." His analysis is worth quoting at length: Where the political state has attained its full degree of development man leads a double life, a life in heaven and a life on earth, not only in his mind, in his consciousness, but in *reality*. He lives in the *political community*, where he regards himself as a *communal being*, and in *civil society*, where he is active as a *private individual*, regards other men as means, debases himself to a means and becomes a plaything of alien powers. The relationship of the political state to civil society is just as spiritual as the relationship of heaven to earth. The state stands in the same opposition to civil society and overcomes it in the same way as religion overcomes the restrictions of the profane world, i.e. it has to acknowledge it again, reinstate it and allow itself to be dominated by it. Man in his *immediate* reality, in civil society, is a profane being. Here, where he regards himself and is regarded by others as a real individual, he is an illusory phenomenon. In the state, on the other hand, where he is considered to be a species-being, he is the imaginary member of a fictitious sovereignty, he is divested of his real individual life and filled with an unreal universality.

The "political state" that Marx refers to here is a modern product: it is only on the basis of bourgeois relations that the state clearly separates itself from civil society. Marx's contrasting description of feudal relations in this essay is helpful in this regard: "The old civil society [of feudalism] had a *directly political* character, i.e. the elements of civil life such as property, family and the mode and manner of work were elevated in the form of seigniory, estate and guild to the level of elements of political life."

There is a connection emerging between Marx's understanding of bourgeois society as a society of competing private producers, and the alien character of this society's general interest, which can only be "unreal." The state is alien and detached from civil society precisely because bourgeois civil society is inherently divided. As Marx would put it in *The German Ideology*, "the *practical* struggle of these particular interests, which *actually* constantly run counter to the common and illusory common interests, necessitates *practical* intervention and restraint by the illusory 'general' interest in the form of the state."

The most important application of this analysis is Marx's vision of social emancipation: "Only when real, individual man resumes the abstract citizen into himself and as an individual man has become a *species-being* in his empirical life, his individual work and his individual relationships, only when man has recognized and organized his *forces propres* [own forces] as *social forces* so that social force is no longer separated from him in the form of *political* force, only then will human emancipation be completed."

Marx speaks of man as a species-being in the sense that human consciousness and social intercourse differentiate humans from animals. Humans engage in purposive, conscious social production, transforming themselves and their environment. But when the social links between people, through which they express their species-character, become a mere means of individual existence, man is estranged, or alienated from this social essence. The analysis Marx develops in the 1840's is a unified critique of human alienation, of the freeing of social production from the control of the producers and the separation of political power from the body politic. In his "Introduction" to Marx's *Early Writings*, Lucio Colletti emphasizes the significance of Marx's critique of alienation for his analysis of capitalist society: "When real individuals are fragmented from one another and become estranged then their mediating function must in turn become independent of them: that is, their social relationships, the nexus of reciprocity which binds them together. Thus, there is an evident parallelism between the hypostasis of the state, of God, and of money."

The essentials of Marx's critique of politics are all elaborated in the 1840's. This is the inescapable foundation of Marx's understanding of proletarian revolution, which is given vivid expression in *The German Ideology*: "For the proletarians... the condition of their life, labour, and with it all the conditions of existence of modern society, have become something extraneous, something over which they, as separate individuals, have no control... they find themselves directly opposed to the form in which, hitherto, the individuals, of which society consists, have given themselves collective expression, that is, the state; in order, therefore, to assert themselves as individuals, they must overthrow the state."

What is clear from the above is that Marx did not hold an instrumental view of the state as a mere apparatus that can be administered by different social classes. It was the bourgeois expression of the illusory general interest in a divided society: the interests of private property given general force. Yet, the reader may be wondering where Marx's theory of the *dictatorship of the proletariat*, a transitional *state* characterized by the "conquest of political power for this class," comes in. In fact, in *The German Ideology* itself, the theory of proletarian dictatorship (not yet given this name) is presented rather clearly: "... every class which is aiming at domination, even when its domination, as is the case with the proletariat, leads to the abolition of the old form of society in its entirety and of domination in general, must first conquer political power in order to represent its interest in turn as the general interest, which in the first moment it is forced to do."

The proletariat must represent its interest as the general interest because it must overthrow the old society in its entirety, transforming not only its own conditions of life, but those of other classes as well. It is not a question simply of equalizing social conditions, but of *overthrowing* a social class relationship that has spread over the entire globe: that of wage-labour and capital.

Though his early writings focused on the bourgeois state as a specific historical form, Marx's transhistorical definition of "the state" in general is also presented in *The German Ideology*, when Marx describes the state as "the form in which the individuals of a ruling class assert their common interests." This definition of course does not describe the specific features of any real state or historical class of states. Any state nonetheless requires some organization of armed force, legislation, justice, etc., and a "worker's state" would be no exception. *What is significant about the above definition, however, is that it makes the concepts of "state" and "class rule" coterminous.* On the same page we find also an excellent description of the *bourgeois* state: "By the mere fact that it is a *class* and no longer an *estate*, the bourgeoisie is forced to organize itself no longer locally, but nationally, and to give a general form to its average interests. Through the emancipation of private property from the community, the state has become a separate entity, alongside and outside civil society; but it is nothing more than the form of organisation which the bourgeois are compelled to adopt, both for internal and external purposes, for the mutual guarantee of their property and interests."

For Marx, popular working class participation in governance is the necessary route to a rationally planned economy, or the abolition of bourgeois civil society. When the workers-the vast majority-reclaim the political power alienated to bureaucratic hierarchies, they subordinate the state power to their economic needs, or elevate civil society to the realm of politics. We will now look at Marx's views on the transition to socialism.

Proletarian Dictatorship

To understand Marx's views on the transition to socialism, it is useful to go back to his 1844 "Critical Notes on the Article 'The King of Prussia and Social Reform,'" where social emancipation is identified as the soul of the proletarian revolution. Marx writes, "All revolution-the *overthrow* of the existing ruling power and the *dissolution* of the old order-is a *political act*. But without revolution *socialism* cannot be made possible. It stands in need of this political act just as it stands in need of *destruction* and *dissolution*. But as soon as its *organizing functions* begin and its *goal*, its *soul* emerges, socialism throws its *political* mask aside." Here we can see the emergence of a distinct conception of transition to socialism. This is developed somewhat as a distinct understanding of *political power* in Marx's critique of Proudhon:

> The working class, in the course of its development, will substitute for the old civil society an association which will exclude classes and their antagonism, and there will be no more political power properly so-called, since political power is precisely the official expression of antagonism in civil society.... Do not say that social movement excludes political movement. There is never a political movement which is not at the same time social. It is only in an order of things in which there are no more classes and class antagonisms that social evolutions will cease to be political revolutions.

Here we see the development of the concept of proletarian political power (or "state power," as Marx sometimes referred to it): it has a social soul unlike any previous form of political power, but this class power necessarily takes a political (state) form because during the process of transition to socialism the antagonisms of civil society have not yet been completely abolished. Later Marx would label this transitional phase the period of the *dictatorship of the proletariat*. This quite simply meant the political rule of the working class. This transitional period, as Marx conceived it, did not entail the existence of a transitional form of society intervening between, and distinct from, capitalism and communism. The transitional period is essentially a period of revolutionary change. "Between capitalist and communist society," wrote Marx, "lies the period of the revolutionary transformation of the one into the other." The *raison d'être* of the proletarian state power is to bring the means of production into common ownership, to bring about the "expropriation of the expropriators," as Marx described the aim of the Paris Commune.

A little-known text by Marx, his 1874 "Notes on Bakunin's Book *Statehood and Anarchy*," explains the concept of proletarian dictatorship more clearly than any other. In his book Bakunin ridicules Marx's concept of the transitional state power of the proletarian dictatorship, and Marx critically responds in his "Notes." Bakunin writes, "If there is a state, then there is domination and consequent slavery. A state without slavery, open or camouflaged, is inconceivable-that is why we are enemies of the state. What does it mean, 'the proletariat raised to a governing class?'" Marx responds, "It means that the proletariat, instead of fighting in individual instances against the economically privileged classes, has gained sufficient strength and organisation to use general means of coercion in its struggle against them; but it can only make use of such economic means as abolish its own character as wage labourer and hence as a class; when its victory is complete, its rule too is therefore at an end, since its class character will have disappeared." The claim that through revolution the proletariat will be "raised to a governing class" thus has nothing to do with creating a dictatorship of a political sect, but is rather a claim that the proletariat will use "general means of coercion" to undercut the bourgeoisie's power (by abolishing the private ownership of the means of production, disbanding the standing army, and so forth). It is the entire proletariat that is to exercise this power. Bakunin asks, "Will all 40 million [German workers] be members of the government?" Marx responds, "Certainly! For the system starts with the self-government of the communities." This statement is certainly striking, but there are other places in the text where Marx more subtly conveys his radical conception of proletarian democracy. When writing about proletarian power and the peasantry, Marx writes that "the proletariat... must, *as the government*, take the measures needed... " , identifying the transitional government with the proletariat as a class. Another example: when quoting Bakunin's critique, Marx inserts a revealing parenthetical comment: "The dilemma in the theory of the Marxists is easily resolved. By people's government they (*i.e. Bakunin*) understand the government of the people by a small number of representatives chosen (elected) by the people." Here Marx is very clearly implying that he does *not* understand "people's government" or workers' government, as the government of the people by a small number of representatives elected by the people. This is a rather clear indication that Marx is still faithful to his 1843 critique of bourgeois democracy.

Clearly, this conception of "proletarian" government is distinct from the bourgeois state, or from any previous form of state power. As Marx makes clear in the above statements, he is referring to a proletarian "government" only in the sense that the working class uses general means of coercion to enforce its aims. Proletarian government is not used by Marx to mean that some elite group (assumedly the intellectuals, as Bakunin argued) would use general means of coercion over the whole proletariat, for that would rule out working class "self-government." Rather, the proletariat *as a whole* would assert its class interests over an *alien* class (by abolishing private property, expropriating the capitalists and socializing the means of production, disbanding the standing army, etc.). For anarchists, who often define these terms somewhat differently, much of the confusion about Marx's claim that the proletariat must wield political power seems to be based on Marx's frequent use of the words "state" and "government." But as we have seen, there is nothing anti-democratic about the meaning Marx attached to these words. Most anarchists, unlike Marx, *define* the state in terms of minority rule. It is easy for someone who uses this sort of definition to read Marx's mention of a proletarian "state" and immediately associate it with oppression and detachment from effective popular control. The problem is that interpreting Marx in this way creates a number of contradictions in his writings that vanish when his basic theoretical framework is better understood.

Another example of Marx's use of the idea of proletarian dictatorship comes in an essay on "Political Indifferentism" that criticizes both the Proudhonists and the Bakuninists. Marx recognizes that the workers must struggle against the *bourgeois state*, but also that a revolutionary form of state is needed before social classes as such disappear. Marx pretends to speak for his opponents:

> If in the political struggle against the bourgeois state the workers succeed only in extracting concessions, then they are guilty of compromise; and this is contrary to eternal principles.... If the political struggle of the working class assumes violent forms and if the workers replace the dictatorship of the bourgeois class with their own revolutionary dictatorship, then they are guilty of the terrible crime of *lèse-principe*; for, in order to satisfy their miserable profane daily needs and to crush the resistance of the bourgeois class, they, instead of laying down their arms and abolishing the state, give to the state a revolutionary and transitory form.

This passage illustrates fairly clearly that proletarian dictatorship is simply the political power of an armed working class. The essence of a "workers' state," for Marx, was workers' power, not any particular leadership at the helm of the state.

Furthermore, as Hal Draper has pointed out, it is a mistake to assume that the word "dictatorship" in the phrase "dictatorship of the proletariat" is supposed to refer to dictatorial (as distinguished from democratic) policies or forms of government. In fact, it was not until the latter part of the 19th century and more definitively after the Russian revolution that the term "dictatorship" came to have a specifically anti-democratic connotation. The origin of the term is the Roman *dictatura*, which referred to an emergency management of power. After 1848, around the time that Marx began using the term, it became relatively common for journalists to bemoan the "dictatorship" or "despotism" of the people, which posed a threat to the status quo. In 1849, a Spanish politician even made a speech in parliament declaring: "It is a question of choosing between the dictatorship from below and the dictatorship from above: I choose the dictatorship from above, since it comes from a purer and loftier realm." Revolutionaries had even used the word "dictatorship" before Marx to refer to a transition to socialism. Blanqui, for example, advocated an educative dictatorship of a small group of revolutionaries. Marx's use of the word "dictatorship" in the phrase "dictatorship *of the proletariat,*" however, is original and deliberately distinct from Blanqui's usage. Engels emphasizes this point in a passage on Blanqui: "From the fact that Blanqui conceives of every revolution as the *coup de main* of a small revolutionary minority, what follows of itself is the necessity of dictatorship after its success-the dictatorship, please note, not of the entire revolutionary class, the proletariat, but of the small number of those who made the *coup de main* and who themselves are organized beforehand under the dictatorship of one person or a few. One can see that Blanqui is a revolutionary of the previous generation." It is clear that the Leninist model of a particular sect or political party exercising political power is much closer to the Blanquist conception of "dictatorship" than to Marx's, and Engels explicitly criticized this conception of how political power should be exercised. It is also clear that Blanqui's model of rule by a small group of revolutionaries shares more in common with popular fantasies about Marx than with Marx's dictatorship of the *whole proletarian class.*

Storming Heaven

We have seen that Marx's radical democracy formed a major part of his political perspective. Though not as explicit in his economic studies, to which Marx devoted so much of his life, his basic political perspective comes to the fore once again in his analysis of the Paris Commune of 1871, a landmark event in the history of the workers' movement. It is in his analysis of the Paris Commune that Marx's understanding of the transition to socialism is most clearly developed. We will look closely at Marx's famous essay on the Commune, as well as his drafts for this text.

In *The Civil War in France*, Marx lauds the Commune as "a thoroughly expansive political form, while all previous forms of government had been emphatically repressive. Its true secret was this. It was essentially a working-class government, the produce of the struggle of the producing against the appropriating class, the political form at last discovered under which to work out the economic emancipation of labour." In his First Draft, Marx also characterized the Commune as "a Revolution against the *State* itself." Here he was referring specifically to the French centralized executive power, which had not been broken by previous revolutions. Marx focuses on the Commune's break with this state machinery, and the resumption of power by the masses: "It was a Revolution against the *State* itself, of this supernaturalist abortion of society, a resumption by the people for the people of its own social life. It was not a revolution to transfer it from one fraction of the ruling classes to the other, but a Revolution to break down this horrid machinery of Class domination itself."

Although Marx's terminology is somewhat different from other parts of his writings (where he referred to the proletariat's exercise of state power), the main points of his vision of proletarian emancipation remained constant: the proletariat exercises political power through general means of coercion over the capitalist class, and it does this *as a class* rather than through an elite group of individuals raised above the rest of the ruling class, using democratic methods that would be appropriate to the future communist society. The frequent claim that Marx simply adopted the anarchist view of the state after the Paris Commune could not be further from the truth. The parasitic French state of the bourgeoisie was to be destroyed, but in 1871 Marx did not cease to call for working class *state* power.

The method of political organization adopted by the Paris Commune is also described as "the reabsorption of the State power by society as its own living forces instead of as forces controlling and subduing it." This "reabsorption" was accomplished when the Commune did away with "the state hierarchy altogether" and replaced "the haughteous masters of the people" by "always removable servants" acting "continuously under public supervision." The Commune challenged "The delusion as if administration and political governing were mysteries, transcendent functions only to be trusted to the hands of a trained caste." In Marx's writing on the Paris Commune, we can see again Marx's support, expressed as early as 1843, for a public able to "deliberate and decide on public affairs *for themselves*." We see a reappearance of the themes of his Critique of Hegel: direct democracy through responsible delegates, the elimination of bureaucracy and its attendant mysteries. Marx even called the Parisians of the Commune "heaven-stormers" and contrasted them with "the slaves to heaven of the German-Prussian Holy Roman Empire." It is possible that Marx was using his 1843 identification of the bourgeois state as the "heaven" of civil society. The Parisians *stormed heaven* in that they conquered the political power that had previously been sharply separated from their profane existences. The Commune easily became Marx's model for the transitional proletarian state. Marx praised the workers of Paris for having "taken the actual management of their Revolution into their own hands and [having] found at the same time, in the case of success, the means to hold it in the hands of the People itself, displacing the State machinery, the governmental machinery of the ruling classes by a governmental machinery of their own." Here we see that the process of transition itself must be self-managed by the workers. The opposition to Blanquist conceptions could not be more self-evident.

In his Second Draft, Marx makes an even clearer statement of the prefigurative nature of the proletarian dictatorship: "the working class cannot simply lay hold on the ready made State machinery and wield it for their own purpose. The political instrument of their enslavement cannot serve as the political instrument of their emancipation." Derek Sayer has emphasized this aspect of proletarian dictatorship. He writes that breaking down the separation between the state and civil society is "not for Marx one of communism's remote objectives, but an indispensable part of any conceivable *means* for its attainment. What needs to be understood is that Marx is being every bit as materialist here as in his critique of the Anarchists. If the objective is labour's self-emancipation the means *have* to be 'prefigurative', because they are the only ones which will work." For Marx, this form of power can be a "state" from the perspective of its *political*, coercive function of uprooting the foundations of the rule of capital. It cannot be a "state" in the sense of a "parasitic excrescence" usurping power from the mass of workers.

A passage from the Final Draft focusing on the *organization* of the Commune is worth examining closely: In a rough sketch of national organization which the Commune had no time to develop, it states clearly that the Commune was to be the political form of even the smallest country hamlet, and that in the rural districts the standing army was to be replaced by a national militia, with an extremely short term of service. The rural communes of every district were to administer their common affairs by an assembly of delegates in the central town, and these district assemblies were again to send deputies to the National Delegation in Paris, each delegate to be at any time revocable and bound by the *mandat impératif* (formal instructions) of his constituents. The few but important functions which still would remain for a central government were not to be suppressed, as has been intentionally misstated, but were to be discharged by Communal, and therefore strictly responsible agents. The unity of the nation was not to be broken, but, on the contrary, to be organised by the Communal Constitution and to become a reality by the destruction of the State power which claimed to be the embodiment of that unity independent of, and superior to, the nation itself, from which it was but a parasitic excrescence. While the merely repressive organs of the old governmental power were to be amputated, its legitimate functions were to be wrested from an authority usurping pre-eminence over society itself, and restored to the responsible agents of society. Instead of deciding once in three or six years which member of the ruling class was to misrepresent the people in Parliament, universal suffrage was to serve the people, constituted in Communes, as individual suffrage serves every other employer in the search for the workmen and managers in his business. And it is well known that companies, like individuals, in matters of real business generally know how to put the right man in the right place, and, if they for once make a mistake, to redress it promptly. On the other hand, nothing could be more foreign to the spirit of the Commune than to supersede universal suffrage by hierarchic investiture.

Marx saw the mandated and revocable delegates of the Commune as an example of working class state power in action. Recall Marx's 1843 description of the bourgeois state: "The separation of the political state from civil society takes the form of a separation of the deputies from their electors." Marx clearly thought that the Commune exhibited the opposite tendency. Here we see a vivid contrast between the bureaucratic French state machinery and the "governmental machinery" of the workers. Richard N. Hunt, in writing about the Commune, highlights what he called Marx and Engels' "double usage" of the word "state," which can function as a stand-in for a parasitic bourgeois state machinery, or as a general description of organized class rule: "The full-time army as parasite disappeared, but the part-time National Guard remained as the coercive instrument of the workers' state. Here in sharpest focus one can perceive Marx and Engels' double usage: the parasite state is to be smashed immediately; the state as instrument of class coercion is to remain until the need for it fades away."

Marx makes another important distinction between the Commune and normal bourgeois government: "The Commune was to be a working, not a parliamentary, body, executive and legislative at the same time." The delegates were generally to be responsible for carrying out legislative decisions, instead of simply voting on them. As Marx put it in his Second Draft of *The Civil War in France*, "The modern bourgeois state is embodied in two great organs, parliament and the government [the executive]." Parliamentarism is not identified with effective control from below, but rather with professional politicians who are not truly responsible to the public. In an 1888 letter to Laura Lafargue, Engels spoke of French political illusions: "Why, if the French see no other issue than *either* personal government, or parliamentary government, they may as well give up." Clearly the solution is not greater power for one of the two "great organs" of the bourgeois state, but rather an integration of their functions under the control of the revolutionary workers. In the Commune Marx saw the destruction of a bourgeois state and the democratization of executive power. Hal Draper writes on this theme:

> It was Marx's view that the abolition of the separation of powers, far from being a temporary or provisional expedient, was a basic necessity for a truly democratic government. He reiterated this view in his 1851 article on the French constitution, after quoting its statement that "the division of powers is the primary condition of a free government." [Marx:] "Here we have the old constitutional folly. The condition of a 'free government' is not the *division* but the *unity* of power. The machinery of government cannot be too simple. It is always the craft of knaves to make it complicated and mysterious."

We have seen how, in the 1840's, Marx described the bourgeois state as "a separate entity, alongside and outside civil society." We have also seen how the Commune represented the "reabsorption" by the people of a "parasitic" state power. In a remarkable 1891 passage, Engels draws together some of these different ideas to make a valuable contrast between proletarian state power and previous forms of state power. It is worth quoting at length: From the very outset the Commune was compelled to recognise that the working class, once come to power, could not go on managing with the old state machine; that in order not to lose again its only just conquered supremacy, this working class must, on the one hand, do away with all the old repressive machinery previously used against it itself, and, on the other, safeguard itself against its own deputies and officials, by declaring them all, without exception, subject to recall at any moment.

What had been the characteristic attribute of the former state? Society had created its own organs to look after its common interests, originally through simple division of labour. But these organs, at whose head was the state power, had in the course of time, in pursuance of their own special interests, transformed themselves from the servants of society into the masters of society. This can be seen, for example, not only in the hereditary monarchy, but equally so in the democratic republic. Nowhere do "politicians" form a more separate and powerful section of the nation than precisely in North America.... It is precisely in America that we see best how there takes place this process of the state power making itself independent in relation to society, whose mere instrument it was originally intended to be. Here there exists no dynasty, no nobility, no standing army, beyond the few men keeping watch on the Indians, no bureaucracy with permanent posts or the right to pensions. And nevertheless we find here two great gangs of political speculators, who alternately take possession of the state power and exploit it by the most corrupt means and for the most corrupt ends-and the nation is powerless against these two great cartels of politicians, who are ostensibly its servants, but in reality dominate and plunder it. Against this transformation of the state and the organs of the state from servants of society into masters of society-an inevitable transformation in all previous states-the Commune made use of two infallible means. In this first place, it filled all posts-administrative, judicial and educational-by election on the basis of universal suffrage of all concerned, subject to the right of recall at any time by the same electors. And, in the second place, all officials, high or low, were paid only the wages received by other workers.

This passage emphasizes very strongly the special character of proletarian state power. Richard N. Hunt ably describes a "central thread" of Marx and Engels' analysis of the Paris Commune as "the desire to debureaucratize or, more broadly, deprofessionalize public life, to create a democracy without professionals. This is the really crucial and distinguishing characteristic of the workers' state as conceived by Marx and Engels.... Deprofessionalization is the remedy to the parasitic tendency which has existed in all previous states. It is exactly what is involved in 'smashing' the state machinery and 'reabsorbing' state power." The payment of workers' wages to officials, mentioned by Engels, is a clear example of this deprofessionalization.

Some critics may look at a focus on the Paris Commune as bound to make Marx and Engels look very hostile to the bourgeois state, when in fact their politics were much more ambiguous. Did they not advocate participation in bourgeois elections, and the election of workers' candidates into parliament? In fact, in certain countries, they even thought that a working class parliamentary majority could be used for a peaceful transition to socialism. For many anarchists, this is the defining aspect of Marx's political thought, and his supposed authoritarianism is considered proven on this evidence. Leaving aside the question of the relative value of electoral politics, it is worth asking whether there is necessarily any contradiction in advocating the use of bourgeois parliaments while hoping for their eventual replacement by Communal-type organization, in other words whether one can insist on the fullest possible democratization while participating in governmental forms that are less than ideal. The anarchist assumption, of course, is that participation in bourgeois governmental forms can only help sustain such institutions. But the error comes when it is assumed that since Marx advocated such participation, he also believed in keeping the governmental forms of the bourgeois state for the period of proletarian rule.

As we have seen, Marx in fact foresaw a fundamental change occurring when the workers reabsorb their alienated political powers, and the state becomes servant instead of master of society. Unsurprisingly, this change entails certain formal changes such as the extension of the principle of democratic control to more areas of public life, the maximization of popular control over elected delegates, a deprofessionalization of public life and an end to bureaucratism, a simplification of governmental functions and the end to the division between executive and legislative power. As Richard N. Hunt has put it, "... Marx and Engels never imagined that the leaders of the workers' movement would simply step into the high offices of the state and govern as a professional cadre in much the same manner as their bourgeois predecessors."

Marx always believed that some democracy was better than none at all, and even that a limited bourgeois democracy can point beyond itself just by allowing some degree of popular participation in politics. As he put it in *The Eighteenth Brumaire of Louis Bonaparte*: "The struggle of the parliamentary orators calls forth the struggle of the scribblers of the press; the parliamentary debating club is necessarily supplemented by debating clubs in the salons and alehouses; the deputies, by constantly appealing to the opinion of the people, give the people the right to express their real opinion in petitions. The parliamentary regime leaves everything to the decision of majorities, why then should the great majority outside parliament not want to make the decisions?" With regard to the use of parliament, Marx was clear that the problem of social transformation is not solved in parliament, and that the workers cannot simply rely on the wisdom of their leaders. Hal Draper relates one instance in which Marx criticized Lassalle on these issues:

In 1863 Lassalle sent Marx a pamphlet of his in which he made his bid for leadership of the German workers' movement. Marx commented in a letter to Engels: "He behaves-with an air of great importance bandying about phrases borrowed from us-altogether as if he were the future workers' dictator. The problem of wage-labour versus capital he solves like 'child's play' (literally). To wit, the workers must agitate for *universal suffrage* and then send people like him 'armed with the unsheathed sword of science [*Wissenschaft*]' into the Chamber of Deputies." Here is how Lassalle had put it in the pamphlet, addressing himself to the workers: "When that [universal suffrage] comes, you can depend upon it, there will be at your side men who understand your position and are devoted to your cause-men, armed with the shining sword of science, who know how to defend your interests. And then you, the unpropertied classes, will only have yourselves and your bad voting to blame if the representatives of your cause remain in a minority...."

Marx's critique of Lassalle is especially valuable, as it was a critique of a simplistic notion of revolution-from-above in a contemporary of Marx. Marx also criticized the harmful influence of Lassalle's perspective on the Gotha Programme: "Instead of the revolutionary process of transformation of society, the 'socialist organization of the total labour' 'arises' from the 'state aid' that the state gives to the producers' co-operative societies and which the state, not the worker, '*calls into being*.' This is worthy of Lassalle's imagination that one can build a new society by state loans just as well as a new railway!" Building a new society is for Marx a process of self-emancipation. The wielding of political power is an important part of this: the workers must take charge, re-organize society, and exercise the social power previously denied them. This is why Lassalle's socialism-from-above is totally inadequate.

Many people think of Marx as an advocate of socialism-from-above because they hear the word "centralization" and assume that Marx advocated some sort of authoritarian arrangement. Marx did not view the functions of a central government as a pure limitation on autonomy, but rather saw the "unity of the nation" as being realized (not destroyed) by uprooting those who administer the state as a sphere separate from civil society. Bakunin's approach, for example, lacks this critique, as he praised the Parisian workers for proclaiming "the complete abolition of the French state, the dissolution of France's state unity as incompatible with the autonomy of France's communes." Here we can see Bakunin's debt to the Proudhonian socialism with which Marx so vehemently disagreed. While Bakunin was a sworn enemy of all political and economic centralization, Marx had a very different perspective, but one that was in no way more "authoritarian": "*National centralization of the means of production* will become the natural basis of a society composed of associations of free and equal producers, carrying on the social business on a common and rational plan." Marx thought that both centralism (a *common* plan) and democratic control from below were necessary for building socialism.

Conclusion

Marx's political theory is indeed widely misunderstood. Yet anyone who has studied Marx's writing on the Paris Commune is led to agree with Hal Draper when he observes, "... the Commune state, any genuine workers' state, is not merely a state with a different class rule but *a new type of state* altogether." This assessment is entirely consistent with Marx's emphasis on the proletariat as the bearer of a revolution with a social soul, a unique historical class in this regard. Its political rule is likewise unique as far as political rule goes. As Marx put it in the *Manifesto*, "All previous historical movements were movements of minorities, or in the interests of minorities. The proletarian movement is the self-conscious, independent movement of the immense majority, in the interests of the immense majority."

The myth of Marx's authoritarian statism flourished in the 20th century. The Soviet state, for example, wished to clothe itself in Marx's theoretical mantle-in particular, the shibboleth of proletarian dictatorship. Furthermore, Bakunin's conception of Marx's political theory came to life, so to speak, with Stalinism. It is unsurprising, then, that Marxism and anarchism have developed strikingly similar erroneous ideas about Marx's theory of the state. The mythical version of Marx's theory is indeed discredited. Marx's actual political theory, however, still deserves serious consideration.

9

Marxism and Feminism

The re-emergence of feminism in the 1970s, itself the product of a whole generation of militants imbued with Marxism-at least in Europe-contributed to the development of two types of currents: those advocating a pure and simple rejection of Marxism, others the surpassing of Marxism through some methodology supposed to be better suited to the new subject matter. This paradoxical phenomenon can be explained by factors both internal and external to Marxism. The desire to analyse the relations between sexes is not a new thing in this century, contrary to widespread belief.. It could even be said that the generalisation of the capitalist mode of production and the ideological revolution of the Enlightenment marked the starting point of a blurring of the real relations between sexes but also opened up the possibility to transcend them. In fact, the observation of ancient slave societies and medieval societies shows a strikingly abundant theoretical or phantasmagorical production justifying women's oppression, far greater than the production aimed at maintaining class divisions. The mythology of Ancient Greece, Confucian China and Vedic India was largely based on conflict between the sexes. The medieval Church erected a massive set of concepts on women's inferiority.

On the other hand, bourgeois ideology remains full of contradictions. Taking the existence of Man as a universal, a-historical and classless subject as its starting point, it finds it more difficult to ascertain some inherent inferiority of any given human group-the same problem arose with colonised peoples whose elite used the official bourgeois values against the colonial power. Thus, even if over the last two hundred years it has constantly attempted to demonstrate scientifically the inferiority of women-from the size of the brain to modern aptitude tests-bourgeois thinking has chosen to justify the institutions through which oppression is exerted rather than establish the existence of sub-human groups.

The fascist doctrine which starts from the supposed inferiority of women represents the exception confirming the rule. Middle Ages clerics described "The Woman" as diabolical whilst bourgeois ideology stated the need for families and the equivalence between femininity and maternity. Moreover, as the class most often under attack (since its inception was paralleled by the emergence of the workers' movement), the bourgeoisie's ideological production concentrated essentially on the defense of its class interests : valorization of labour, of the individual, legitimization of the State... Women's oppression, so widely used, is hardly mentioned. While it was so highly claimed in other modes of production, it has been virtually erased under capitalism. Women have become a sort of "Black continent". Feminism in the 1970s started by reaffirming the oppression of women and its manifestations. It was a break with the past.

I consider that Marx and Engels remained dependent on the intellectual context of their time when neither relations between men and women nor the global situation of women within the capitalist system and within the different classes they belonged to were analysed. Only the institutions reproducing bourgeois society and in which women were involved came under scrutiny. Thus women happened to be in the subject of the analysis but never represented its starting point; the explanation of their oppression remained partial as no global understanding was aimed at; consequently, it was opened to misinterpretations and fuzzy theories. Women were dubbed "proletariat of the proletariat", "slave", "serf", all striking terms that did not clarify the real function of their oppression in the system. This explains why, in the last decade, Marxism was rejected as intellectually barren : "Marx did not say anything sensible on the woman question, Engels got it wrong on the origins of oppression..." is often heard together with dualistic statements that Marxism is still useful for class analysis but useless for relations between the sexes. As if a new area of study required a new methodology !

There is no need to precise that this rejection is not purely theoretical. For decades-apart from brief revolutionary periods-the reformist labour movement with its social-democratic or Stalinist traditions has been reciting bourgeois ideology on this question. This did not lend credit to Marxism. Moreover, current feminism found its origin in the United States often relying on psychoanalysis or relating women's oppression to other forms of oppression (national or racial question) which did not encouraged a Marxist approach. Finally, as feminism was posed in terms of a social group suffering from segregation and inscribed in the framework of otherness (the man is the norm, the woman is the other), it could hardly escape the fashionable plague of philosophies of the Difference from the "New Philosophy" to the "New Right" including all sorts of interpretations claiming a psychoanalytical origin.

In this article, I would like to show what I believe to be correct in Marx' and Engels' texts and what is erroneous. I would like to demonstrate the inability to explain women's oppression as a global phenomenon of those theories that claim to reject or surpass Marxism which, despite some statements here and there, remains the only methodological approach for understanding the question.

MARX, ENGELS AND THE QUESTION OF WOMEN'S OPPRESSION

The great merit of Marxism is that it denounced the subjugation of women at a time, in the 19th century, when other "socialists" went as far as advocating its deepening (Proudhon in particular). Marx and Engels continued the tradition of the Saint-Simon and Fourier schools of thought-to which Flora Tristan belonged-which demanded sexual equality and the subversion of the bourgeois family. Going beyond the Utopians who limited themselves to a description of women's inferiority and asked for equality in the name of justice, Marxism started from a fundamental presupposition : that women's oppression is not a permanent feature in history but the result of a certain social formation and that relationships between sexes are not a natural but a social construct. This historical and materialist basis remains nowadays the dividing line from structuralist ethnology (Lévi-Strauss) which takes the exchange of women as the constituent element of human societies or from the psychoanalysts who believe that sexual differentiation is the driving force in the structuring of psyche.

In this field however, Marx derived his historical approach from a postulate, itself a logical outcome of historical materialism, rather than from a belief borne out of accurate studies of the status of women throughout the centuries. Only Engels' last book-40 years after Flora Tristan's death !-offered a systematic approach to the question. The Origins of the Family distinguished 3 main periods in women's history : classless societies in which women held leading positions (original matriarchy); non-capitalist class societies in which women are devoted to domestic reproduction as "slaves"; capitalism which reintroduced women into the productive sphere thereby providing an objective basis for their emancipation. This highly simplified division in periods is acceptable; what is not acceptable is the analysis of the status of women during some of the periods.

First, it is undisputed that societies without private ownership of the means of production, without state apparatuses, and with kinship social systems, showed examples of women's oppression infinitely more violent than that of 19th century imperialist countries. Many tribes of this type lived almost exclusively on female labour controlled by men; women were exchanged like goods, went and resided in the husband's village where they lost all rights; the ideological and religious production of those societies was intensely misogynist.

Why did Engels get it wrong ? Trapped in the ethnological findings of his time, which were much more limited than today's, Engels mixed two very different types of societies : matrilineal and matriarchal societies. Most of the known primitive or archaic societies undoubtedly operate or operated on the basis of matrilineal descent, but power belonged to maternal uncles and not women. Engels did not understand the importance of the place of residence of the family. Gender relations were totally different whether the husband went to his wife's clan (matrilocality) or the wife went to the husband's (patrilocality). The generalisation of patrilocality was much more significant in the "historic defeat of the female sex" (this concept is ambiguous for it evokes pitched battles rather than a contradictory process spreading over milleniums inside transitory social formations) than the emergence of slavery, the State, patrilineality or the patriarchal family. Moreover, Engels based the origins of the changes in the status of women on a primitive division of labour with men hunting and women foraging and farming, which enabled men to appropriate the social surplus. I believe that there is no "natural" and universal division of labour. Men did what women did and vice versa, depending on the society they belonged to. Even such archetypically female activities as spinning and weaving are carried out by men in some North African tribes. It is not the nature of the work that matters but social relations. I do not intend here to discuss the research hypotheses on the status of women in pre-class societies and even less those on the historical "origins" of women's oppression for which there is no widely accepted final answer. But the most productive method derives from the most classic Marxist concepts. Even for societies where relations of production are built on kinship relations, the most useful questions are the following : who produced, who controlled production ? Who benefited from the kinship system?

I defend the idea that the known pre-class societies, which were almost all patrilocal, whether matrilineal or patrilineal, functioned on the principle of collective appropriation by men of women's labour force. This situation is confirmed by present primitive societies; it can be inferred from the study of archaic social formations, dominated by female slavery and where femininity and slavery were linked as a constant ideological feature. I therefore think that the slavery "revolution" and the private appropriation of the means of production stemmed from lineage societies, representing a break or continuity, as in those societies the collective appropriation of female labour and the devaluation of a human group within a clan supplied a model for later forms of exploitation. Nevertheless, although I believe that the first type of class struggle opposed women to men, I do not deduce from it the primacy of gender struggle for later modes of production.

Women, however, are not "redistributed" inside the main classes as men are; it is not difficult to allocate women from the exploited layers to a class, though they are never exploited "in the same way" as men; the question is much more delicate for women of the ruling classes in certain historical periods. To which class, for example, should we allocate the wife of an Athenian aristocrat in antiquity, who was married at 12, locked up in the gynaeceum, deprived of any control over her wealth and working with the servants ?

Engels characterized the second period in women's history by their exclusion from production. From the emergence of slavery to that of manufacture, women would have been devoted to reproduction in both senses of the word. "The wife became the first domestic servant, pushed out of participation in social production. Only modern large-scale industry again threw open to her-and only to the proletarian woman at that-the avenue to social production." This assertion is still widely adhered to by Marxists. J.-L. Moynot wrote that in history "the male labour force played the main role", women being devoted to child-raising and domestic tasks.

Such a thesis is both anachronistic and unacceptable. It is nachronistic because it implies a marked division between the productive and reproductive spheres which was only introduced by capitalism. Let us take the example of a village community at the height of feudal mode of production. The sexual division of labour was absolute and immutable. But it did not correspond to the productive/reproductive division. Women were involved in some agricultural tasks, the hardest; men did the rest; all produced. Women spun, another activity which, as spun wool was sometimes sold, was as productive as work in the fields essentially for self-consumption. Domestic work ? It was quite limited given the types of habitat and eating habits, and were often left to an elder woman or youngsters. This thesis is also unacceptable because no known social formation in history has ever been able to do without the massive use of female labour for production.

Only a precise study of a given society at a given time can determine the respective roles of male and female labour, and these vary greatly. So, to assert that women have been excluded from production is a feature of patriarchal ideology that claims the non-existence of women's work. Were the slaves of Asian monarchs or of Mycenae who were textile workers or cultivating the large estates of kings and temples really unproductive? Not productive, the medieval female peasants ? On the contrary, the use of female labour was characterized by a combination of the most devalued productive tasks and reproductive ones, the first being often presented as an extension of the latter. In non-capitalist class societies, only the women of the ruling classes were excluded from production. Here again, it is important to differenciate them from men of the exploiting classes insofar as they nearly always worked : they were "the first servant" in the gynaeceum or in the feudal manor whilst their husband was totally "idle", devoting his time to politics, war or hunting, according to the period concerned.

Thus, the distinction between production and reproduction does not enable us to understand the condition of women in slave or feudal modes of production. More interestingly, if we start from the real individual status of women, we then discover that the use of their labour force, whatever the type of work, was never the same as that of men but took place in the context of specific social relations of domination. At the origins of slavery, there were more female slaves; while a numerical equality was later attained, however, the chances of women gaining their freedom were reduced, particularly given the fact that they brought the additional advantage of their children. In medieval societies, the father or husband, by custom the owner of her labour and her body, remained the automatic go-between the peasant woman and her lord. Let us take the example of the villain (free peasant in Western Europe): he owned the "use" of his land, could sell it or leave it; he had to pay numerous taxes but remained a free man. For the female villain, there was no freedom : land did not belong to her as she rarely inherited, nor did the produce of her labour; she could not leave because she depended on her father or husband's authority.

The male and female villains both belonged to the same fundamental class : their interests were the same against that of the lord and their role in the production process was similar. But it is obvious that, within the exploited class, women represented a layer defined both by their class but also by their personal status inside the family, a status not dissimilar to that of slaves. A woman did not belong to herself. Whatever their own oppression, father and husband kept economic power (controlling her labour) and political power (maintaining hierarchy) over her in these societies where authority mattered at all levels of the social structure.

Marx and Engels correctly sensed that capitalism introduced a major break in the condition of women and in the nature of the family. With brilliant intuition at the time of "savage capitalism" when women's situation seemed more appalling than the peasants', they were able to understand the logical evolution of the new mode of production which would create the objective conditions of her emancipation. With its tendency to involve more women in the sphere of social production, with the proletarianisation of an ever increasing number of workers, and by depriving the family of its role in the transmission of property, capitalism (partially) undermined the basis of male domination. Even if this conception now appears too unilateral, even if Marx and Engels made mistakes in the pace, late capitalism partly justifies their analysis. This is convincingly demonstrated by a comparison between the status of women in the imperialist countries and that of women in the third world which-all things being equal-are very similar to the condition of our great grand-mothers. Similarly, the positive role that Engels assigned to the insertion of women in capitalist production (despite some ambiguous formulations) had the merit of providing some legitimacy to the right of women to work at a time when the majority of the labour movement was condemning them for "stealing jobs". Today, this position remains with some nuances (access to wages does not guarantee freedom as the women join the proletariat as women) the dividing line with those who question, in theory or in practice, the need for women to work outside the home. Marx and Engels did not praise domestic labour or motherhood, which is quite remarkable given that the utopian socialists were demanding rights for women in the name of motherhood. "I repeat that the woman is everything in the life of a worker : as a mother, she influences him while a child; it is from her and from her only that he learns the first notions of this vital science which is the science of life...". This quote by Flora Tristan could possibly be understood as an acknowledgement of the reality. But Prosper Enfantin, in the tradition of Saint-

Simon, and others following on from Fourier have constantly praised the Mother and her duties, with mystical high-flown language perfectly in line with the current bourgeois ideology that had been developed on that question at the end of the 18th century. Engels was more modern when he wrote : "The modern individual family is based on the open or disguised domestic enslavement of the woman."

Nevertheless, as I explained above, neither Marx nor Engels tried to formulate a theory of women's oppression. Das Kapital details the conditions of production in the capitalist system but virtually never mentions those of reproduction. This stems from the system itself which, by establishing the most radical separation of history between the sphere of production and that of reproduction, makes it possible to analyse each on their own. In that way, Marx only looked at women as far as their work in manufacturing was concerned and did not understand their condition as a whole. Marx and Engels did have a theory of the family, but the structure they described belonged to the past : they included in the fundamental characteristics of the monogamous family its role in the transmission of inheritance through legitimate children and the increase in wealth brought about by the wife's dowry. "The rule of the man in the family, the procreation of children who could only be his, destined to be heirs of his wealth-these alone were... the exclusive gains of monogamy." They were right to consider that this function of the family was condemned to wither away by the spread of capitalism. It is no longer its main function-at least for the vast majority of the population-even though research conducted in France on the creation of wealth showed that, inside the ruling class, inheritance plays a significant role in its transmission. The family however is still thriving and so is women's oppression.

Marxist theory has three major flaws for us: the differentiated use of male and female labour power by capitalism; the emergence of a bourgeois family adapted to the economic and political needs of the system; and the nature of social relations between sexes.

Marx and his contemporaries could only sez the determining role played by female labour in the accumulation of surplus profits at the origins of industrial capitalism. "When capital got hold of machines, it cried : women's work, children's work". The explanation seemed simple : unlike the members of corporations, women had no skills and could adapt far more easily to new working conditions; their upbringing and their extremely precarious lives made them docile.

This explanation arose from the economic situation, as it was explained by Marx. But in fact, the overexploitation of women until late capitalism is a structural phenomenon. No one denies that professional inequality, at all levels of the social pyramid, is the rule. The lack of qualification is no longer the cause but a consequence of the need for capital to have at its disposal an overexploited labour force. In France, we have reached the paradoxical situation that because women do better at school they end up less qualified : they take their high school exams whilst boys (given their failure at school) are redirected towards technical training which makes them more suited to the market. In any case, as soon as women enter a profession, even a highly skilled one, it become very rapidly devalued. Moreover, what Marx noticed for the first industrial revolution, has been verified with the present technological changes. New working conditions-computing, bureautics, restructuring of working rythms-are tested on women. This constant shows how superficial any parallel with immigrant labour is. Foreigners have always eventually managed to get "integrated', so that at each new wave of expansion, more immigrants were needed. Women never get "integrated" and raise the question of what enables Capital to maintain the devaluation of their labour force.

The composition of the wage is a major element, and is different for men and women. Marx gave this definition of the wage : "The value of the labour force was determined by the expenses needed for the worker's and his family's upkeep." This composition of the wage has been generally correct, with the exceptions of periods of acute crisis of capitalism, and of the lumpen-proletariat. But it is only true of the male labour force. On the other side, it looks as if the female wage was cut by the part which men receive to maintain their family, on top of themselves. This differentiation in wages operates for all, the system assuming that all are married. The best proof can be seen in the social measures for women in developed capitalist countries as these measures are largely meant to compensate for the absence of a husband : benefits to widows, single mothers or divorcees; pensions that widows receive immediately whilst widowers have to wait until their own retirement (the latter being very recent !), etc. Society prefers to "support" millions of women rather than paying them an equal wage. Contrary to appearances and to bourgeois legislation, the gap is still widening: women are, proportionately, increasingly numerous as skilled and unskilled workers.

It is obvious that this pin-money wage exists because of the need to accumulate profits; whether it constitutes a structural or conjunctural element remains an abstract question since the realisation of profit always occurs in concrete historical circumstances (and relationships of forces). The fact that this phenomenon survived three industrial revolutions, from the origins of capitalism to today, would indicate its structural nature. The specificity of this overexploitation comes from the fact that it derives its legitimacy from an institution experienced as external to the relations of production, the family, and beyond the family, from the whole civilian society which sets women as an oppressed group.

Marx and Engels prophesied the short-term disappearance of the bourgeois family. They have been very often blamed for that, some historians and some Marxists concluding the opposite, its reinforcement, as a parallel to the growth of the bourgeois State. Marx' and Engels' prediction has to be explained in their historical context : the frenzied exploitation of "savage capitalism" had split the worker apart from his/her peasant family and upset previous roles. Engels has given a good description of the English situation, though sometimes in an ambiguous manner."In many cases, the family is not totally destroyed by work, but everything is upside down. It is the woman who feeds the family, the man who stays at home, cleans the house and cooks. This is very frequent. In Manchester only, hundreds of them can be found who are condemned to domestic work. One can easily imagine the legitimate indignation that this de facto castration creates for workers and the sort of upheaval in family life resulting from it, alhough the other social conditions remain unchanged." The family thus appeared as a remnant of pre-capitalist social relations, which only retained a useful function for the ruling classes. Marx and Engels were mistaken where they took a structural phenomenon for a conjunctural one. This mistake-which can be explained as I have said by its historical context-prevented them from seeing the need for a theory of the bourgeois family; it also enabled the reformist ideologists of the labour movement to defend the "worker's family" without seeming to break too openly from Marxism. Indeed, after the first phase of savage capitalism, the bourgeoisie felt the need to introduce the model of its family inside a working class that was too mobile and untamed.

Numerous studies published in France in the last ten years which show the new interest of historians for these questions (in parallel with the rise of the feminist movement) reveal how this process was started from 1870-80 with more "decent" dwellings for workers, suited to the nuclear family (mining villages replacing the promiscuous caves), with the ideology of motherhood extended to the female worker. The bourgeoisie's interests were clear : the reproduction of the labour force that capital did not want to socialise was accomplished in a private framework : the worker became more settled and more responsible through the family; women kept on being defined by their role in the family which enabled their overexploitation and use as a reserve army of labour. The bourgeoisie was actively helped by the organised workers' movement, composed essentially-as we know-of skilled male workers. Several explanations can be given : the strength of a "return to the past" Proudhon-style, which praised the merits of the patriarchal family against capitalist immorality; the stabilisation of workers which facilitated their unionisation; and above else, the fight against female competition by keeping the majority of women in the home and by hoping to send the others back home !

So, progressively, the model of the bourgeois family was generalised to the whole of society as a unit devoted to reproduction (and cut from the sphere of production), to the socialisation of children and to the equivalence between femininity and motherhood. Marx and Engels have not stressed that early capitalism was not able to socialise most of the domestic tasks. Their mistake did not come from the fact that they believed it possible, but from their lack of analysis of the concrete conditions, in their time, of reproduction of the species and the labour force. But the status of women derives precisely from the dialectical link between their reproductive work done in the family and their insertion in work for the market, each linked to the other. By limiting the analysis of women to their link with production, one fails to understand what makes them "special". As long as the system cannot transform domestic tasks into products for the market, it will save an enormous amount of capital by having them performed in a private framework. Marx had not clearly perceived this aspect, stating that the worker found on the market the means to reproduce his labour force. In the classic Marxist theory, housework appeared as non-work, which is in contradiction with Engels' statement on domestic slavery. Domestic tasks are easily described as free, which they are not entirely. The male worker receives a part of his wage to enable his family to live (or survive) on and so, in a certain way, to pay for his wife's domestic work. This is not contradictory to the function of saving capital. The male "surplus-wage" (difference with the female wage) never reaches-by far-the numbers of housework hours even paid at a minimum wage level.

Should we conclude that Marx and Engels were completely wrong and that capitalism provoked a strengthening of the family? The often used word "strengthening" is not accurate. The bourgeoisie did not impose a strengthening of pre-capitalist family bonds, but another type of family. Is it new because of the consolidation of the economic base of this new family which would come from assigning reproduction to a private framework ? It is new, as we have seen, because of the geographical and economic separation between production and reproduction. But in non-capitalist societies, the so-called reproductive tasks were also accomplished within the family by women, which the present system used. It could even be said that capitalism has a tendency to socialise more and more of the work previously done in the private framework. From the first industrial revolution onwards, in the towns, the family production of a number of basic food products disappeared (bread, vegetables, meat); clothes progressively became available on markets... As for late capitalism, it demonstrates the ability of the system to spread the reign of merchandises to large sectors of the reproductive sphere : lightning growth of the ready-to-wear market, pre-cooked dishes, laundry... Even consumption is losing (a little) of its family trait to become more individualised. This new stage in capitalism corresponds logically to a new wave of women's entry on the labour market. In France their percentage of the active population has been regularly increasing since 1970. "If the worker's wife, in the past earning no wage, is now joining the mass of producers supplying work in the capitalist industry, she directly increases the production of additional goods and of surplus-value. If a part of the goods thus produced is then consumed by the workers' families replacing domestic services previously accomplished free by the housewife, all this is profitable for capital as it facilitates the realisation of surplus-value, the accumulation of capital and enlarged reproduction."

Two elements of this process are essential : the taking of responsibility for housework by the private sphere is not structurally indispensable to the functioning of the system, but is a necessity over a long period; the status of women takes shape in the link between labour market/family, but in the last analysis the determining factor which can change their condition is the need for accumulation of surplus value, at the very heart of the system. What then is so specific to the bourgeois family compared to previous types ? It is the political, of course ! It materialises the split between the private man on the one hand, and the producer and citizen on the other. It embodies efficiently bourgeois individualism (inward-looking nuclear family) whilst guaranteeing the indidual a place for a mimimum of emotional support. More than ever before, it ensures the socialisation of children despite compulsory schooling. All sociologists stress it : marriage is based on love and not interest, and thus, the Family remains the number 1 value in any opinion poll. This social and political function is efficient enough and independent enough from the economic structures to be integrated without any change by the Eastern Europe countries where it renders similar services to the ruling layers. Everywhere, the internalisation of this model is very strong and contributes to the alienation of those who, as mothers, are its pillars. But the process is contradictory. In fact, in non-capitalist societies, the family undoubtedly operates as the place of women's oppression; in those social formations with their fundamental inequalities where the State is weaker, authority is spread throughout the different layers of the social body based on hierarchies determined by birth, function, age, gender, and accepted as permanent. Men dominate women because God (or Mother Nature) wanted it as such. The modern State, as the embodiment of Law above classes and groups, had to break those intermediate hierarchies and claim the freedom and equality of the individual in front of it; this change reflects the needs of Capital in a "free" labour force. In this change, the old family which was the place of codified male authority slowly and partially lost this role for objective reasons (the logic of the system) and subjective ones (women's struggles). The participation of women in production for the market, access to studies similar to the men's, the bourgeois discourse on formal equality between all individuals, clashed with the oppressed status of women at work and in the family. Marx and Engels sensed the phenomenon because it was fundamentally logical for the system, but it manifested itself much more slowly and in a more contradictory fashion than they predicted. This phenomenon has not reached its ultimate form and the conscious intervention of organised women will play a decisive role in shaping it.

The third gap in Marxist theory concerns the nature of social gender relations. Marx and Engels used much stronger words than their various epigones who strove to deny women's oppression by men in the name of workers' unity. "The (family) contains in miniature all the antagonisms which later developped in society and its State." (Marx) "(Conjugal marriage) appears as the subjugation of one sex by the other, as the declaration of a conflict between sexes." (Engels)

However, what neither of them really understood, is the foundation, in the capitalist system, for why gender conflicts are still going on. Some feminists have talked about the oppression of women by men through domestic work. This notion of appropriation of women's labour force for productive and reproductive tasks by men seems correct for pre-class societies; it has to be looked at on its own merits for each individual case for non-capitalist, class social formations. It does not work for capitalism. Exploitation means appropriation of surplus-value within production for the market and absolute separation between the owner of capital and the worker. Nothing like this in domestic work. Its destiny is to be accomplished in a private framework, outside any idea of profitability, and thus cannot be productive in the Marxist sense of the word. One can accept that a husband buys the labour force of his wife with his wage, but their interests are not fundamentally opposed; both are legally equally entitled to the husband's wage, to the objects produced at home, and none has any interest in diminishing the share of the other. Moreover, the spouse expects a service; he is not directly interested in his wife's production : does it matter if ironing is done in one or two hours ? No, as long as it is done; and once it is done, he will not go and get additional ironing from his neighbour, just to keep her busy!

By excluding the concept of exploitation, I do not mean that male dominance is "just backwardness in the mentalities". We have seen how capitalism functions on the basis of the over-exploitation of the female labour force and with savings obtained on the upkeep of the total labour force. It is obvious that this achievement necessitates a devalued status to all women at all levels in civilian society. Extraordinary creative powers were not required for that : it only needed to maintain and adapt an oppression several thousand years old, with the active support of those who clearly benefit materially and morally from it, whatever their class. Men were granted the collective status of oppressors with crumbs of surplus-value (higher wages) and social privileges (not to do housework) and ideological ones. This produces "poor white" type of feelings among the most exploited and represents a major factor in the loss of class consciousness. Obviously men and women belong to different classes in the capitalist system. Within each class, their historical interests are the same (though one could discuss the contradictory interests of bourgeois women). Concretely and conjuncturally, it is another story : competition for jobs, particularly high during periods of crisis; competition for access to high positions; competition in the political or trade union world, which is a male bastion especially well protected... These social relations between men and women do not easily fit in pre-established concepts. Terms of slavery or serfdom do not account for the juridical freedom, the "equality" which women enjoy today. Men are endowed by birth with privileges compared to the women of their own class and in some aspects compared to all women. A partial similarity can be drawn with racial minorities such as in the USA though with a big difference that oppression is not exerted individually with each white having his Black to oppress.

Adding to that the fact that this oppression is so ancient, but also constant in the relations between men and women, and plays a major part in structuring each individual character, one can only conclude that it will survive beyond the capitalist relations of production and even beyond the present family. Sexual conflicts exist, we encounter them every day. It is evident that the internal evolution of capitalism has partially supplied an objective and contradictory basis for overcoming them, and that the destruction of the system will broaden this objective basis. What remains determinant-and which Marx and Engels could not easily see-is the subjective factor of the independent women's struggle.

Can Feminism go beyond Marxism ?

Some rejected Marxism as inadapted in the name of women's independent struggle. These new methodological approaches can be broadly classified into two main currents : the first criticising Marxism as "economist" and incapable of explaining gender conflicts; the other wanting to add to Marxism a theory of the patriarchal mode of production that would run parallel to capitalism. It is impossible here to detail the various positions. We will concentrate on those which structure the currents of organised feminists in France.

The Psychanalyse et Politique group claimed, right from the start, to have developed a new theory with a fusion of Marxism and psychoanalysis. Marxism was supposed to offer a reserve of concepts : exploitation, State power, class struggle, imperialism... and an analysis of men's relations between themselves. Psychoanalysis, reinterpreted and socialised by the group's gurus, was to provide the methodological base for the analysis of gender relations. The approach is the following : Sexual Differentiation induces a different relationship to one's own body, according to one's gender, which in turn induces a relationship to the antagonistic Symbolic. The registered MLF [the Psyc et Po group registered "women's liberation movement (MLF)" as their name) believes, along with Lacan, that the domain of Power, of Making and of the Word is male whilst resistance to Power, the inarticulated discourse of the Body and the immediacy of Life are female. This symbolic polarity gives the social sphere its backbone; in order to insure their dominance, men led women to renounce their own identity and to accept the model of patriarchal values (rationality, power, etc.). So that present society witnesses two parallel conflicts, though one determines the other: class struggle between men, as an illustration of their immoderate wish to enslave their neighbour; and the symbolic revolution of the most conscious women to rediscover their identity, subvert partriarchal order and, consequently, the capitalist society deriving from it. This struggle can only be accomplished through a radical separation from men, "erotic and political independence".

How is it that this current, now losing momentum for political rather than theoretical reasons, has been able to attract women, particularly amongst the intelligentsia ? Without any doubt, it gives an answer to gaps in Marxist texts : how to justify the depth to which both sexes internalize women's oppression? How to explain the persistency of sexual polarity in symbols and values beyond the modes of production? Marxism lacks, it is true, a theory of the Subject taken as a whole, and of its alienation, not only as an economic agent. Psychoanalysis is the instrument for a study of alienation with its deciphering of individual and collective behaviour. Access to language, the structure of language, the world of symbols... are deeply marked by sexual dichotomy which plays a significant role in structuring the character. To unearth and analyse this can either act as a critique or a reinforcement of social order. But it is the later possibility that takes place when one draws psychoanalysis towards a Philosophy of Being. The "content" of the unconscious then becomes a permanent feature of the human species instead of the internalization by both the individual and the collectivity of a given situation in history. Jung's school (Jung Man in search of his soul) and his recent epigones who claim to read the universal fantasms of humankind in the myths of archaic and primitive societies, do not fail to postulate the dual structuration of the Unconscious between the Male and the

Female (animus-anima). Translated into the field of values, this provides, as one could expect, a collection of patriarchal prejudices. Woman = Passivity, Irrationality, Matter... G. Devereux' recent book Woman and Myth, is typical of the kind. In its search for a female identity, Psychanalyse et Politique can only reproduce the same commonplaces and the same reactionary ideology. What can the female identity really be? A different relationship to the body and sexuality from that of the men's? Well, then we cannot forget that the relationship to the body is not immediate but has always been put in a historical context for the human species. From this relationship to the body should we deduce a Difference in the psyche of the individual? To believe this is to fall in the trap of some biological determinism and/or in the old idea that women are nothing but their body. "Tota mulier in utero."

Marxists cannot but challenge this interpretation of psychoanalysis as they cannot but denounce the Philosophies of the Difference which have been flourishing for the last decade. Among women, the same attempt to rediscover "feminine values" can also be found in the American neo-feminism (Betty Friedan). As far as the "New Right" is concerned, they start polemics against "monist" philosophies guilty of thinking in universal concepts when earth enjoys diversity (understand inequality) of ethnic groups, regions, sexes, individuals. A diversity which cannot be understood but for specific criteria for each human group. This approach rejects thinking beyond Marxism, but also rejects classical philosophy. For women, it is deadly since, whatever the registered MLF thinks of it, it is the very discourse of the oppressor. It is true that this current does not fully adopt the logic of Difference since it gives to the symbolic world a determining and totalizing function : it is this world which reproduces social relations and determines them. However, to render the historical process dependent on an invariant which fixes two human groups in a radical otherness, is to pose the existence of two fields of thought and above all, two fields of action : symbolic subversion for women, class struggle for men.

The strength of Marxism comes from its methodology which enables a reconstitution of fragments of women's oppression (work, family, values...) into a meaningful whole. It sets women in matters historical and matters social from which patriarchal ideology (and not reality) had rejected them. By doing so, it places them not on the side of classes but at the heart of the class struggle. Not because of some preoccupation with their sordid life, nor because they are the most exploited, oppressed... but because their oppression enable the capitalist mystery to function at all levels and that, once reshaped and regenerated, this oppression can be transmitted to other oppressive societies.

Symbolic subversion ? Who opposes it ? One cannot see how it could operate outside a social framework involving all relations of production and outside the insertion of women into that process. On the content of the symbolic subversion, disagreements are obvious. To standardize male and female values is reactionary, to impose them in the name of a rediscovered Identity reeks of totalitarism. Men are not women and vice versa? Some are oppressed and some are oppressors : their relationship to the world is different... Would the reduction of differences between the sexes would impoverish humankind as anti-feminist ideologists and some women claim? So what should we think about mutilations imposed on all the individuals forced to accept the sexual norms of their society, of the body-centred attitude to ideas and behaviour? The victim's resentment and the satisfied stupidity of the oppression are automatic consequences of ethnic or sexual "racism'. One can have serious doubts about their enriching value.

The other criticism made to Marxism concerns its allocation of women to classes which erases the unity of their oppression. Some stick to a description : women are all discriminated against, and bourgeois women remain oppressed. "Women as a group objectively exploited by men's society form a separate social category with common characteristics whatever their class" wrote Anne de Pisan and Anne Tristan in Histoire du MLF (History of the Women's Liberation Movement). As far as the description is concerned, it is relatively easy to answer that oppression differs slightly between the public housing estates and bourgeois areas.

Others, to create women's unity, put the family as the determining factor for the functioning of capitalism. This thesis is developed in Being Exploited produced by an Italian collective, in Women's Power and the Subversion of the Community by Maria Rosa Della Costa and Selma James, and in France, in the articles of the journal Nouvelles questions féministes (New feminist issues). The idea is the following : the reproduction of the labour force, vital for capitalism, is accomplished by women; the system cannot give it up without destroying itself. The family reproduces the relations of production : "The existence of the world as a market for goods is based on the existence of a mode of domestic reproduction excluded from this market" (Being exploited). In this way, women are all defined by this precise function, while men are in classes.

This theory is wrong on two counts : it confers autonomy on the bourgeois family to the point of making it a determining factor in the durability of the system (hence for those women the revolutionary nature of the demand for a domestic wage...). Is capitalism possible without family? It would be absurd to answer in the abstract, outside a historical and geographical context. At certain periods, for certain social layers, the system destroyed the framework of the family, if only to rebuild it later : dislocation of the working class family at the beginning of capitalism, interdiction to establish a family. Moreover, we have seen that the third industrial revolution tends to socialise domestic tasks.

It ignores women working outside the home. To which class do they belong ? What are the links between their paid work and their domestic functions ? It remains a mystery...Other feminists go even further. Marxism describes one production system when in fact there are two : capitalism relying on the exploitation of man by man (as in male person), and the family mode of production based on the exploitation by men of the free labour of housewives in a relation of slavery. These two systems, according to Christine Durand (old article in Partisans Nos 48-49; more recent articles in Questions féministes) are "theoretically" independent of each other. There again, we have two major objections : one cannot talk about exploitation for domestic work, at least in the Marxist sense of the term. If the fact of belonging to the "women" class comes from the housework done for a man, then is not it possible for women to free themselves from this condition by remaining single?

The coexistence of two modes of production at this stage of capitalism is simply theoretical. One would have to demonstrate that the family is an economic unit operating on its own logic, apart from capitalism. However, everything proves that this structure evolves in close relation to the demands, the evolution and the transformations of the system.

In reality, all theories claiming to surpass Marxism have one common feature : they propose a vision of reality which is unchanging, deprived of historical perspective.. Here is women's oppression as Eternity fixed it...

If, on the women's question "reading Marx" is insufficient, the Marxist methodology-history unfolding in the resolving of successive contradictions-remains an irreplaceable asset.

10

Critical Theory and Limits of Sociological Positivism

THE DEVELOPMENT OF CRITICAL THEORY

The foundations of the critical theory of society are in the early philosophical manuscripts of Karl Marx (Marx, 1963). Prior to the 1840's, social theory, political theory, "scientific" sociology, and classical political economy existed as coherent intellectual traditions, but a critical theory of society had not yet emerged. Utopian socialism, scientific political economy, and critical philosophy existed, but were not yet combined in a critical theory of society which could reflect the class struggles and social revolutions which were transforming Europe in the middle of the 19th century.

Theories of history have existed at least from the time of Plato's dialogues, in which his notion of the telos or goal of human society resided in the striving for infinite perfection. In Aristotle's Politics (Aristotle, 1962), nature of a just society as a goal for humans is rigorously analysed. Following in each of these traditions is a continual philosophical dialectic between various idealist and materialist schools of thought. A philosophy of history was elaborated in Aristotelian form by Ibn Khaldun (1963) in November of 1377 in his treatise, Introduction to History, and was further developed in Italian by Giambatista Vico (Vico, 1968). But the most comprehensive theory of history and society in Europe was formulated by George Hegel in the 19th century. Hegel elaborated the first systematic philosophy of history or social theory to emerge in human thought, and to establish itself as an intellectual tradition (Hegel, 1956).

But social theory in the work of Hegel, political theory in Rousseau (1950), and positivist and "scientific" sociology in Comte (1966) and Spencer (1969) were either grounded in a criticism of the human condition in political society, or in faith in the possibility of a natural science of the enduring laws of society. Criticism of society was reduced by these theorists to criticism of the state, and critical thought was reduced to a search for formal laws of social structure and development. Equally bound to a positivist image of science were the classical political economists—Adam Smith (1909) and David Ricardo (1965), who analysed the laws of motion of the economic categories of civil society as if they were the laws of nature.

It was not until Marx that the basis for a truly critical and social theory was established. In his early work, Marx sought release of humanity from the bonds of alienation—from the domination by a society of wage labour and economic exploitation. This society was neither understood nor controlled, neither *by* the captains of industry nor by the leaders of the state apparatus. The whole society was alienated from the human actors who produced and reproduced it. An alienated society is a social formation which is beyond control of the human beings who have produced it. In that sense, both European capitalism of the 1840's and American capitalism of the 1970's are alienated societies. These are both social formations which were created by human beings and their labour, but for a series of very specific reasons have grown out of control of the human beings who constructed them in the first place. Social theory which does not recognize the alienated relations of capitalist society does not understand human beings as the essential reality of society, nor does it comprehend the totality of the social formation. Past, present and future are reduced to a one-dimensional time frame, and rather than being able to come to terms with the nature of social reality as a whole, alienated social theory simply comprehends its parts.

The methodological basis of the critical theory of society is the dialectical logic of George F. Hegel (1956). According to the principles of dialectical logic, "That which is cannot be true,". In other words, our existing society of racism, genocide, and possible nuclear holocaust cannot be the "truth" of human existence. Truth must lie somewhere else, not in the facts of the given reality, but in the negation or transcendence of those facts. Truth lies in the attempt to go beyond this reality to a better world. Thus, truth lies in our attempt to change the world, in our critique of the established reality,. A critical sociological analysis is true insofar as it helps change the world and make it a more human place in which to live. So while reality may lie quite beyond human comprehension and can never be reduced to words, truth is the living of each moment of human life to its maximum potential, the unfolding of reality from its potential to a lived practice or actuality of human existence. In contrast to a.critical analysis, much of sociology remains at the level of the "facticity of the given,". The difference between reality as it presently appears and its essential Qualities is not distinguished. Such analysis has the effect of justifying the status quo whether it intends to do so or not.

There are no textbooks on the "methodology" of critical theory. Rather, critical analysis refuses to acknowledge the reduction of epistemology to methodology. Where most sociology asks "how is it possible to prove this fact?", a critical analysis asks "what is a fact?" Facticity resides in the whole for critical theory while it is a mere fragment for others. The criterion of verification can never be applied to critical sociological analysis. Only the criteria of transcendence and praxis apply. Does the sociological analysis go beyond our taken-for-granted assumptions about the established reality? Does the analysis extend our knowledge of the established reality, totality (Lukacs, 1971), or totalization (Sartre, 1963) by transcending it, that is by making it an understood part of a larger whole? Even conventional positivist sociology would usually agree to the criterion of transcendence. For what is sociology if it does not go beyond the taken-for-granted assumptions of the status quo...just another form of journalism with more statistical data? Transcendence of the status quo should be a criterion of all sociology worthy of that name.

The criterion of transcendence may be thought of as the degree to which the analysis uncovers the potential for social change and human liberation inherent in any social institution. The "unactualized potential" of a social system implicitly acknowledges that social change is continuous. A second criterion for judging the truth of a theory is praxis, or the degree to which sociological analysis is responsible to human values (Habermas, 1971).

Praxis is the key concept that differentiates the critical sociologist from the ahistorical gatherer of "common sense facts" and cataloguer of mathematical abstractions whose activities characterize contemporary sociological positivism. Praxis refers to the ideal of conscious practical action—of making the critique of alienation speak for popular needs and lead to concrete actions against the capitalist commodity relationships—within historical possibilities. Knowledge serves "real world" interests whether it is encyclopedic (Foucault, 1970) knowledge aimed at cataloguing the status quo so that someone else may act to maintain it as in the case of sociological positivism, or contemplative (Kirkpatrick, 1973) knowledge which assumes a special status from which to view social reality, status that claims to be apart from that reality. Sociology is part of society, and does not objectively stand above it. No matter what pains are taken for "objective value-free analysis," (Weber, 1949) knowledge cannot be divorced from social reality and values. Critical theory establishes truth as that which negates or opposes the status quo. The mere description of the status quo, whether it be statistical or interpretative, can never by itself qualify as critical theory.

Historical Emergence of Critical Theory

Two developments are responsible for the emergence of critical sociology. First, intellectual theories from England, France, and Germany had been put forth in specialized form. Marx attributed his analysis to a synthesis of English political economy, French utopian socialism, and German idealistic philosophy. Second, the class struggles and social revolutions within capitalism became so intense that the working class could not be prevented from becoming conscious of its exploitation within the capitalist social relationships (Korsch, 1970). Marx became part of the articulation of a new world view—a world view of the exploited wage workers, rather than a world view of the aristocracy or the rich bankers as had previously prevailed. Critical theory of society emerged in the criticism of capitalism from the point of view of the wage worker or proletariat.

Critical theory of society developed along with the dominance of the capitalist social relations of production. In the 19th century the antagonism between workers and capitalists became so intense that the workers were in actual danger of being exterminated; they were not given enough wages to even reproduce themselves. Prior to the 1840's other basic social antagonisms were brought to the consciousness of the human race and written about in a critical way—the antagonism between master and slave, and between men and women—but it was only in the 1840's that critical thinking about society was able to reflect on the social relationships in the society as a whole.

The development of capitalism created the preconditions for the demystification of social forces formerly conceived as natural or God-given for all of eternity—such as the feudal systems of social inequality which rested on the divine rights of the nobility. All that humans had created, from the gods to the social structure, became subject to the critique of human reason in the aftermath of the Enlightenment and the French Revolution of 1789. However, capitalism generated its own system of mystification, that of "eternal" or "natural" economic relationships of exploitation, competition, and hierarchy.

Science and technology have become the new religion of capitalist society. The dualistic form of the religious world view, the dichotomy of subject and object (Greenberg, 1971) formerly expressed as the alienation of humans from their constructed deities, was mechanistically replicated in the secularized version of religion which today is called science. The fall of religious metaphysics became a necessary step in the rise of a new God—science and technology—overriding the individual's belief in the primary of human thought, creativity, and energy. As the theological or metaphysical epoch of history was seen by August Comte, the founder of scientific sociology and positivism, to be giving way to the rise of the scientific era, so the high priests of the new society were, for Comte, to be sociologists and other social scientists (Comte, 1966).

The critical theory of society, at least in the 20th century with Lukacs (Jacoby, 1971), Korsch, and the Frankfurt School

(Connerton, 1976, Wellmer, 1971), has been locked in a polemical dialectic with the heirs of Conte's social positivism (Kellner, 1975-76). According to Max Horkheimer, the demand that the positivists make that sociology must conform to the "facts" is similar to the demand in the medieval society that theories conform to religious dogma. According to Horkheimer (1971:91): "The positivist command to conform to facts and common sense instead of to utopian ideas is not so different from the call to obey reality as interpreted by religious institutions, which after all are facts too. Each camp undoubtedly expresses a truth, under the distortion of making it exclusive... Both schools are heteronomous in character. One tends to replace autonomous reason by the automatism of streamlined methodology, the other by the authority of a dogma."

In trying to explain why people in modern society worship science and technology as they once worshipped Gods, Marx looked at the sociological organization of labour in the capitalist society. He found that in capitalist society, labour is so organized as to make work involuntary for the vast majority of the population. They were wage workers or wage "slaves" who had to work in order to eat. Marx was trying to make the point that work in a capitalist society is essentially forced labour. According to Marx (1963:125): "The worker, therefore, feels himself at home only during his leisure time, whereas at work he feels homeless. His work is not voluntary but imposed, forced labour. It is not the satisfaction of a need, but only a means for satisfying other needs. Its alien character is clearly shown by the fact that as soon as there is no physical or other compulsion it is avoided like the plague... the external character of work for the worker is shown by the fact that it is not his own work but work for someone else, that in work he does not belong to himself but to another person.

"We arrive at the result that man (the worker) feels himself to be freely active only in his animal functions—eating, drinking, procreating, or at most in his dwelling and personal adornment —while in his human functions—creativity and craftsmanship— he is reduced to an animal."

The reality of alienated labour under capitalism is more than a simple issue of economic exploitation or the "cheating" of the worker out of some of the value of his/her labour time.

It is fundamentally a degradation of human life, of the qualitative inequality of the worker's exchange of her or his life energies for the things necessary merely to survive. In capitalist society, human beings are alienated from their social nature as species beings (Marx, 1971) and the liberation from this alienation is the historical problem of human existence.

Critical theory was first developed by Karl Marx (1963) in the Economic and Philosophical Manuscripts of 1844. In the work of one North American exponent of the critical theory of society—Trent Schroyer (1973)—it is called the Critique of Domination. Other scholars have referred to the critical theory of society as Hegelian/Marxism, or dialectical Marxism (Klare and Howard, 1971). Having located the historical context within which the critical theory of society was first articulated, we will now trace its development in order to briefly contrast it with modern scientific technology.

The Rediscovery of Critical Theory

After its formulation in the era of the class struggles of 1848, critical theory lay dormant and undeveloped until the eruption of the European revolutionary social movements around 1917, when it was revived by Georg Lukacs in his History and Class Consciousness (Lukacs, 1971). Lukacs was appalled by the barbarism and depravity of World War I and inspired by the Russian Revolutions of 1917 and the Hungarian Commune of 1919 (of which he was the deputy commissar of culture). At the time that he finished his major contribution to critical sociology History and Class Consciousness, Marx's economic and philosophical manuscripts were gathering dust in Moscow, unpublished and unnoticed for nearly seven decades.

In the aftermath of the victory of the Bolshevik revolution, Lukacs' History and Class Consciousness and Karl Korsch's Marxism and Philosophy (Korsch, 1970, an historical attempt to explain the development of Leninism from marxism) were subjected to intense criticism from both the Social Democratic and Communist Parties of Europe. At this point, Lukacs compromised with the Marxism of Stalin. He eventually recanted the critical concepts in History and Class Consciousness, thereby becoming another (if not the most articulate) apologist for the bureaucratic elite in the Soviet

Union. Under fire from his former comrades, Korsch left the German Communist Party to independently continue his polemics against the "mechanical materialism" of Lenin and the Communists and Kautsky and the Social Democrats. He taught sociology at Tulane University in New Orleans, Louisiana, and for a while, he taught Marxism informally to the playwright Bertolt Brecht. He died in Massachusetts in 1961. Lukacs again became active in political struggle and critical theory in his later life, participating in the Hungarian Rebellion of 1956 against the Stalinist Bureaucracy of the Soviet Union.

Beginning in Germany, a tradition has extended and enriched the critical theory of society which includes the persons associated with the Frankfurt Institute for Social Research—Marcuse, Adorno, Horkheimer, Benjamin, Neumann and Habermas, among others (Jay, 1973). The rise to power of Hitler and National Socialism in Germany nearly destroyed the Frankfurt School. It was only by leaving Germany that they survived.

Walter Benjamin, thinking he was about to be captured within occupied France, resisted by committing suicide—a tragic casualty during one of the greatest human catastrophes of all times. The Frankfurt School, as it is most often called, is historically traced in Martin Jay's book, The Dialectical Imagination. While Jay's treatment suffers from having been originally developed within the academic constraints of a Ph.D. dissertation at Harvard, it is nonetheless an excellent history of the school. Critical theory has two goals: to bring to consciousness the awareness of capitalist exploitation and bureaucratic domination; and to create a popular demand for liberation—a demand, desire, and need for a better world. Critical theory is critical in two senses: it brings to our consciousness oppression of which we may or may not have been aware, and it calls for "criticism of life" to resist and change the existing system of domination and exploitation. Some versions of Marxism are critical theory and some are not: other theories are used critically from time to time such as phenomenology, psychoanalysis and existentialism.

In Herbert Marcuse's analysis of the Economic and Philosophical Manuscripts of 1844, the connections between the Frankfurt School's critical theory and the Hegelian humanism of Marx are perhaps most clear. It is also clear from this exposition by Marcuse that the old Marx who wrote Capital and is the scientist and economist par excellence, developed his scientific categories for the analysis of capitalism from philosophical foundations.

According to Herbert Marcuse (1973), the critical theory of the young Marx already contained revolutionary praxis-"The theory in itself is a practical one; praxis does not only come at the end but is already present in the beginning of the theory." Praxis is the philosophical basis of the theory presented by Marx, which includes a demand for the overthrow of the capitalist social relationships involved in production (like wage work and capitalist investment and profit) by an economic and political struggle of the working class (people who work for wages or salary).

The critical theory of Marx implies much more than just a political revolution, and certainly it does not imply an authoritarian tyranny of state capitalism. It does imply a revolution in the very being of humankind. Marcuse quotes Marx as follows: (1973:5): "This communism... is the genuine resolution of the conflict between man and nature and between man and man—the true resolution of the strife between existence and essence, between objectification and self-confirmation, between freedom and necessity, between the individual and the species. Communism is the riddle of history solved, and it knows itself to be this solution."

Marx criticized the categories of political economy because those categories were posed as the "scientific" explanation of the economy which exploited and oppressed people through forced wage labour, economic exploitation, and the commodification of social relationships into exchange relationships. Capitalist economic relations required misery, hunger and toil. The oppression that people feel in capitalist society is not caused by naturally-given "laws" of capitalism which can be discovered scientifically, but by political and social structures which were created by human beings. What humans have created, humans can change, not simply "discover." According to Herbert Marcuse (1973:5-6): "This kind of political economy scientifically sanctions 'L-,he perversion of the historical/social world of man into an alien world of money and commodities; a world which confronts him as a hostile power and in which the greater part of humanity ceases to be anything more than abstract' workers (torn away from the reality of human existence), separated from the object of their work and forced to sell themselves as a commodity."

Attempting to follow Marx's methodology in criticizing the "Natural Laws" of capitalism, the critical theory of society conceives of itself as critique (Howard, 1971). Rather than accepting the categories of social being as they exist in the East or West, critical theory posits the possibility and potential of a freedom which has yet to be realized. The rapid standardization and bureaucratization of the Communist countries and the rise of consumerism and mass society in the capitalist countries make the Frankfurt School demand for critique in the tradition of Hegel's dialectical logic a rational theoretical means to the negation of a status quo which has, while proclaiming the rationality of its own system, actually "eclipsed" reason and established irrational domination. Therefore, much of the work of the critical theory of society has been generated from a critique of the established practices of contemporary social science.

Both positivist sociology and classical political economy are grounded in a faith in the scientific method, or in the "episteme" of Western rationalism (Foucault, 1970). The critical theory of society, as a moment of self-reflection of western culture, achieves its most progressive intellectual insight with its criticism of the Enlightenment (Goldman, 1971), and of the Western concept of reason and rationality from which scientific ideology develops (Marcuse, 1964). The advances of technology and science have themselves undermined the humanistic roots of science. Science and technology are today "alien creations" out of popular control or understanding. They are ideology— the new God which, combined with the State's power, appears to be "omnipotent, omnipresent, and omniscient" like the God of Moses. The social sciences, in an attempt to appear as powerful and true as science and technology, have attempted to adopt their methods and rules of verification. By developing a philosophical critique of science, critical theory unravels a hidden essence of capitalism—the system of "rational" domination. The ideology of science is a means to this hierarchy of domination which is then perpetuated in the social sciences, as we will discuss in a moment.

CRITIQUE OF SOCIOLOGICAL POSITIVISM

Sociological positivism was originally systematized by Auguste Comte in reaction to the French Revolution of 1789 as an alternative to the "anarchic force of purely revolutionary principles." By renouncing the legacy of transcendental philosophy and subordinating the imagination to observation, Comte's positive philosophy hoped to concern itself with "facts", not speculation; with scientific laws, not fanciful contemplation; "with organization and order instead of negation and destruction," (Marcuse, 1941:345). Positivism attempts to equate the understanding of social reality with the scientific explanation, prediction, and control of natural reality as practiced by the "hard" sciences of physics, physiology, chemistry, or biology. Using the methods of natural science to study social relationships and human beings, however, requires that one reify or make abstract and static living human beings, necessarily distorting them from the outset. Although.the scientific method is successful in manipulating and controlling natural reality, natural reality is also constantly chancing, so the positivist conception of the natural universe is also likely to be reified and static compared to the underlying natural "reality" out of which the positivist constructs his/her models.

Social and natural reality are conceived by the positivist as "objectively" quantifiable and measurable. What appears on the surface is conceived as the full extent of reality, in opposition to a critical conception of essence and appearance which understands the necessity of qualitatively new forms.of being continually coming into existence. Critical theory and critical sociology, as we elaborate them, are concerned with the theoretical examination of social structure—kinship, economic structure, political structure and class structure—guided not only by a theory of society but also by a critique of the established social reality including the taken-for-granted assumptions about these social phenomena. By comparing the existing kinship, economic, political and class structures with alternative possibilities present within the status quo, sociology can be a force for social change rather than technical resource for bureaucratic administration and capitalist domination.

There is one key difference between Nature and History and that is that human beings have created one, but not the other. That which humans have the power to make, they have the power to change. These are key insights into the nature of society which first emerged in Western Europe during the Enlightenment and the French Revolution.of 1789, a revolution in social thought as well as in political power. This important insight, however, was cut short by the sociological positivism of A. Comte and his followers (Zeitlin, 1969), perhaps best exemplified today by the standard "high science" or mathematical sociology which is characteristic of the majority of the articles in the American Sociological Review, the major sociological journal for positivists in North America.

The early positivists like Comte attempted to equate the study of society with the study of nature and tried to discover laws of societal development on a par with the structural principles of human anatomy in Biology. Comte even went so far as to compare families, social classes and political structures in society with cells, tissues, and organs of the human body. Such simplistic organismic analogies soon gave way to a neo-positivism which eclipsed social theory altogether. Positivism has today been reduced to the gathering of statistical information about fragmentary aspects of social reality by using the precise procedures of natural science. The modern neo-positivists argue for the necessity of gathering "facts" to either construct (Stinchcomb, 1967) or to test (Chavetz, 1977) "sociological theories" without allowing a reflection on or examination of the social theory which defined and constituted the "facts" in the first place.

Sociological positivism negates the basis upon which the human production and transformation of societies might be understood. By postulating the prior existence of "facts" out there in the world, prior even to the human action of thinking about or conceptualizing the world, positive thought falls to comprehend how even the formation of those "facts" is an act of the human mind. In short, within the positivist world view, the facticity of the world of immediate appearances is an a priori assumption. Subjectivity is abolished and society engulfs the individual. Yet at the same time, the facts assumed to be "real," "objective" and manipulated with mathematical precision, are facts concerning, in the majority of cases of sociological positivism, subjective states within individuals. So sociological positivism abolishes the subject as an active creative human mind: in many cases, it abolishes objective reality by reducing it to subjective states quantitatively measured and manipulated. Positivism is a form of objectivistic idealism.

Positivism concentrates on the object of knowledge, abolishing the human actor doing the knowing, thereby attempting to hide the "subject" of knowledge from critical examination. Knowledge is presented by the positivist as a thing which jumps out of nowhere. The human being who created the "knowledge" is not recognized as being part of the society which is being studied. There are at least two problems which positivism encounters at this point: one of methodology and, more importantly, an ethical problem.

On the level of method, Aaron Cicourel and others have pointed out that the human beings who label social reality with numbers are themselves making judgments about the reality they quantify. In Method and Measurement in Sociology, Cicourel develops a critique of Ithiel De Sola Pool's reliance on the common sense of the coder (the technician who gives numbers to human relationships) (1964):

"And if we must rely on human judges, then we should know as much as possible, to paraphrase Pool, about how the 'human computer' goes about encoding and decoding messages... Instead it is often assumed that such meanings are self-evident, that native-speakers of a language are more or less interchangeable, that the manifest content is sufficient for study, or that judges are interchangeable. The structure of common-sense knowledge remains a barely recognizable problem for sociological investigation."

Pool's reliance on the "human computers" to put his data together and analyze it has built-in methodological problems. His ethical problem becomes clear when the nature of what he studies is looked at. During the Vietnam war, for example, Pool analysed the results of numerous interrogation sessions of "suspected Viet Cong." Along with Samuel Huntington, he helped design the "forced urbanization" strategy in Indochina—the saturation bombing of the rural areas which forced millions of peasants to leave their ancestral homes and move to the cities or "strategic hamlets," a misnomer for concentration camps.

The refusal of positivists to comprehend themselves and their work as subject to examination helps shield them from ethical considerations. Their attitude seems useful because it may keep the work of social science out of the danger of conflict with authoritarian governments and exempt from the ethics of responsibility for the support of genocide, as in Pool's participation in such policies in Vietnam. Superficially then, social science becomes "value-free", but it certainly does not explain the changing nature of society as a whole, as sociology originally intended, and its "freedom" exists only within the values of the status quo. "Objective" social science can operate on a grant from the U.S. State Department to do an "objective" study of class consciousness among lower class workers in slums in Chile and indirectly give the results of the study to the CIA through professional publications (which are also "objective and value-free"). These sociologists do not see the relationship between themselves and the murder and torture of people under the fascist dictatorship which overthrew the democratically elected socialist government of Chile in 1973 with the aid of the CIA. Hundreds of social scientists were involved in Project Camelot gathering data about numerous underdeveloped countries and computerizing their findings in a form only accessible to government agencies. The assumptions and methodology of positivism contain within them additional practical repercussions which merit further discussion.

The Practice of Positivism

Fundamentally, positivist knowledge is knowledge alienated from both the social scientist and the society studied. The relationship between the positivist and the social world they study has often been termed a "contemplative stance." The only role that is acceptable for the positivists to play is one of contemplating the world they study. Their information can be given or sold to the powers that be and used for administration of anything from welfare to "criminal justice," but the role of sociologist can only be that of observer of the given reality. Positivist thought is called "one-dimensional" by Herbert Marcuse because positivist sociology is reduced to the contemplative observation of what is, and the ethical impulse to judge the social world and transform it into one in which humans may be free of domination is suppressed by the positivist concept of knowledge. As Emile Durkheim (1938), the French positivist sociologist, said, "social facts are things." This statement expresses the attempt of positivism to commodity knowledge and to reify or "thingify" social reality which is actually composed of changing living human relationships.

The term reification literally means "thingification". It means that positivists treat the concrete flux of social experience as if it were reducible to their abstract models of it. Soon empirical experience becomes little more than an excuse to "test" an abstraction, or to use a sophisticated mathematical model such as "path analysis" or the various types of "systems analysis." Sociological positivism, at its most sophisticated, becomes abstract, reified objectivistic idealism. Positivism hides from the social world it claims to study, in the relative security of cumulative statistical obscurity. Furthermore, all system's analysis and statistical sociology operate on the assumption that what appears to exist is the extent of reality. The model of the system's analyst has no room for "new variables" and conceptualizes reality from the point of view of the status quo. The very categories of analysis are developed under the assumption of the existence of reality as it is, not as it could be. This is a built-in bias to system's analysis which the technicians and theorists (Horkheimer, 1972) alike do not question.

Is positivism merely an ideology designed to justify the practice of corporate monopoly capitalism (U.S.A.) and bureaucratic state capitalism (U.S.S.R.) or does the "knowledge" of the positivist really have a use value in the technology of domination? Both the work of liberal positivists like Blalock and "scientific" Marxists like Louis Althusser (Althusser, 1971) are shaped by this framework of objective idealism. They both reduce knowledge and philosophy to a contemplative stance from which to gaze upon the world, eliminating praxis from the realm of thought, and philosophy from the realm of politics.

Both the liberal positivist professor and the Communist party intellectual are free to pursue knowledge in the university or in the Party, but the direction of society and social life is left to the authoritarian leadership of the "democratic" or "Communist" government. Such governments legitimate themselves to the general population through symbolic plebiscites (elections) and social welfare programs (socialized medicine, food stamps, etc.), all administered by a technocratic elite. The meaningful participation of intellectuals, to say nothing of popular participation, is eliminated from social reality in both theory and practice by the "scientific" methodology.

In short, although the interest implicit in positivist social science is the technical control of human behaviour, the effect is also ideological, since the method eclipses popular power and justifies the legitimacy of scientific experts. But when, as in Vietnam, the vast majority of people refuse to submit to the power of technocratic domination, the impotency of mobilizing material resources without moral justification becomes clear. Over half a million U.S. troops, untold billions of dollars, and more bombs than were used throughout all of World War II could not defeat the power of the people in Vietnam.

Although the positivists set out to explain and control the social world, they actually take a back seat to the people who control the social wealth and the social relations of production—the Rockefellers, Morgans, DuPonts and the rest of the monopoly capitalist class (Domhoff, 1967; Mills, 1956) in league with the Pentagon and the White House—a structure which composes The Power Elite. The people whose interests the positivists serve are the owners or capital or corporate stock, the Generals in the Pentagon, the President and the managers of the corporate capitalist state apparatus. In order to continue their work within the society they study, social scientists must preserve, both through the topics studied and the methodology employed, the power structure of the status quo. This mode of producing knowledge then becomes all the more ideological and dogmatic "truth."

If a critical sociologist were to raise the issue of the illusory nature of value neutrality to a sociological positivist, and to point out that objective value-free knowledge is being used by the CIA and the State Department to help suppress popular democratic governments in Latin America, the sociological positivist might declare that such a question itself is "political" and not "sociological". Sociology from the positivist viewpoint treats only scientific questions which can either be verified or be subject to disproof by operationalized measures, and has no room for ethical statements about the propriety of democracy, exploitation, hunger or torture. In reply to this bias, a critical sociologist might suggest that the ties of sociologists in Latin America and Vietnam to American imperialist domination and hegemony can indeed be empirically demonstrated, measured and quantified. In short, it finally becomes clear even to these scientists that the ideology of "value-free" science serves as a mask for complicity with the powers that be, that "value-free" science is a value-laden operation.

American anthropological studies of Native Americans on "Indian reservations" and British anthropological studies of black Africans in "Bantustands" and Australian aborigines in "game preserves" also provide examples of social science's complicity with colonial and racist powers. In these cases, as in the case of sociological studies of internally colonized peoples such as the Blacks or Chicanos in North America, the social scientists are members of the imperialist oppressor nation and cultural grouping while the object of study is the oppressed community (Harris, 19). Without any self-reflexive critical perspective, these studies simply describe and therefore legitimate the oppressive power relations of the status quo. Sometimes it seems that only a fine line can be drawn between sociological positivism and counter-insurgent espionage posing as "value-free science." These sorts of abuses occur from within a methodology which refuses to reflect on the social position of the agents who employ it, focusing solely on the "rules of procedure" for attaining "truth" and "knowledge."

The demand for a critical sociology is the demand that people who engage in the study of society stop serving the forces of imperialism, genocide, and colonization, and become a force for positive social change and the dignity of human beings—a demand that they refuse to work for Fascist governments in Latin America (Chile, Brazil, etc.), Africa (South Africa, Rhodesia), Asia (South Korea), and the Mideast (Iran), and to define a public or historical constituency in whose interests they can ethically and responsibly act. Otherwise, sociology, in a long term historical perspective, might appear to be little more than an intelligence arm of a repressive capitalist state apparatus.

During the period in which this [essay] is being written, fascist organizations in the United States such as the Nazis and the Ku Klux Klan have organized and demonstrated in cities all across the country. In Southern California, the KKK has organized and recruited from within the police departments and Marine Corps bases. They have defaced the residence of one of this book's authors with a white cross in response to a public position taken against him. The Frankfurt School's landmark studies of the fascist character during World War II helped in the struggle against Fascism then, but seem inadequate today the task of resisting fascist tendencies within the North American social structure (Adorno, et al., 1973). The study of the authoritarian-submissive personality structure as an attitudinal prejudice does not illuminate the ideological mechanisms of dissemination and acceptance of fascism or the face-to-face processes of recruitment and organization of fascist movements. It is the immediate task of North American critical sociology to overcome these inadequacies and to understand fascism as a contemporary social tendency. In countries such as Greece and Chile, fascist dictatorships have banned sociology as an academic discipline because of its critical potential in undermining their regimes.

What is a Fact?

Sociological positivism bases the verification of its knowledge on a notion of facts as irreducible units of truth which are to be discovered by the social scientist. But facts do not fall to us from heaven. They are a constructed part of the society and the intellectual context within which we live and work (Berger, 19). For the positivist, some fragments of reality are "facts", others are "values". Who decides what is what? This problematic of sociological positivism—that is, the collection of assumptions, suppositions taken for granted, and factors omitted (or critical sciences)—is seldom if ever examined by the positivists themselves. The positivists are content to elaborate their rules of methodology, either ignoring the social theory on which they are based or refusing to admit that they have a theory. The assumption behind the technocratic facade of "high science" sociology is the claim of the scientific method to a cognitive monopoly on truth (Habermas, 1971). This is an essentially religious or dogmatic claim of truth, not an enlightened and open pursuit of truth. Positivism's claim to truth is most often expressed in the ideology of "value-free" social science. The claim to be value-free is one of the more value-laden defenses given in response to social scientists who question the fundamental rationality of the academy and society in the modern world. Especially in an era when more than 50% of the sociology Ph.D.s work for the federal government, it is inaccurate to discuss the idea of a value-free science of society in practice, let alone in theory. The claim to value-free sociology depends upon adherence to a dogmatic belief in the objectivity of "facts."

One of the things that unites all of the various types of positivists in both the social and natural sciences is the taken-for-granted intersubjective agreement on the "factual" nature of reality (Horkheimer, 1972:208). Horkheimer calls it "traditional theory": "In traditional theoretical thinking, the genesis of particular objective facts, the practical application of the conceptual systems by which it grasps the facts, and the role of such systems in action, are all taken to be external to the theoretical thinking itself. This alienation, which finds expression in philosophical terminology as the separation of value and research, knowledge and action, and other polarities, protects the savant from the tensions we have indicated and provides an assured framework for his activity."

The separation of value and fact, made credible when the sociological positivist ignores the origin of his/her facts, the consequences of theory, and the context of sociology in society, serves to protect university professors by giving them a safe zone in which to protect their narrow specialty, "free" from ethical questions and social struggles. The organization of sociology embodies the organization of the monopoly capitalist division of labour of which it is a part. Horkheimer suggests this (1972b:191): "The assiduous collecting of facts in all the disciplines dealing with social life, the gathering of great masses of detail in connection with problems, the empirical inquiries, through careful questionnaires and other means, which are a major part of scholarly activity, especially in the Anglo-Saxon universities since Spencer's time—all this adds up to a pattern which is, outwardly, much like the rest of life in a society dominated by industrial production techniques."

There are many disagreements among traditional sociological theorists about methodological procedures. For example, there are disagreements about the best way to gather facts—such as the experimental method versus the phenomenological (Cicourel, 1964). There are general disagreements between the positivists who consider themselves primarily "empiricists" (Homans, 1964), and those who consider themselves primarily "theorists" (Parsons, 1951). Furthermore, there are disagreements between "grand" theorists (Parsons, 1951) and "middle range" theorists (Merton, 1954). Such disagreements concern inductive versus deductive methods, quantitative versus qualitative, micro versus macro, and questions of scope and range, but there is essential implicit agreement on the "factual," empirical or verificational nature of theory itself. According to Horkheimer (1972b), traditional theory is anchored in the view that theory is the conglomeration of propositions and "facts" about an object ordered in a form (usually mathematical forms are given the highest prestige as in the natural sciences), such that all facts may be deduced from a few basic postulates. No matter which system of traditional theory we may consider, their common belief in the systemization of "facts" belies a fundamental objectivistic idealism. As T.W. Adorno puts it in Negative Dialectics (Adorno, 1974): "The system, the form of presenting a totality to which nothing remains extraneous, absolutizes the thought against each of its contents and evaporates the content in thoughts. It proceeds idealistically before advancing any arguments for idealism."

As a systematization of the "facts," traditional theory relies, as Marcuse (1964) points out, on the "facticity of the given." The main problem with neo-positivism from a sociological point of view is that it assumes that the social world is given as a fact of nature, just like mountains or the ocean, and ignores the "historical" character of the social world which is created by human actors, some with great resources in power and wealth, some very much at the mercy of men, police, and other agents of the status quo...all in social interaction with cultural symbols to which they themselves give significance.

The social world did not spring out of nowhere. It is the historical product of human beings and should be understood and criticized in its historical and cultural context, not simply described in a "factual" manner. The most obvious flaw of traditional theory is that it is ahistorical. The objects we find in our social environment—cities, towns, fields and factories—are not simply given to us by Nature, they are historical products of human labour. Not simply "reality in itself," but also the way in which we perceive reality is historically conditioned. Horkheimer notes this insight in the following phrases (1972a:200)

"The facts which our senses present to us are socially performed in two ways through the historical character of the object perceived and through the historical character of the perceiving organ. Both are not simply natural; they are shaped by human activity, and yet the individual perceives himself as receptive in the act of perception."

The individual perceives "facts" in a passive way since the humanly and historically produced society that we live in is an alienated one, as we have described it above—one which is essentially out of control of the ones who produce it. The social relationships of modern society are founded directly on oppression and exploitation, and therefore appear to us as objects not of our own making, but as given natural phenomena.

For example, in Southern California the decisions about how to plan and develop the cities of San Diego and Los Angeles were not arrived upon by the members of the whole communities in a democratic way. They were not planned by artists, architects, and city planners working for the people of those communities. Giant multinational corporations, bankers, and developers made all of the important decisions about how the "given facts" of Southern California were to be produced, and they made these decisions as prisoners of the dictates of increased profits and capital accumulation.

Moreover, the workers whose labour actually builds the Jack-in the Box and MacDonald's hamburger joints lining the streets with garish neon and who build the little boxes of privatized social isolation called condominiums, have no power to determine what housing will look like, who will live in them, and where they will be located. These aesthetic atrocities which desecrate the beautiful coasts of Southern California with corporate blight in no way respond to the needs and desires of the people who eat, live in, and build them. They are built solely according to the dictates of maximum profit, as any capitalist developer will cheerfully admit. The automobile, the smog, the freeway, the oil slicks, billboards, and neon signs complete the physical presence of the corporate state.

A sociologist's "objective" description of such an affront to the human need for beauty and ecological harmony as a "fact" of urban sociology, rather than as an historically produced form of uncontrolled capitalist expansion, is comparable, on the theoretical level at least, to Samuel Huntington's call for and description of the effects of saturation bombing of the countryside of Vietnam as "urbanization" (Slater, 1970). The napalming of villages in Vietnam, the development of pellet bombs by U.S. multinational corporations such as Westinghouse, Honeywell, Texas Instruments, and others as specifically anti-personnel devices designed to mutilate the human body and "tie up the medical resources of the enemy" and even the saturation bombing of Hanoi by U.S. B-52's on Christmas Day, 1972, can be evaluated by the positivist in "factual" terms; body counts and equipment losses become the exchange equivalents of capitalist genocide (Sartre, 1967).

11

Marxism and Political Economy

Marx's materialistic investigation of bourgeois society is based from the very beginning on a recognition of the cardinal importance of Political Economy. While but a few weeks before, he had written to his bourgeois-democratic friend Ruge, the characteristic words that the critic of modern society may start from "any given form of theoretical and practical consciousness" and that more especially the "political State" expresses within its form all social struggles, needs, and truths *sub specie rei publicae*, he now definitely transcended that intermediate stage of his materialistic moulding process by the conclusion that "the anatomy of civil society must be sought for in Political Economy." Nor was this merely an advance toward a better method of scientific investigation. The theoretical transition to Political Economy coincided with a practical transition from the Jacobinic bourgeois revolution, which had aimed at solving the social problems and needs of the working classes *sub specie rei publicae*, to the independent action of the modern proletariat, which is resolved to seek for the specific roots of its oppression and for the specific path to its emancipation in Political Economy. "The economic emancipation of the working class," say the Rules of the Working Men's International Association drawn up twenty years later by Marx, "is the great end to which every political movement is subordinated as a means."

The theoretical programme of the youthful Marx, to "seek for the anatomy of civil society in Political Economy," does not, however, mean a simple acceptance of the accomplished results of the preceding period of economic science. Political Economy was, historically, the new science of the bourgeoisie, brought forth by the rising industrial class in its revolutionary fight against feudalism. Now, in a new historical epoch, that revolutionary struggle has come to an end.

The bourgeois class rules, both politically and economically, in present-day society. Thus, Political Economy, dealing with the material foundation of the existing bourgeois State, is for the proletariat first and foremost an enemy country. Nor does it lose this character by the fact that parts of the ground held by its outposts are being occupied by the theoretical vanguard of the proletariat. The first task for the representatives of the new revolutionary class in this field is, therefore, to reconnoitre the enemy's position.

In striking contrast to the illusions cherished by many socialists in their time and up to the present day, Marx and Engels never accepted the idea that this same economic science which the proletarian class inherited from the bourgeoisie, could now, by a mere elimination of its inherent bourgeois bias and a consistent working out of its own premises, be transformed into a theoretical weapon for the proletarian revolution. Wherever such an opinion was expressed by the first socialist Ricardians of 1820-30, by the Owenists, or by Proudhon, Rodbertus, and Lassalle, they declared it an "economically false theory," an idealistic application of morality to economics and in its practical consequence a reactionary *Utopia*.

They pointed out that the equality-idea resulting from the epoch of bourgeois "commodity-production" and expressed in the economic "law of value" is still bourgeois in its character. It is therefore only ideologically incompatible with the exploitation of the working class through capital, but not in actual practice. The socialist Ricardians imagined that they could attack the economists on their own ground and with their own weapons. On the basis of the *economic* principle that "it is Labour alone which bestows value," they wanted to transform all men into actual workers exchanging equal quantities of labour. In order to obviate this state of affairs one must not apply a different interpretation to bourgeois economics but rather, through a real change in society, bring about a practical situation in which those economic laws will cease to hold good and thus the science of economics will become void of contents and ultimately vanish altogether.

Political Economy then, according to Marx, is a bourgeois science. This applies even to Marx's own contributions to the further development of its main doctrines. Marx fought to the end against the mistaken idea that his economic analysis of *Value* applied to any other than bourgeois conditions. Even the Marxian doctrine of *Value and Surplus Value* is only the final outgrowth of a conceptual process which, in content, had been almost completed by the classical bourgeois economists. Friedrich Engels, immediately after Marx's death, made it quite clear, and the posthumous publications from Marx's papers exhaustively proved, that Marx at no time in his life countenanced the opinion that the new contents of his socialist and communist theory could be derived, as a mere logical consequence, from the utterly bourgeois theories of Quesnay, Smith, and Ricardo.

How then are we to understand the leading part which, in spite of all this, Political Economy played in the genesis of Marx's theory of society, and maintained through all its subsequent developments? This in itself shows again the superiority of the *materialistic* standpoint. Marx kept aloof from that superficiality by which many revolutionary theorists in his time and today imagined that by a mere theoretical effort, wishful thinking, or a simple "change of heart" they could ignore such objective facts as those investigated by economic science — the very fundamentals of all existing social relations. The modern working class in its independent social movement inevitably starts from the historical results of the bourgeois revolutionary movement. At the same time this bourgeoisie and the new mode of production it brought forth, its State and all its other institutions and ideas, are the very antagonist from whom the proletariat must completely separate its own action and whom it must ultimately conquer in a decisive battle. So must the proletariat, in evolving its own revolutionary thought, start from the results achieved by bourgeois economic investigation. It cannot skip over, in its own materialistic theory, the definite forms of economic science existing historically in the present epoch any more than it can neglect, in its revolutionary practice, the existence of the modern capitalistic mode of production. Only by means of a practical and theoretical action persistently continued for a considerable time through several intermediate phases, can the proletariat carry through the necessary change in the existing conditions of material production and thereby ultimately surpass the social forms of consciousness which are at present bound up with those conditions.

Long before he applied this consequence of his materialistic principle to economic science, Marx had applied it to philosophical thought in the battles waged in the forties between the various groups of young Hegelians, on the question of the impact of "philosophy" (i.e., Hegelian philosophy) on the imminent political revolution. He had opposed the attitude of the philosophical party which derived the revolution immediately from the principles of philosophy just as much as he had opposed that of the anti-philosophical party which turned its back on philosophy. Just as he had done in his previous criticism of philosophy, so now in his criticism of Political Economy, Marx seemed to call out to the socialistic Ricardians, etc., who wished to derive socialism from bourgeois economics: *"You cannot realize Political Economy* (in practice) *without doing away with it* (by theoretical action)"; and to the "pure" historians, "pure" sociologists, "pure" revolutionary activists, who ignored all economics, *"You cannot do away with Political Economy* (by practical action) *without realizing it* (in theory)."

CLASSICAL POLITICAL ECONOMY

Classical Political Economy, as distinct from the adulterations of the "vulgar" economists of the 19th century and from the more recent attempts at an entirely new start, originated historically as an integral part of the *new science of civil society*, created by the bourgeoisie in its revolutionary struggle to establish this very society. It formed a realistic complement to the great philosophical, political, juridical, moral, aesthetic, and psychological upheaval, through which during the period of the so-called "Enlightenment" the ideological representatives of the rising bourgeois class first expressed the new bourgeois consciousness which corresponded to the change in the real conditions. Even in its purely theoretical form, the new science of Political Economy during this early period, as well as in the first great systems of the Physiocrats, was bound up with the whole of the new bourgeois social science in a natural and ingenuous unity. It is true that Adam Smith separated his economic *Inquiry into the Nature and Causes of the Wealth of Nations* from the "general principles of law and government, and of the different revolutions they have undergone in the different ages and periods of society," as discussed in his academical lectures, just as he had already split another part from that bulky whole in his earlier *Theory of Moral Sentiments*. Yet in his economic work he embraced once more, along with the fundamental economic relations, the whole of the new political and social conditions arising from the development of industry, exchange of commodities, and the division of labour within the new bourgeois order of society. Even in the work of Ricardo, in which the classical epoch of Political Economy reaches its close, this "organic" connection between Political Economy and the whole of society is preserved. At the same time, it can be said that the system of Ricardo which, as a true "anatomy" of civil society, formally restricts itself to an ingenious dissection of the material foundations — the skeleton, as it were, of the social body — shows the first symptoms of an impending disintegration. Still more does the subsequent theoretical development of bourgeois economics reveal the inevitable results of the change which during the ensuing period was to strip the bourgeois "production-relations" more and more of their original positive functions as incomparable stimulators and encouragers of the productive forces inherent in the new, industrial society.

This historical process, through which the hitherto progressive forms of the bourgeois production-relations were finally transformed into so many fetters, has since, in spite of temporary interruptions, asserted itself with ever increasing strength. It finds its economic expression in those periodically recurring dislocations of all existing proportions of capitalist production which, since their earliest characteristic occurrence in the first modern economic crisis of the year 1825, have assumed ever greater dimensions and ever more acute forms during the whole of the following century, challenging at their culminating points the whole existence of bourgeois society. There is no need to deal in this connection with the manner in which the curve of "social unrest" during the last hundred years continuously reflected the course of economic development, if not exactly at each point yet in its entire movement. The only point to be discussed here is the difference which prevails between the repercussions on the labour movement of the periodic business cycle, and those more permanent alterations within the whole economic system of modern society which have been described by recent explorers as a "structural change."

While the recurring phases of the "normal" industrial cycle are followed by corresponding ups-and-downs in class warfare, there is no such "cyclical" rhythm discoverable in the underlying secular movement. In spite of the intervening longer periods of an apparently undisturbed upswing and prosperity brought about by the temporary defeats, iron-handed oppression, and effective crushing of all existing workers' organizations, the proletarian struggle against the existing capitalist order of society has grown from its first elementary beginnings to embrace ever greater numbers, and to assume ever more efficient, more conscious, and more threatening forms.

It has become a veritable war between the oppressing and the oppressed classes, a war conducted on many fronts simultaneously, which sometimes breaks out in open revolts. The first World War, 1914-18, and the first wave of the proletarian world revolution released by the war, challenged the very premises on which during the "restful" intervals of this restless development, the bourgeois economists, and in their wake the moderate socialists, had based their "historical refutation of the Marxian prognoses." The first shock was followed by even stronger charges. The protracted economic crisis and the new series of wars and civil wars terminating the short-lived momentous upswing which had resulted during the 20's from the first apparent recovery of post-war capitalist equilibrium, reflected once more the utter absence of cohesive forces within the present economic system, and finally refuted the illusions by which the economic optimists had conjured up for themselves a complete abolition of crises in "organized capitalism," and of all class oppositions and class struggles in the "*democratic*" or, more recently, in the "*totalitarian State.*" Even such things as *machinery* and *money*, formerly so undoubtedly good and useful, have been robbed of their virtue as forces productive of social wealth and turned into forces destructive of social existence. The political and intellectual superstructure of society follows the change in its material conditions. The democratic forms of the State, the liberal ideas of the ascending phase of capitalist commodity production, have everywhere begun to totter. One after another of the safety-valves of the economic and political system is suspended. Emergency and martial law are the rule of common law. War and civil war on a world-wide scale have become the "normal" form of existence of present-day society.

A minor consequence of this universal destruction of the positive social function of bourgeois production-relations manifests itself in the gradual decay of the encyclopaedic spirit which had been so conspicuous during that earlier period when Political Economy embraced the whole of the social progress of the community. It is only from a formal point of view that Ricardo's economic system can be regarded as an advance on that of Adam Smith. While Smith had worked out his ideas on an epic scale and, little troubled by logical contradictions, developed the subject matter of Political Economy to a vast totality, Ricardo logically subordinated the whole of the bourgeois system to a unique principle, tracing back all its economic laws to the definition of value in terms of labour-time. The theoretical satisfaction offered in Ricardo's *Principles* (and more especially in its first two chapters which, as is demonstrated by Marx, virtually contain the whole book) by their originality, unity of the basic view, simplicity, concentration, profundity, novelty, and pithiness, is purchased at the expense of a loss of substance foreshadowing an impending emaciation. The generality aimed at by Ricardo is only the generality of scientific form; there is nowhere in his work, as there had been in that of Smith, the urge of a wider political aim. Its historical function consisted in summing up the great positive achievements of the classical period of bourgeois economic science and in the formal conclusion of an actually completed epoch.

While thus in Ricardo the turn to formalism was historically necessary and, thereby, theoretically justified, the progressive formalistic anaemia of the later period brought none of the great theoretical advantages of which the sceptics and the cynics of present-day "pure" Economics are so proud. They are so convinced of their superiority over the "unscientific" methods applied by the classical economists that they even accept without demur the reproach that their new theoretical science has become a mere plaything, purged of any political significance and of any possibility of application. Following the example of some modern mathematicians, logicians, and physicists, but without in any other respect keeping pace with the achievements of those real sciences, they want to carry on, in a field which cannot otherwise boast of any particular purity, the business of "pure" science, not for any useful purpose but merely "for the greater glory of God."

The actual outcome of this later development of Political Economy was a gradual decay. At the same rate as under the impact of the changed conditions of bourgeois production, bourgeois economic theory abandoned its original comprehensive social tendency, it abandoned also its formal scientific qualities, its impartiality, its logic, and fecundity. "From the year 1830 dates the finally decisive crisis." Henceforth any genuine development of Political Economy was precluded by the real historic development of bourgeois society.

Marxism restored, consciously and on a higher level, the connection between Political Economy and social science which had spontaneously and unconsciously evolved with the bourgeois classicists at an earlier stage. Only for this reason had the science of Political Economy any interest, only thus did it assume its important place in the whole of the Marxian social research. For this reason alone, it appears absurd that so many people should rack their brains to find out why Marx never paid the slightest attention to that "new departure" which, since the middle of the 19th century, is assumed to have been made by an altogether new economic science based on subjective value and the theory of so-called "marginal" utility. Marx did take cognizance of every new word, true or false, which was contributed to any economic question during his lifetime, even by the least important Epigone of classical Political Economy. His adherence to the classicists did not make him neglect the work of another school which, to a certain extent, preceded the theorists of "marginal value" in an attempt to reconstruct economic research by stressing "subjective" value (value in use) rather than classical "objective" value (value in exchange). He did not shrink, though he sighed under the burden, from the task of refuting the many inconsistencies of the leaders of the so-called "kathedersozialistische" school, from Rodbertus to Adolf Wagner. His apparent neglect of the new questions raised by the theorists of marginal utility sprang from an entirely different source. By the very principle of his *socio-economic research,* Marx was not interested in the thoughts of people who, though still calling their science "Economics," did not have anything in common with that research into the material foundations of society which had formed had formed the theme of classical Political Economy, any more than he would have been interested in some other auxiliary inquiry into a group of natural and technical facts not particularly important for the historical change of society. An economic doctrine indifferent to its social implications aroused the attention of Marx only when in spite of its purely "theoretical" concern, it afterwards did serve to draw practical application from its purely theoretical contents, and thus, like Duehring's "socialist" doctrine in the 70's, found supporters within the ranks of the workers' movement. This, however, did not take place with the theory of marginal utility until some years after Marx's death when, in Engels's phrase, G. B. Shaw and his followers endeavoured to base a plausible kind of "vulgar" socialism upon "Jevons's and Menger's use-value and marginal-utility theory," in order "to build on this rock the Fabian church of the future." That is why Marx in all his comprehensive criticism of traditional economic theory never considered the theory of marginal utility while, on the other hand, Friedrich Engels, when editing the third volume of *Capital*, bestowed a critical after-thought upon this newest theoretical attempt, if only in that somewhat curt and deprecatory remark.

POLITICAL ECONOMY TO MARXIAN CRITIQUE OF POLITICAL ECONOMY

As the revolutionary bourgeoisie had enlightened itself as to the principles of the new industrial society in the new science of *Political Economy*, so did the proletarian class assert its revolutionary aims in the *Critique of Political Economy*. This is not a critique of single results of bourgeois economics from within. It is, fundamentally, a critique of the very premises of

Political Economy based upon the new standpoint of a social class which, theoretically as well as practically, goes beyond bourgeois economy. It investigates the tendencies inherent in capitalist commodity production which in the course of their further development produce the necessary basis for the economic, political, and ideological struggle of the proletarian class, and which will ultimately overthrow the bourgeois mode of production and advance to the higher production-relations of a socialistic and communistic society.

The Marxian "critique" is not the first appearance of a genuine principle of criticism as a driving force in the development of economic science. Already in the earlier phases of Political Economy the Mercantile system had been criticised by the Physiocrats, the Physiocrats by Adam Smith, and Adam Smith by Ricardo. Nor was that earlier economic criticism a matter of pure theory. Each new phase of the theoretical development implied a new phase in the real historical development of the capitalistic mode of production. There was no clear distinction; in fact, every historical phase was in itself a criticism of the preceding phase. For all that, the actual historical and theoretical "subject" of economic science remained unchanged through all these stages. The bourgeois class in its revolutionary struggle against the obsolete forms of feudal production, could not, and did not, distinguish its particular interests as a class from its general interest in the whole of historical progress. Even after the defeat of feudalism, it could still for a considerable time quite honestly regard itself as promoting the general welfare of society. During this phase Political Economy was even striving to cooperate, with the utmost impartiality, in the solution of the new economic problems emerging from the increasingly unsatisfactory conditions of the real people, that is, the actually working section of the as yet undivided industrial society.

That state of things was profoundly changed by the new historical development which set in with the economic crisis of 1825 and with the great political changes of 1830. Henceforward, the new conditions established within bourgeois society no longer permitted an impartial analysis of the economic principles underlying those conditions. A strictly scientific investigation of social development was possible only from the standpoint of that class whose task in history is to transcend the narrow bourgeois horizon and, ultimately, to do away with classes altogether. The theoretical system of Ricardo marks the turning point.

The complete impartiality of the genuine scientific investigator which appears everywhere in the work of Ricardo, had seemed miraculous already to his contemporaries. "Mr. Ricardo seemed to have dropped from another planet," said Lord Brougham. With faultless clarity, this English banker of the beginning of the 19th century, who nowhere goes beyond the boundaries of the bourgeoisie, presented in his system the inherent disharmonies as well as the harmonious and progressive features of the bourgeois mode of production; more particularly he revealed the inevitable opposition arising between the two industrial classes. He declared from the outset that the principal problem in Political Economy is to state the proportions in which the whole produce of society is allotted to each of the three social classes: the proprietors of land, the owners of capital, and the propertyless labourers. Thus "the contrast of class interests, of wages and profits, of profit and rent," became indeed, as was later stated by Marx, the very "pivot" of Ricardo's economic investigation.

The position of Ricardo in the history of economic science is precisely analogous to that occupied by Hegel in philosophical thought, just as in a preceding phase the economics of Adam Smith had corresponded to the philosophy of Kant. This analogous historical position appears most clearly in Ricardo's important contribution to what we have described in an earlier chapter as the "bourgeois self-criticism." The scientific criticism of the existing capitalistic system, which pervades the economic system of Ricardo, surpasses the occasional comments of the earlier economists on the unpleasant sides of the new bourgeois conditions even more than the earlier philosophical critics had been surpassed by Hegel. While in dealing with Hegel we had to disregard the mystifying form of his statements in order to find out his realistic advance on his predecessors, the superiority of Ricardo's criticism over that of his forerunners is clear like day. His critical statements not only surpass all previous criticism in their sweeping power of generalization and in the irresistible logic of their reasoning. A more decisive difference appears in their very premises, namely, in the fact that they rest no longer on that naïve faith in the fundamental perfection or the unlimited perfectibility of the new world order, which had prevailed among the economists of the preceding period quite as much as among the philosophers.

Political Economy in its first period had been optimistic and confident to the extent that along with the blessings of the new bourgeois mode of production it could afford to acknowledge their purchase price. "Not for a single moment did it deceive itself as to the birth pains of wealth, but what is the use of crying over historical necessity?" Even for Adam Smith it had still been fairly easy, in his great inquiry into the best possible ways to raise the general wealth of society, to regard the interests of the "inferior order" of the wage-labourers as well as those of the two "superior orders" (profit and rent). He had even endeavoured to oppose the tendency of the newly arrived bourgeoisie to monopolize for itself the advantages won in a common battle and to bring definitely to the front the neglected interests of the common man. He did not thereby endanger, but rather tightened the apparent unity of the two industrial classes which were at that time still busy conquering the last surviving prerogatives of the landed aristocracy. A different situation was faced by Ricardo when in a supplementary chapter added to the third edition of his *Principles* he did not uphold the favourable view on the effects of machinery which he had expressed in the preceding chapters of his work but which in the meantime had been proved to him by Sismondi to be erroneous both in fact and in theory. While he had then emphasized the "general good" which must of necessity be brought about by "these mute agents which are always the produce of much less labour than that which they displace," he now carefully re-examined his earlier position. A more realistic consideration of the "influence of machinery on the interests of the different classes of society" led him to the conclusion that the opinion entertained by the labouring class, that the employment of machinery is frequently detrimental to their interests, is not founded on prejudice and error, but is conformable to the correct principles of Political Economy.

No wonder that the later pseudoscientific apologists of capitalism should denounce him on this count as the Father of Communism. Said a leading American economist in 1848: The system of Mr. Ricardo is one of discord. . . it tends to foster enmity between classes and nations. . . His book is the right textbook for the demagogue who aims at power through agrarianism, war, and plunder.

All post-Ricardian developments of Political Economy testify to the fact that the historical struggle waged between the progressive industrial class and the obstructive forces of feudal oppression had now been finally superseded by a new revolutionary conflict arising within bourgeois society between the two hitherto united classes produced by modern industry itself — bourgeoisie and proletariat.

The first of the various schools to work out the scientific results of classical Political Economy under the changed historical conditions of the 19th century sprang up immediately after Ricardo's death. From this school started the attempt with which we have dealt above, to use the Ricardian theory as a weapon against the existing economic system of society and thus to derive anti-bourgeois conclusions from bourgeois principles. But in the main the spokesmen of this new school contented themselves with celebrating the victory of the Ricardian principles over all pre-Ricardian economics in a series of splendid tournaments which were for the most part displayed in scattered review-articles, occasional papers, and pamphlets and were, after long oblivion, rediscovered and recognized in their historical importance, mainly by the endeavours of Marx. This last polemical intermezzo preceding the final collapse of the fighting spirit in bourgeois economic theory — a skirmish resembling, as Marx said, the "Sturm und Drang" period of economic science that had raged in France after Dr. Quesnay's death, but not more than "Indian summer reminds us of the spring" — covered roughly the decade 1820 to 1830. After that it dragged on in ever weaker manifestations to the Repeal of the Corn Laws in England in 1846 and to the outbreak of a new revolution on the continent in 1848-49.

Another tendency of post-Ricardian economics is represented by a school of pseudoscientific writers who flattened, diluted, and gradually entirely dispersed the theoretical results reaped from the work of classical economists. The theoretical contents of the prolific writings of this school are most aptly, if somewhat cruelly, described by Marx as a mere "vulgarization" of the scientific achievements of Political Economy. The "vulgar" successors of the great classical economists have, indeed, not added any new contribution to that genuine work of discovery by which their scientific predecessors had discerned the inner relations of the modern bourgeois mode of production and thus brought forward the necessary premises for its genetic presentation. Scientific analysis was everywhere replaced by mere conceptual reflection.

That simple reproduction of the given external conditions, which for the classicists had been merely one of the constituents of their theory — its "vulgar" element — was now finally set up as a separate existence. Yet this was not the lowest point reached in the gradual decay of a formerly vigorous and vital science. A still more complete loss of scientific character was seen, when later, along with the further development of the real oppositions inherent in the life of bourgeois society, economic science itself split in mutually opposing parts. Bourgeois economists, when no longer confronted with their own internal dissensions, but with a group of socialistic dissenters opposing them from without, promptly threw over all semblance of unbiassed theoretical research.

From a mere neglect of the progressive tasks of true science, they turned to a conscious defence of existing bourgeois conditions against the impending socialistic menace embodied in the writings of Sismondi, Owen, Fourier, Saint-Simon. The more the stern outlines of the class strife asserted themselves in the actual development of capitalist society, the more the economists applied themselves to a misrepresentation and, ultimately, to an entire negation of these new historical tendencies. At each further step in the unavoidable development of "class" and "class discord" within reality, they strengthened their desperate efforts to keep these embarrassing topics entirely out of their theoretical picture. They even endeavoured to purge the classical concepts of any such impurities wherever they had already been introduced into economic theory by their great scientific predecessors. Thus bourgeois economists became even incapable of a faithful registration of external facts. By the combined effect of all these self-established obstructions, the "vulgarized" economic theory of the 19th century became poorer and poorer in theoretical content. There is, however, a difference between the earlier stage when, for instance, Say had "vulgarized" Adam Smith, and the latter stage when MacCulloch, Bastiat, and others had "vulgarized" Ricardo. In the earlier phase the "vulgarizers" had found their material as yet unfinished, and thus had been compelled to contribute, though in a diminishing degree, to the solving of real economic problems. In the later phase they dropped all independent theoretical effort and occupied themselves with a mere plagiarizing of the doctrines of Ricardo and with an arguing away of the unpleasant aspects.

The deductions which the socialist Ricardians had been unable to draw, and which the "vulgar" economists had deliberately dodged, were formulated fifty years later by a new school of economic research. The true conclusions of classical Political Economy were drawn by Marx. The "critical" tradition of the classical epoch of Political Economy was revived by the Marxian "Critique" of Political Economy in *Capital*. This new criticism, however, was more than a transition from a given phase to a further developed phase of economic science. It implied a change of the class which henceforth was to be the historical as well as the theoretical "subject" of all Political Economy. While previous criticisms had for their practical aim a further "development" of the bourgeois mode of production, the Marxian criticism aims at its complete overthrow. "Critique" of Political Economy, then, is the theory of an impending revolution.

Not only Marx and Engels, but all revolutionary Hegelians of the 40's and 50's of the last century, had used the word "critique" in this large historical sense. The terminology fell into complete oblivion during the sad period of decline which set in after the collapse of the Chartist movement and the triumph of the counter-revolution in the whole of Europe consequent upon the defeat of the Paris proletariat in June, 1848. Thus a complete abandonment of all revolutionary "critical" tendencies in theory coincided with the abandonment of the last residues of a practical revolutionary tendency. Marx and Engels were the only ones who rescued from oblivion both the practical and the theoretical aspects of a truly revolutionary "critique."

SCIENTIFIC VERSUS PHILOSOPHICAL CRITICISM OF POLITICAL ECONOMY

Marx's approach to Political Economy was from the outset that of a critical and revolutionary student of society rather than that of an economist. Yet a long period was still required before, from the first discovery of Political Economy as an "anatomy of civil society" through a series of intermediate phases, he arrived at his final scientific and materialistic investigation and critique of the whole complex of ideas and facts constituting the historical existence of "Political Economy."

Marx was already an outspoken revolutionary and even a proletarian socialist at the time when he regarded a really developed "Political Economy" as it existed in England and France as being in itself revolutionary progress, and practically identified the aims of Political Economy with the aims of socialism. He contrasted this modern form of relating industry to the State, or the "world of wealth" to the "world of politics," with the reactionary form in which that "main problem of modern times" had then begun to occupy the attention of the Germans. "While the problem in France and England is worded Political Economy, or wealth controlled by society, in Germany it is termed National Economy, or nationality controlled by private property." If we apply to Marx the terms which he, but a short time later, was to apply to a similar standpoint, we may say that during this short first period Marx had criticized politics only from the standpoint of economics, but had not yet extended his revolutionary criticism to the economic basis itself; or that up to now he had merely "criticized Political Economy from the standpoint of Political Economy."

By the time when he had raised this objection to his first socialist antagonist, Proudhon, Marx himself had adopted an altogether different standpoint which utterly transcended all economic science in an apparently final manner. His *economico-philosophical manuscripts* dating from this second period, and the economic fragments inserted in a mainly philosophical work written at the same time, anticipated all the critical and revolutionary conclusions which were later embodied in *Capital*. Yet this new critical insight was couched in a highly philosophical language and appeared much more as a materialistic continuation of the old philosophical struggles among the different Hegelian schools than as a scientific criticism of the contents and premises of Political Economy. Instead of dealing directly with the theories and concepts of the great classical economists, Marx dealt rather with the idealistic, that is, insufficient reconstruction and criticism which these concepts had in the meantime found in the philosophy of Hegel and of the right and left Hegelians of the 1830's and 40's. For example, he disposed of the socio-economic phenomenon which he was later to solve in a rational way in his critical exposure of the "Fetishism of Commodities," by a reference to the then most fashionable Hegelian term of "human self-alienation." He summed up his criticism of Proudhon in the sentence: "Proudhon conquers economic alienation only within the bounds of economic alienation." In the same manner his criticism of other fundamental economic phenomena started from the assumption that "Hegel takes the position of modern Political Economy" and that, therefore, a materialistic exposure of the idealistic shortcomings of Hegel's philosophical criticism of the economic terms is equivalent to a final refutation of Political Economy itself.

Marx began to free himself from the remaining vestiges of his former philosophical creed by a comprehensive criticism of all post-Hegelian philosophy. In this he was joined by Engels. As a first result of their life-long cooperation, which after some more or less frustrated earlier attempts was now really beginning, Marx and Engels during the next two years worked out in detail the contrast prevailing between their own materialistic and scientific views and the various ideological standpoints represented by their former friends among the left Hegelians (Feuerbach, Bruno Bauer, Stirner) and by the philosophical belles-lettres of the "German" or "true" socialists. Thus, they finally broke with what Marx later called their "former philosophical conscience." From this thoroughly changed standpoint Marx now cruelly criticized the somewhat bewildering manner in which his former philosophical criticism of Political Economy in the meantime had been further worked out by Proudhon. He showed that Proudhon did not treat the economic categories as theoretical expressions of historical conditions, corresponding to a definite stage in the development of material production, but as "pre-existing eternal ideas," and thus ultimately fell back on the standpoint of bourgeois economics. Such criticism of Proudhon's philosophical mystification of economic concepts was undoubtedly justified. But Marx's new anti-philosophical tendency was now so strong that, instead of supplanting Proudhon's bad philosophy by a better and more scientific criticism of Political Economy, he rather confronted Proudhon's unscientific criticism with the science of Political Economy itself, i.e., with Ricardo's theory of value. Thus he no longer reproached Proudhon for not having passed critically beyond the narrow bounds of economic science. He now reproached him for sharing, as an economist, the "illusions of speculative philosophy" and for not yet having entered the realm of a really scientific Political Economy.

Only with the next stage of this long and somewhat circuitous development do we reach the period, during which Marx finally worked out his own *critical economic theory* which is, at the same time, the basic part of his materialistic theory of the historical development of society and of the proletarian revolution. The first mature fruit of this new stage is contained in the masterly lectures which Marx delivered to the German Workers' Educational Association at Brussels in 1847 and later published, in a revised form, in his own revolutionary paper during the 1848 revolution. Outline and contents reveal that we have here the first fragmentary statement of that comprehensive exposition of the "economic conditions underlying all present-day class wars and national struggles," which, later, after being further worked out and many times entirely recast was to appear as *Das Kapital*. The most conspicuous difference is that Marx in the earlier work does not yet start from the analysis of "commodities" in general but from a particular kind of commodity — *wage-labour*, and from the opposition between the two main classes of modern capitalistic society which directly springs from the appearance of that commodity. We find, moreover, in this first scientific exposition the striking description (pivotal for all subsequent developments and unsurpassed, in trenchant power, even by Marx's own later formulae) of "capital" itself, which is defined as not being a relation between *men and nature*, but as *a relation between man and men based on a relation between man and nature* — a specific historic form of a social relation arising and decaying with the rise and decay of modern industrial or "capitalistic society."

The working out of this first scientific exposition of Marx's revolutionary criticism of Political Economy was interrupted by the outbreak of the February Revolution, just as in a later period of world history, Lenin's presentation of "The Marxian Doctrine of the State and the Task of the Proletariat in the Revolution" was interrupted by a situation calling for the performance of that very task.

After the final defeat of the abortive European revolution of 1848-49, Marx made the most of the long years of involuntary leisure which were forced upon him as an exile in London, by making "an entirely fresh start" in his economic studies. The ultimate form of his materialistic theory, which resulted from that new and prolonged period of economic and social research, is at the same time Political Economy and a criticism of Political Economy. It works out the classical system of bourgeois economy and ultimately transcends all phases and forms of bourgeois economy. It shows the most general ideas and principles of Political Economy to be mere fetishes disguising actual social relations, prevailing between individuals and classes within a definite historical epoch of the socio-economic formation.

TWO ASPECTS OF REVOLUTIONARY MATERIALISM IN MARX'S ECONOMIC THEORY

There appears in the successive phases of Marx's theory, besides the main line of a continuous growth of the critical revolutionary standpoint, another line of development which, to a certain extent, runs contrary to the first. Hand in hand with increasing stress on a strictly materialistic and scientific approach, goes a greater emphasis on economic theory itself, as against a mere critical attack on its philosophical, historical, and practical premises. It seems as if Marx during the further study of the vast unexhausted material accumulated during the classical epoch of Political Economy that he found heaped up in the vaults of the British Museum, was more and more strongly impressed by the lasting significance which the scientific results of classical Political Economy were bound to have for the new revolutionary class, for a really materialistic theory of bourgeois society, and for a practicable way to its revolutionary overthrow. Just as the tremendous depression and stagnation following the defeat of the Paris workers in 1848 had imposed upon the materialistic investigator a long period of leisure for his ever-expanding, ever-deepening economic studies, so at the same time many revolutionary impulses within the actual workers' movement were forcibly repressed in their genuine practical function.

A new stage of development seemed to be opened for Capitalism with the discoveries of gold in California and Australia — discoveries which attracted the most active members of the working class and thus further paralyzed even the faintest attempts at recovery within the European revolutionary movement. All those historical changes were reflected in the later development of Marx's revolutionary theory. The social revolution of the proletariat was now mainly represented as a necessary development of society, during which capitalistic production by the working of an inevitable economic law brings forth its negation with the inexorability of a natural process.

He did not for this reason commit himself to the so-called fatalist tendency "discovered" over and over again in some of Marx's phrases by the later bourgeois critics and by their supporters within the labour movement. A closer investigation reveals that even in that gloomiest period, both of the proletarian movement and of his own career, Marx kept himself far away from any fatalism. Still, it is a definitely changed pattern of revolutionary action which was henceforward sketched out by the materialistic theory for the historical movement of the workers' class.

The question as to whether that change resulted in a strengthening or a weakening of the revolutionary movement can only be answered by taking into account the historical circumstances prevailing at the time, or rather, through the entire historical period. We merely note that the new phase of Marx's revolutionary science and the increased importance which was now assigned to economic theory within its frame, arose from a particular historical situation and suggested a form of behaviour adapted to that particular situation. Marx's materialistic theory, grounded on firm economic foundations, seemed to point out a new way to the workers, who had now passed the period of their first Utopian enthusiasm and spontaneous aggressive activity. Though this new way might not ensure a quick and easy advance to victory, nor even a direct approach to decisive battles, yet in comparison with the meagre chances of the earlier period, it afforded a distinctly better opportunity, nay even a practical certainty of success.

This element of disillusionment and dearly-bought sobriety which is inherent in the later phases of Marx's "materialism" and is largely responsible for the tremendous effect which Marxism was to exert upon the workers' movement during the ensuing historical period, was produced by the historical conditions of the 50's. It is, at the same time, both historically and theoretically connected with another and much more general chain of historical events.

The proletarian revolution of the 19th century, which so far had found its most powerful and most conspicuous theoretical expression in the revolutionary materialism of Marx, appears, under a secular aspect, as being itself a mere *second phase* within the whole of the modern revolutionary movement. Thus it shares, to a certain extent, the more general "disenchantment" which after the conclusion of the great French Revolution was first proclaimed by the early French theorists of the counter-revolution and Romanticists.

This idea of disenchantment has, in fact, exerted a considerable influence upon Marx mainly through Hegel, and has thus directly entered into the "materialistic" Marxian theory of the modern workers' movement. Nay, more, we may go still further back and find within the materialistic theory of the proletarian revolution some traces of the revolutionary tradition of the Jacobinic Convention of 1792-94. This particular phase of the French revolution which was afterwards exalted over and over again by Marx, Engels, and Lenin as a model of the highest political sagacity and energy, had, likewise, been a "second" and sobered phase in contrast to the exuberant and illusionary phase of 1789-92.

On all these grounds the Marxian materialistic and economic theory bears the specific characteristics of a *theory of the second phase of the proletarian revolution*, and has actually made its first entrance in all countries where it became the dominant revolutionary theory at the very time when an analogous historical situation had arisen in that particular country. Even in *Russia*, where revolutionary Marxism was to make world history by a first great victory of its principle, similar historical circumstances accompanied its reception.

The revolutionary social democratic, i.e., "Marxist," principle was inaugurated in Russia since 1883, according to the testimony of the best authority on the subject, mainly by a pamphlet of Plechanov which, under the heading *Socialism and Political Struggle*, endeavoured to "open up a new way for the *defeated* revolutionary movement through which it could secure for its cause *a certain, if not immediate, victory*."

Instead of following by a conscious and violent action the model set by the preceding generation of Russian revolutionaries, it was to rely on the socio-economic process of development which would "slowly but unavoidably undermine the old régime" and through which the Russian working class "in an historical development proceeding just as inexorably as the development of capitalism itself," would finally "deal the death blow to Russian absolutism" and would then "join, as an equal member, the ranks of the international proletarian army."

In a similar way, Marx and Engels themselves upon several occasions expressed the idea that the different degrees of "maturity," or the preparedness of the workers' movement in various capitalistic countries to accept the Marxian materialistic theory, more or less depended upon the experience gained by each section of the workers concerned during a preceding phase of Utopian illusions and immediate revolutionary attempts. This assumption of two definite phases, one "Utopian," the other "scientific," through which every modern labour movement must pass in its historical development, was finally stated by Friedrich Engels in his well-known pamphlet on *The development of Socialism from a Utopia to a Science*.

Since its first appearance in France, in 1880, this pamphlet was spread under this and under various other titles in large editions throughout the world and became as significant for the various *Social-Democratic Movements* preceding the World War, as have been, for other historical phases of the modern workers' movement, *The Communist Manifesto* of 1848, Marx's *Address and Rules of the Working Men's International Association* of 1864, and Lenin's pamphlet on *State and Revolution* of 1917.

Whatever the reasons, there is no doubt that Marx, during his later development, linked himself more and more closely with the scientific results of classical Political Economy. The Marxian "Critique" as contained in the second and third books of *Capital* (which after his death were edited by Engels), and even in the first book edited by Marx himself, not infrequently gives the unwary reader the impression of being no longer directed against the whole of the preceding bourgeois economic science, but only against those superficial and apologetic forms into which the truly scientific statements and concepts of the great classical thinkers had degenerated with the post-classical or "vulgar" economists. Yet this is by no means the real significance of Marx's economic and social theory. It is easy to clear up some ambiguous statements by reference to those sections of the first Chapter of *Capital* in which Marx stated with the utmost precision the difference between his critical economic theory and the doctrines presented by even the greatest and most advanced thinkers of the classical epoch of bourgeois Political Economy.

ECONOMIC THEORY OF CAPITAL

In our presentation of the economic theory of Capital, we shall confine ourselves to one or two results of the Marxian teaching, extremely abstract in appearance, which include, in our opinion, the revolutionary kernel of the Marxian theory and thus constitutes its fundamental and epoch-making importance. It is this, in fact, which explains why the teaching of Marx has gained and retained, for almost a century, the active support of millions of revolutionary workers in all parts of the world, and which even today forces from the most bitter opponents of the proletarian class movement an unwilling tribute, in that they announce as the aim of their reactionary and counter-revolutionary endeavours — *War against Marxism*.

Marx himself, in a letter which he wrote to Engels soon after the appearance of *Capital*, designated as the "three fundamentally new elements" of his book, the following:

(1) that in contrast to *all* earlier economics which from the outset had dealt with the detached fragments of surplus

value in their fixed forms of Rent, Profit, Interest, as given entities, he first treated the general form of Surplus Value, in which all those elements are still comprehended in an undivided unity like the uncrystallized components in a chemical solution;

(2) that, without exception, economists had missed the simple fact that if a commodity is the sum of the "value in use" and the "value in exchange," the labour entailed in the production of the commodity must possess the same twofold character, while the mere analysis for "labour sans phrase," as in Smith, Ricardo, etc., must inevitably stumble upon something inexplicable. *This is indeed the whole secret of the critical conception;*

(3) that for the first time wages are shown to be an irrational manifestation of some other relation hidden behind them.

All these innovations are of decisive importance with regard to the ultimate aim of the Marxist theory, the critical transformation of economics into a direct historical and social science dealing with the development of material production and of the class struggle.

That goal, however, is not reached by an immediate disintegration of economics as a particular form of knowledge but by a further theoretical development which brings into relief the inherent contradiction between the economic categories and principles and the actual facts which had hitherto been presented in their guise. While Marx seems merely to proceed with the work begun by the great bourgeois economists, his further development of their theories is guided in every case by a definite critical purpose. A more refined, more comprehensive, more thorough, and more consistent analysis serves to advance the traditional economic concepts and theorems to that point where the practical reality behind them, i.e., their historical and social contents become tangible and subject to a critical attack.

Thus the Marxian definition of value in terms of labour differs from the classical definition not by its conceptual form but rather by a closer connection with the underlying social conditions. Similarly, the advance made by the famous Marxian doctrine of surplus value, as stated by Marx himself, is new only because of the more comprehensive synthesis, by which he reduced to a common denominator the various phenomena of profit, interest, and rent as described by the classical economists.

Nor does the new Marxian definition of wages, not as the "price of labour" but as the price of labour-power, amount to a major scientific discovery since the best classic writers, and, indeed, Marx himself in his earlier period had already applied the former term in exactly the same sense which was later more fully expressed by the more elaborate description. Both these apparent technicalities and, in fact, the whole of the Marxian improvements upon classical economic theory are important, not for their purely formal advance over the classical concepts, but for their definite transfer of economic thought from the field of the exchange of commodities and of the legal and moral conceptions of "right" and "wrong" originating therein to the field of material production taken in its full social significance.

For example, the economic concept of a *surplus value* existing in the form of goods and money and competed for by its rival claimants is now transformed into the concept of a *surplus labour* performed by the real workers in the workshop under the social domination exerted upon them by the capitalist owner of the workshop. Furthermore, the "free labour contract" of the modern wage labourer is, by an apparent change of terminology only, now revealed as a real sale of the labour-power of the wage-labourer to the capitalist in return for wages, and thus as a social oppression and exploitation of the labouring class persisting within an assumedly "free" and democratically ruled society.

Marx begins the further theoretical development of the economic categories at the point where classical political economists had ended, i.e., with an analysis of "value" based on the distinction of a "value in use" and "value in exchange," and with the reduction of "value" to "labour." These two scientific discoveries of the last stage of bourgeois classical economics, of which, as they were then represented, the one was bound to remain entirely sterile, and the other led only to a one-sided and formalistic further development, were used by Marx to work out his new concept of "*commodity-producing labour*" which was henceforth to serve as a pivot for a new understanding of the whole conceptual system of Political Economy.

The distinction between use-value and exchange-value, in the abstract form in which it had been made by the bourgeois economists, (and had, in fact, already been applied by Aristotle to the commodity production of Antique Society) did not provide any useful starting-point for a materialistic investigation of bourgeois commodity production as a particular social form. It was insufficient also for theoretical reasons. The concept of use value was only perfunctorily mentioned by them as a presupposition of exchange value, and exchange value alone was treated as a real economic category.

With Marx, as we have seen in a former chapter, use value is not defined as a use value in general, but as the *use value of a commodity*. This use value inherent in the commodities produced in modern capitalistic society is, however, not merely an extra-economic presupposition of their "value." It is an element of the value, and itself is an economic category. The mere fact that a thing has utility for any human being, does not yet give us the economic definition of value. Not until the thing has social utility (i.e., utility "for other persons") does the economic definition of use value apply.

Just as the use value of the commodity is economically defined as a "*social use value*" (use value "for others"), so is the specifically useful labour which goes into the production of this commodity defined economically as a "*social labour*" (labour "for others"). Thus, Marx's "*commodity-producing labour*" appears as a social labour in a twofold sense. It has, in common with labour in other stages of the historical development of production, the *general social character* of being a "specifically useful labour," which goes to the production of a definite kind of social use value.

It has, on the other hand, the *specific historical character* of being a "generally social labour," which goes to the production of a definite quantity of exchange value. The capacity of social labour to produce definite things useful to human beings (a general condition of the Circulation of Matter going on between Man and Nature) appears in the *use value* of its product. Its capacity for the production of a value and a surplus value for the capitalist (a particular characteristic of labour which derives from the particular form of the social organization of the labour process under the conditions of the capitalistic mode of production within the present historical epoch) appears in the *exchange value* of its product. The fusion of the two social characteristics of commodity-producing labour appears in the "value form" of the product of labour, or the "*form of commodity*."

Only thus critically modified, is the *theory of labour value* a suitable starting-point for an economic theory in which labour is considered not merely formally and in one of its aspects but in its full material realization.

The earlier bourgeois economists when speaking of labour as a source of wealth, had likewise thought of "labour" in terms of the various forms of real work, though they did so only for the reason that their economic categories were as yet undeveloped, and still in the process of separation from their original material contents, vague and indeterminate. Thus, the Mercantilists, the Physiocrats, etc., successfully declared the true source of wealth to lie in the labour expended in the export industries, trade and shipping, in agricultural labour, etc. Even with Adam Smith, who from the different branches of labour definitely advanced to the general form of commodity-producing labour, we find that concrete aspect retained, along with the new and more formalistic definition which is also expressed in his system and was later to become the exclusive definition of value in the work of Ricardo, and by which labour is defined as an abstract and merely quantitative entity. This same abstract form of labour, which he correctly defined as exchange-value producing labour, he at the same time, irrationally enough, declared to be the only source not only of value (exchange value) but also of the material wealth of the community, or use value.

This doctrine which still obstinately persists in "vulgar" socialism, and which is unjustly imputed to scientific socialism by its bourgeois critics, is according to Marx economically false. In so far as "labour" is regarded in its specific character as useful labour, and, in the same way, "wealth" its material form as an object of utility, labour is *not* the only source of wealth. (If this were so, it would be difficult to explain why in present-day capitalistic society just those persons are poor who hitherto have had that unique source of wealth at their exclusive disposal, and even more difficult to account for the fact that they remain unemployed and poor, instead of producing wealth by their labour.)

But it is just here, in the very inconsistency of his economic theory, that a remembrance of the concrete reality of human labour lingers in the mind of Adam Smith. In praising the creative power of "labour" he was not thinking so much of the forced labour of the modern wage-labourer, which appears in the value of the commodities and produces capitalistic profit, as of the general natural necessity of human labour, which produces things useful and beautiful.

Likewise, his naïve glorification of the "division of labour" achieved in these "great manufactures," by which he understood the whole of modern capitalist production, does not so much refer to the extremely imperfect form of present-day capitalistic division of labour (arising through commodity production and exchange) as to the general form of human labour vaguely fused with it in his theoretical exposition. "Adam Smith's contradictions," said Marx later, "are significant in so far as they contain problems which he indeed does not solve, but which he reveals just by contradicting himself."

In the further development from Smith to Ricardo, Political Economy becomes more consistent — and one-sided. Even now, bourgeois economists do not deny that there are two characters inherent in the commodity, use value and exchange value. But they deal only with "value of exchange" as the true economic value. While immersed in their "economic" definition of "value" in terms of labour, they appear to have quite lost sight of the other aspect of labour which had, at least unconsciously, been taken into consideration by the older economists, that is, of labour as a specifically useful activity, which brings forth as its product a definitely useful object (a use value). "Political Economy," said Marx, "nowhere explicitly and consciously distinguishes between labour represented in value and the same labour so far as it is represented in the use value of its product."

Marx has reintroduced in a new form real, concrete labour into Political Economy. He deals with "labour" not in the indefinite, ambiguous, and vacillating form as it had appeared in the writings of the older bourgeois economists; not as the labour of the commodity-producer, or as the materially and formally free labour of the independent master craftsman, who had control over his own material means of production, and who exchanged the product of his labour in the form of a commodity for another kind of commodity, or the product of another form of an equally free and independent labour.

Marx deals with labour in its present unambiguous, and definite, form of *labour producing a commodity for another person*, i.e., of labour formally paid to its full value but actually exploited; formally free, actually enslaved; formally the independent labour of an isolated worker, actually collective labour performed by proletarian wage-labourers who are separated from the material means of production and to whom their own tools and the *social character of their own labour* — that is, the productive power of what would be under otherwise similar conditions the produce of an isolated worker, now increased a thousandfold by the social division of labour — stand opposed in the form of *capital*. Political Economy is now no longer a science of commodities, and a science of labour only indirectly, and in an abstract and one-sided manner.

It becomes a direct science of social labour, of the productive forces of that labour, of their development and afterwards their enslavement by the fixed forms of the production-relations prevailing in present-day bourgeois society and, finally, of the emancipation of the productive forces in present society by the revolutionary action of the proletarian class. A glance at the first volume of Marx's *Capital* will suffice to convince us of the completely changed character of this science of economics.

From the very beginning the meticulous analysis of the most general economic categories ("Commodity," "Money," and "Transformation of Money into Capital") in the first chapters of Marx's work, adheres only in appearance to "that turbulent sphere of the exchange of commodities which is taking place on the surface of commodity-producing society, open and visible to all." In truth, from the opening sentence to the final conclusion, the Marxian analysis serves to make us look through those highly abstract and sophisticated categories of the bourgeois economists, to disclose their "fetish character," and to demonstrate the specific social character of bourgeois commodity production lying behind them. It becomes highly transparent while dealing, in its later parts, with the sale and purchase of a commodity of a very special composition, labour-power.

It finally passes from the realm of commodity-exchange into another sphere entirely, the "hidden haunts of production, on whose threshold we are faced with the inscription: No admittance except on business." From now on the *labour process*, or what is according to Marx but another name for the same thing, the *process of material production*, both in its material and historical aspects, constitutes the subject matter of the economic theory of *Capital*.

12

Marx's Labour Theory of Value

As an economist, Marx is generally situated in the continuity of the great classical school of Adam Smith and Ricardo. He obviously owes a lot to Ricardo, and conducts a running dialogue with that master in most of his mature economic writings. Marx inherited the labour theory of value from the classical school. Here the continuity is even more pronounced; but there is also a radical break, For Ricardo, labour is essentially a numeraire, which enables a common computation of labour and capital as basic elements of production costs. For Marx, labour is value. Value is nothing but that fragment of the total labour potential existing in a given society in a certain period (e.g. a year or a month) which is used for the output of a given commodity, at the average social productivity of labour existing then and there, divided by the total number of these commodities produced and expressed in hours (or minutes), days, weeks, months of labour.

Value is therefore essentially a social, objective and historically relative category, It is social because it is determined by the overall result of the fluctuating efforts of each individual producer (under capitalism: of each individual firm or factory). It is objective because it is given, once the production of a given commodity is finished, and is thus independent from personal (or collective) valuations of customers on the market place; and it is historically relative because it changes with each important change (progress or regression) of the average productivity of labour in a given branch of output, including in agriculture and transportation. This does not imply that Marx's concept of value is in any way completely detached from consumption. It only means that the feedback of consumers' behaviour and wishes upon value is always mediated through changes in the allocation of labour inputs in production, labour being seen as subdivided into living labour and dead (dated) labour, i.e. tools and raw materials. The market emits signals to which the producing units react. Value changes after these reactions, not before them. Market price changes can of course occur prior to changes in value. In fact, changes in market prices are among the key signals which can lead to changes in labour allocation between different branches of production, i.e. to changes in labour quantities necessary to produce given commodities. But then, for Marx, values determine prices only basically and in the medium-term sense of the word. This determination only appears clearly as an explication of medium and long-term price movements. In the shorter run, prices fluctuate around values as axes. Marx never intended to negate the operation of market laws, of the law of supply and demand, in determining these short-term fluctuations.

The 'law of value' is but Marx's version of Adam Smith's 'invisible hand'. In a society dominated by private labour, private producers and private ownership of productive inputs, it is this 'law of value', an objective economic law operating behind the backs of all people, all 'agents' involved in production and consumption, which, in the final analysis, regulates the economy, determines what is produced and how it is produced (and therefore also what can be consumed). The 'law of value' regulates the exchange between commodities, according to the quantities of socially necessary abstract labour they embody (the quantity of such labour spent in their production). Through regulating the exchange between commodities, the 'law of value' also regulates, after some interval, the distribution of society's labour potential and of society's non-living productive resources between different branches of production. Again, the analogy with Smith's 'invisible hand' is striking.

Marx's critique of the 'invisible hand' concept does not dwell essentially on the analysis of how a market economy actually operates. It would above all insist that this operation is not eternal, not immanent in 'human nature', but created by specific historical circumstances, a product of a special way of social organisation, and due to disappear at some stage of historical evolution as it appeared during a previous stage. And it would also stress that this 'invisible hand' leads neither to the maximum of economic growth nor to the optimum of human wellbeing for the greatest number of individuals, i.e. it would stress the heavy economic and social price humankind had to pay, and is still currently paying, for the undeniable progress the market economy produced at a given stage of historical evolution.

The formula 'quantities of abstract human labour' refers to labour seen strictly as a fraction of the total labour potential of a given society at a given time, say a labour potential of 2 billion hours a year (1 million potential producers, each supposedly capable of working 2000 hours a year). It therefore implies making an abstraction of the specific trade or occupation of a given male or female producer, the product of a day's work of a weaver not being worth less or more than that of a peasant, a miner, a house-builder, a milliner or a seamstress. At the basis of that concept of 'abstract human labour' lies a social condition, a specific set of social relations of production, in which small independent producers are essentially equal. Without that equality, social division of labour, and therefore satisfaction of basic consumers' needs, would be seriously endangered under that specific organisational set-up of the economy. Such an equality between small commodity owners and producers is later transformed into an equality between owners of capital under the capitalist mode of production.

But the concept of the homogeneity of productive human labour, underlying that of 'abstract human labour' as the essence of value, does not imply a negation of the difference between skilled and unskilled labour. Again: a negation of that difference would lead to the breakdown of the necessary division of labour, as would any basic heterogeneity of labour inputs in different branches of output. It would then not pay to acquire skills: most of them would disappear. So Marx's labour theory of value, in an internally coherent way, leads to the conclusion that one hour of skilled labour represents more value than one hour of unskilled labour, say represents the equivalent of 1.5 hours of unskilled labour. The difference would result from the imputation of the labour it costs to acquire the given skill, While an unskilled labourer would have a labour potential of 120,000 hours during his adult life, a skilled labourer would only have a labour potential of 80,000 hours, 40,000 being used for acquiring, maintaining and developing his skill. Only if one hour of skilled labour embodies the same value of 1.5 hours of unskilled labour, will the equality of all 'economic agents' be maintained under these circumstances, i.e. will it 'pay' economically to acquire a skill.

Marx himself never extensively dwelled on this solution of the so-called reduction problem. This remains indeed one of the most obscure parts of his general economic theory. It has led to some, generally rather mild, controversy. Much more heat has been generated by another facet of Marx's labour theory of value, the so-called transformation problem. Indeed, from Böhm-Bawerk writing a century ago till the recent contributions of Sraffa (1960) and Steedman (1977), the way Marx dealt with the transformation of values into 'prices of production' in Capital Vol. III has been considered by many of his critics as the main problem of his 'system', as well as being a reason to reject the labour theory of value out of hand.

The problem arises out of the obvious modification in the functioning of a market economy when capitalist commodity production substitutes Itself for simple commodity production. In simple commodity production, with generally stable technology and stable (or easily reproducible) tools, living labour is the only variable of the quantity and subdivision of social production. The mobility of labour is the only dynamic factor in the economy. As Engels pointed out in his Addendum to Capital Vol. III, in such an economy, commodities would be exchanged at prices which would be immediately proportional to values, to the labour inputs they embody.

But under the capitalist mode of production, this is no longer the case. Economic decision-taking is not in the hands of the direct producers. It is in the hands of the capitalist entrepreneurs in the wider sense of the word (bankers-distributors of credit-playing a key role in that decision-taking, besides entrepreneurs in the productive sector properly speaking). Investment decisions, i.e. decisions for creating, expanding, reducing or closing enterprises, determine economic life. It is the mobility of capital and not the mobility of labour which becomes the motive force of the economy. Mobility of labour becomes essentially an epiphenomenon of the mobility of capital.

Capitalist production is production for profit. Mobility of capital is determined by existing or expected profit differentials. Capital leaves branches (countries, regions) with lower profits (or profit expectations) and flows towards branches (countries, regions) with higher ones. These movements lead to an equalisation of the rate of profit between different branches of production. But approximately equal returns on all invested capital (at least under conditions of prevailing 'free competition') coexist with unequal proportions of inputs of labour in these different branches. So there is a disparity between the direct value of a commodity and its 'price of production', that 'price of production' being defined by Marx as the sum of production costs (costs of fixed capital and raw materials plus wages) and the average rate of profit multiplied with the capital spent in the given production.

The so-called 'transformation problem' relates to the question of whether a relation can nevertheless be established between value and these 'prices of production', what is the degree of coherence (or incoherence) of the relation with the 'law of value' (the labour theory of value in general), and what is the correct quantitative way to express that relation, if it exists.

We shall leave aside here the last aspect of the problem, to which extensive analysis has recently been devoted (Mandel and Freeman, 1984). From Marx's point of view, there is no incoherence between the formation of 'prices of production' and the labour theory of value. Nor is it true that he came upon that alleged difficulty when he started to prepare Capital Vol.III, i.e. to deal with capitalist competition, as several critics have argued.

The sum total of value produced in a given country during a given span of time (e.g. one year) is determined by the sum total of labour-inputs. Competition and movements of capital cannot change that quantity, The sum total of values equals the sum total of 'prices of production'. The only effect of capital competition and capital mobility is to redistribute that given sum-and this through a redistribution of surplus value-between different capitals, to the benefit of some and at the expense of others.

Now the redistribution does not occur in a haphazard or arbitrary way. Essentially value (surplus-value) is transferred from technically less advanced branches to technologically more advanced branches. And here the concept of 'quantities of socially necessary labour' comes into its own, under the conditions of constant revolutions of productive technology that characterise the capital mode of production. Branches with lower than average technology can be considered as wasting socially necessary labour. Part of the labour spent in production in their realm is therefore not compensated by society. Branches with higher than average technology (organic composition of capital) can be considered to be economising social labour; their labour inputs can therefore be considered as more intensive than average, embodying more value. In this way, the transfer of value (surplus-value) between different branches, far from being in contradiction with the law of value, is precisely the way it operates and should operate under conditions of 'capitalist equality', given the pressure of rapid technological change.

As to the logical inconsistency often supposedly to be found in Marx's method of solving the 'transformation problem'-first advanced by von Bortkiewicz (1907)-it is based upon a misunderstanding in our opinion. It is alleged that in his 'transformation schemas' (or tables) Marx calculates inputs in 'values' and outputs in 'prices of production', thereby omitting the feedback effect of the latter on the former. But that feedback eject is unrealistic and unnecessary, once one recognises that inputs are essentially data.

Movements of capital posterior to the purchase of machinery or raw materials, including the ups and dawns of prices of finished products produced with these raw materials, cannot lead to a change in prices and therefore of profits of the said machinery and raw materials, on sales which have already occurred. What critics present as an inconsistency between 'values' and 'prices of production' is simply a recognition of two different time-frameworks (cycles) in which the equalisation of the rate of profit has been achieved, a first one for inputs, and a second, later one for outputs.

THEORY OF VALUE, KARL MARX

In analysing the value-determining forces at work in the capitalist economy, Marx distinguishes clearly between two kinds of value: "use value" and "exchange value." The former means the usefulness a thing has to its possessor, its utility, or the pleasure or satisfaction derived by its possessor from its utilization. Use value is a purely subjective thing, an abstraction that can exist quantitatively only in the mind of the user or prospective user of the thing, and then only as a plus or minus quantity relative to the similarly realized use value of some other thing. By exchange value Marx means the power of a thing to command all other things in exchange for itself, or "the proportional quantities in which it exchanges with all other commodities." Since it is only exchange value that he seeks to analyze, he commonly drops that prefix and uses just value. By value Marx means precisely the same thing the orthodox economist of today means when he uses that term in economics textbooks.

Marx points out that use value and exchange value are obviously vitally related, since no exchange value can exist unless some use value is present. Only in very primitive forms of economy could a thing have use value without having exchange value. If little specialization prevailed and little exchange took place, most things would have use value and yet no exchange value. Since Marx is analysing the determinants of value in a capitalist economy characterized by specialization and intricate exchange processes, the masses of things commonly produced are destined to be exchanged by their producers for other things and therefore have not only use value but exchange value as well. Things having both of these values he terms commodities. It is the determination of the exchange value of commodities that he attempts to explain. Marx uses the term price, just as do modern orthodox economists, to mean the power of a commodity to command money in exchange for itself. As he puts it, price is the "money name" of the value of a commodity.

KARL MARX, NORMAL VALUE AND MARKET VALUE

Marx, like modern economists, points out that there are several kinds of exchange value (from this point on to be called merely "value"). He distinguishes between what he calls "natural" values (and the corresponding natural prices) on the one hand and "market" values (and the corresponding market prices) on the other. By the former, which Marx also calls "real" value, he means the "normal" value in modern economic terms. This is the normal long-run level of the value of a commodity, on the average, about which short-run values of the commodity oscillate. Deviations from normal value or real value, Marx held, were caused by supply and demand forces, while the normal value itself, which became the market value when supply and demand were in perfect equilibrium, was determined by another force to be described presently. He therefore makes numerous references to market value or prices being out of line with normal values or prices. Like modern economists, who devote their principal efforts to explaining the determinants of normal value, Marx was primarily interested in this. "The question is what determines the amount which becomes the amount at which supply and demand are in equilibrium."

Marx phrased this distinction between normal or real value and market value in several clear paragraphs in his Value, Price and Profit: You will find that the fluctuations of market prices, their deviations from values, their ups and downs, paralyse and compensate each other; so that apart from the effect of monopolies and some other modifications I must now pass by, all descriptions of commodities are, on the average, sold at their respective values or natural prices.

At the moment when supply and demand equilibrate each other, and therefore cease to act, the market price of a commodity coincides with its real value, with the standard price round which its market prices oscillate. In inquiring into the nature of that value, we have therefore nothing at all to do with the temporary effects on market prices of supply and demand. It is interesting to note how closely this distinction follows the words of Adam Smith, whom Marx quotes in Value, Price and Profit as follows: The deviations of market prices from values are continual, but, as Adam Smith says: "The natural price is the central price to which the prices of commodities are continually gravitating.

Different accidents may sometimes keep them suspended a good deal above it, and sometimes forces them down even somewhat below it. But whatever may be the obstacles which hinder them from settling in this centre of repose and continuance they are constantly tending toward it."

Labour as the Value-Determining Element Common to All Commodities

A basic tenet of Marx and other economists of the "labour-cost" school of that time was that whatever the value-determining force was, it had to be something common to all commodities. This meant that an adequate explanation of value necessitated the discovery of something objective (therefore use value would not be suitable) and common to all commodities, and an analysis of the metamorphosis whereby that common element as it existed in all commodities became value. Marx accepted labour, or muscular and mental human effort, as the one element common to all commodities. In question-answer form, Marx puts it thus: "What is the common social substance of all commodities? It is labour. To produce a commodity a certain amount of labour must be bestowed upon it, or worked up in it." If labour is the one element common to all commodities and therefore the clue to values, what common element can be found in all labour? Clearly no qualitative characteristic, for labour obviously varies much from one specialized occupation to another. The common element must be quantitative, and the only element in this category found in all labour is time. Thus, labour time becomes the value-creating and value-determining element in all commodities. Marx follows this line of reasoning in a concise summary in Capital:

A use value, or useful article, therefore has value only because human labour in the abstract has been embodied or materialized in it. How, then, is the magnitude of this value to be measured? Plainly, by the quantity of the value-creating substance, the labour, contained in the article. The quantity of labour, however, is measured by its duration, and labour time in its turn finds its standard in weeks, days, and hours.

Marxian Theory of Value

Before we take up certain separate portions of this theory of value for further study, it will be helpful to note several of the most concise of its numerous summaries: But what is the value of a commodity? The objective form of the social labour expended in its production. And how do we measure the quantity of this value? By the quantity of the labour contained in it.

A commodity has a value because it is a crystallization of social labour. The greatness of its value, or its relative value, depends upon the greater or less amount of that social substance contained in it; that is to say, on the relative mass of labour necessary for its production. The relative values of commodities are, therefore, determined by the respective quantities or amounts of labour, worked up, realized, fixed in them. In this sense every commodity is a symbol, since, in so far as it is value, it is only the material envelope of the human labour spent upon it.

Theory of Value Includes Past and Current Labour

A complete understanding of this theory of value requires that several points be noted with particular care. Marx makes it clear that by the amount of labour embodied in a commodity he means not only the labour at the final stage of the process, or at that point where the commodity takes on the final characteristics essential to its exchangeability. He emphasizes that the value-determining labour content of a commodity includes all the labour at all stages in its production back through the production of the necessary raw materials, power, and machinery. The labour required to restore whatever portions of the machinery are worn away in the production of a commodity is part of the labour content of that commodity. Similarly, if the raw materials entering a commodity are machine-made, the labour necessary to restore any part of that machinery worn out in producing the materials for that commodity is part of the labour content of that commodity. Thus each commodity becomes the "material envelope" of the human labour that went into it, despite the fact that the component parts of this labour are scattered over many separate uses, producing units, and periods of time. Marx summaries this portion of his theory of value and illustrates it as follows:

In calculating the exchangeable value of a commodity we must add to the quantity of labour last employed the quantity of labour previously worked up in the raw material of the commodity, and the labour bestowed on the implements, tools, machinery, and buildings, with which such labour is assisted. The labour required for the production of the cotton, the raw material of the yarn, is part of the labour necessary to produce the yarn, and is therefore contained in the yarn. The same applies to the labour embodied in the spindle, without whose wear and tear the cotton could not be spun.

Hence, in determining the value of the yarn, or the labour time required for its production, all the especial processes carried on at various times and in different places, which were necessary, first to produce the cotton and the wasted portion of the spindle, and then with the cotton and spindle to spin the yarn, may together be looked on as different and successive phases of one and the same process. The whole of the labour in the yarn is past labour; and it is a matter of no importance that the operations necessary for the production of its constituent elements were carried on at times which, referred to the present, are more remote than the final operation of spinning. If a definite quantity of labour, say thirty days, is requisite to build a house, the total amount of labour incorporated in it is not altered by the fact that the work of the last day is done twenty-nine days later than that of the first. Therefore, the labour contained in the raw material and the instruments of labour can be treated just as if it were labour expended in an earlier stage of the spinning process, before the labour of actual spinning commenced.

Only Socially Necessary Labour Is Value Determining

This theory of values does not imply that labour in itself creates value, no matter what the end product of that labour may be and no matter how inefficient it may be. Marx never argued that the more labour is embodied in a product the more value that product possesses. It is only "socially necessary" labour that is value determining. "In saying that the value of a commodity is determined by the quantity of labour worked up or crystallized in it, we mean the quantity of labour necessary for its production in a given state of society, under certain social average conditions of production, with a given social average intensity, and average skill of the labour employed." Thus if one firm were to turn out a product with greater or lesser efficiency, in terms of labour time embodied in it, than characterized the preponderant run of the firms producing that product, the normal value of that firm's product would be determined not by its labour time but by that of the bulk of the producers. Any unusual conditions experienced by one producer, affecting the labour time embodied in his product but not "socially necessary" to the production of that product, are not value determining. Marx illustrates this point as follows: "Though the capitalist have a hobby, and use a gold instead of a steel spindle, yet the only labour that counts for anything in the value of the yarn is that which would be required to produce a steel spindle, because no more is necessary under the given social conditions." It thus follows that the normal value of an existing stock of durable commodities changes in accordance with changes in the socially necessary labour time required to produce identical commodities. Marx logically holds that the quantities of past labour embodied in existing commodities of a certain kind no longer determine the normal values of those commodities if the socially necessary labour required to reproduce them has changed. In illustrating the determination of the normal value of cotton, he contends that

> if the time socially necessary for the production of any commodity alters—and a given weight of cotton represents, after a bad harvest, more labour than after a good one—all previously existing commodities of the same class are affected, because they are, as it were, only individuals of the species, and their value at any given time is measured by the labour socially necessary, i.e., by the labour necessary for their production under the then existing social conditions.

In Marx's theory there are no limits to what may cause a change in the amount of labour socially necessary to produce a given commodity. He makes it a function of the entire environment within which production takes place; consequently, a change in any element in that environment may be the cause of an increase or decrease in the labour time necessary to produce that commodity.

Time Lags in Value Changes

Marx pictures the forces that change the socially necessary labour time to produce any given commodity as working imperfectly and with time lags. Thus if only one firm were to acquire a machine that would shorten the total labour time required in its plant to produce a certain product, that firm for the time being would derive a benefit from the fact that the value of its commodity on the open market (determined by the socially necessary labour time generally required to produce it) has not changed, while its individual value in this limited sphere (determined by the labour time necessary to produce it in this particular plant) has declined. However, Marx further points out that in such a case there would be a downward pull on the commodity's normal value and that the rapidity of its fall would be determined by the degree of competition prevailing among the firms producing this product, while this in turn might be substantially affected by the ability of the originating firm to keep its invention a secret.

Exchange Proves the Presence of Use Value

The injection of the "socially necessary" element into the theory that labour time determines value serves to show that unless a thing has use value, labour spent on it cannot create exchange value. The determination of whether a given quantity of labour time has or has not created use value occurs within the exchange process. Marx holds that "whether that labour is useful for others and its product consequently capable of satisfying the wants of others, can be proved only by the act of exchange. Thus the final determination of whether labour is socially useful or not is made by the buyers of the articles in which labour is embodied as they encounter them and react to them in their exchange activities. There is still another ramification of the "socially useful" idea. According to Marx, it is possible for the social usefulness of a given quantity of labour to be diminished by applying it to some line of production when buyers of commodities would rather have it devoted to some other line of production. This, of course, is merely different in degree from the possibility just cited, in which it is conceivable that labour may be put into the formation of things that have no use value—the labour thus used becoming socially unnecessary and therefore not value creating. This subtle meaning of the term socially necessary is brought out by Marx in the following illustration:

Lastly, suppose that every piece of linen in the market contains no more labour time than is socially necessary. In spite of this, all these pieces taken as a whole, may have had superfluous labour time spent upon them. If the market cannot stomach the whole quantity at the normal price [that is, at the value corresponding to the amount of labour socially necessary to produce the physical linen],... this proves that too great a portion of the total labour of the community has been expended in the form of weaving. The effect is the same as if each individual weaver had expended more labour time upon his particular product than is socially necessary.

The fact that society was demanding another allocation of its total labour time to the various channels of production thus would become evident through market value or price at a particular time being higher or lower than normal or "natural" value or price. In Marxian theory extra surpluses or losses resulting from these discrepancies would stimulate reallotment of labour time to its respective uses, thus reestablishing the dominance of normal value as determined by the content of socially necessary labour time.

Labour Content in Time Units Determines Value

In relation to value determination, qualities of labour have no significance— only quantities measured in time units are effective value determinants. It is the quantity of labour required for its production, not the realized form of that labour, by which the amount of the value of a commodity is determined. While, therefore, with reference to use value, the labour contained in a commodity counts only qualitatively, with reference to value it counts only quantitatively, and must first be reduced to human labour pure and simple.

Skilled labour counts only as simple labour intensified or, rather, as multiplied simple labour, a given quantity of skilled being considered equal to a greater quantity of simple labour. Marx was vague as to just what "human labour pure and simple" meant. Professor Bober concludes that he meant "homogeneous, abstract, unskilled labour."

Marx conceived of all kinds and degrees of occupational skill as being reducible to standard time units of unskilled labour. Thus, to illustrate, a skilled machinist in one clock hour might contribute to production four of these standard time units of unskilled labour. If an average unskilled-labour hour were the standard unit, the skilled machinist would then embody in the commodity on which he was working four hours of socially necessary (assuming standard efficiency of equipment, etc.) labour time per clock hour worked, while the unskilled laborer would embody in the commodity only one hour of socially necessary labour time per clock hour worked. Since hours of socially necessary labour time, rather than clock hours, are held to be the determinants of value, a commodity produced by the skilled machinist (assuming, to make the case simple, that he was unassisted by other workers or machinery or materials) in one clock hour would have a normal value equal to that of the product produced by the unskilled laborer (assuming he also was unassisted) in four clock hours. In other words, the normal values of commodities bear to each other exchange ratios difectly proportional to the number of socially necessary standard time units of unskilled labour used up in the production of each.

Marx was extremely vague in explaining what determines the number of units of unskilled labour time to which a certain clock time spent by a skilled laborer will be equivalent. It is obvious that the number of ratios necessary to convert all the socially necessary labour in a commodity into a quantity of these hours of unskilled labour time would be not only exceedingly numerous but very complicated in a system characterized by much specialization and multitudinous categories of skill. The conversion of skilled into unskilled units of labour therefore cannot be done by one who might wish to study the production of a given product and make such a calculation. According to Marx, "the different proportions in which different sorts of labour are reduced to unskilled labour as their standard, are established by a social process that goes on behind the backs of the producers, and, consequently, appear to be fixed by custom." In a later reference to the problem of converting units of skilled into unskilled labour, he contends that "whenever, by an exchange, we equate as values our different products, by that very act, we also equate, as human labour, the different kinds of labour expended upon them." Marx apparently felt that the impossibility of objectively calculating these relationships or segregating the forces that act in the markets to determine them does not diminish the reality of their independent existence.

Value Is Inherent in the Commodity

Despite certain limitations already noted, Marx finds it possible to contend that value thus becomes something inherent in the commodity. "It becomes plain, that it is not the exchange value of commodities which regulates the magnitude of their value; but, on the contrary, that it is the magnitude of their value which controls their exchange proportions." As Professor Bober points out, it was in this regard that Marx departed from Ricardo's labour theory of value. "Ricardo had constantly in mind exchange value, relative value. To him, value is the power of one product to command others in exchange. To Marx value is exchange value; but it is also an intrinsic entity incarnated in a commodity, and the substance of this entity is congealed labour." It is in this regard that Marx may have involved his theory of value in some internal inconsistencies (to be discussed later) and come nearest to making his theory of value merely a part of his philosophy rather than an objective explanation of what happens in the exchange processes of a capitalist economy.

Made Instruments to Value Determination

Of course, if value is always merely "congealed" socially necessary labour, neither the man-made nor the nature-made instruments used in production can play any direct part in value determination. As previously noted, Marx considered man-made tools and machinery merely the products of labour, so they became indirectly value determining, in that whatever socially necessary labour had gone into tools and machinery actually used up in the production of a commodity were considered part of the socially necessary labour embodied in that commodity. As far as nature or nature-made instruments are concerned, Marx flatly denies (although there are some minor contradictory statements) that the part they may play in production enters in any way into the value determination of the commodities produced: "Since exchange value is a definite social manner of expressing the amount of labour bestowed upon an object, Nature has no more to do with it, than it has in fixing the course of exchange." "So far no chemist has ever discovered exchange value either in a pearl or a diamond." That is, in the purely natural state they are not commodities, because they have no exchange value. Whatever exchange value they may acquire comes only after the application of labour to the natural materials or in anticipation of the possibility of adding human labour to the natural materials. If labour could not be applied, any such exchange value' would immediately vanish. Nature merely furnishes the environment. Exchange values are in no sense a function of the environment. They exist only when labour time has joined itself with nature, and consequently they are the exclusive product of labour time. So runs the Marxian theory.

Labour Content Determines Value of Money

Marx considered price to be merely the "money name" of value. Whatever the chosen money metal might be, its value was determined by exactly the same forces that determined the values of other commodities— the socially necessary labour time embodied in it. "The value of gold or silver, like that of all other commodities, is regulated by the quantity of labour necessary for getting them." Thus each commodity tended to exchange for the number of dollars or pounds containing the amount of gold or silver that embodied an amount of socially necessary labour equal to that embodied in the commodity. "The value, or in other words the quantity of human labour contained in a ton of iron, is expressed in imagination by such a quantity of the money commodity as contains the same amount of labour as the iron." Money thus becomes a common measure of values, whereas money prices merely express relationships between values—that is, between the respective labour contents of commodities on the one hand and of quantities of the monetary metal on the other.

Significance of Monetary Expression of Value

Although Marx held that money prices were mere reflections of values, he attached much significance to the fact that values were so expressed. The real stuff of which values are composed—that is, labour—thus loses its human aspects and is converted into a sort of inanimate abstraction. "When they assume this money shape, commodities strip off every trace of their natural use value, and of the particular kind of labour to which they owe their creation, in order to transform themselves into the uniform, socially recognized incarnation of homogeneous human labour." In discussing this point Lenin held that "money masks the social character of individual labour, and hides the social tie between the various producers who come together in the market."

Modifications of Theory of Value by Marx

Thus far the Marxian theory of value appears to be clear and simple. But from this point on, abstruseness and apparent contradictions feature the theory or theories of value propounded in Volume III of Capital. In pursuing his thought, Marx apparently became involved in certain difficulties arising out of his "socially necessary labour" theory of value. This theory appeared to him to fall somewhat short of explaining actual price phenomena as they prevailed in markets. A modified theory of value appears in his later writings. Students have disagreed heartily over whether this modified theory is or is not consistent with the original value theory expounded earlier.

For the purposes of this discussion and for an understanding of the basic features of Marxian thought, it is not necessary to trace these modifications and their ramifications in detail. The earlier value theory, which has been outlined, holds that each commodity tends to sell for a value or price determined by its content of socially necessary labour. In his later work Marx injected a concept of averages into this theory. Lenin has interpreted Marx on this point as follows: "Naturally, therefore in a society made up of separate producers of commodities, linked solely through the market, conformity to law can only be an average, a general manifestation, as mass phenomenon, with individual and mutually compensating deviations to one side and the other."

Thus, the socially necessary total labour going to produce all commodities determines their total values in terms of each other, or the average socially necessary labour content determines the average value. Professor Bober interprets Marx as holding that "only the total volume of commodities produced in all industries can be said to sell according to the mass of socially necessary labour incorporated in it. In individual cases, commodities in one branch of production will sell at less, and in another at more, than the value according to the labour theory. But these deviations compensate each other, as we should expect, since the deviations of the items from their average will always cancel out...."

As will appear later, in the discussion of "surplus value," Marx was interested primarily in mass or aggregate phenomena. His whole system deals with the sweep of evolutionary change in social phenomena. It is evident that he considered value theory more pertinent and meaningful when stated in terms of averages or masses than when expressed in terms of individual commodities. "He does not claim that the two theories are identical, but he urges that the first is still the heart and soul of the second, and that therefore the labour theory enunciated in the first volume is not abandoned in the third."

MARX'S THEORY OF RENT

The labour theory of value defines value as the socially necessary quantity of labour determined by the average productivity of labour of each given sector of production. But these values are not mathematically fixed data. They are simply the expression of a process going on in real life, under capitalist commodity production. So this average is only ascertained in the course of a certain time-span. There is a lot of logical argument and empirical evidence to advance the hypothesis that the normal time-span for essentially modifying the value of commodities is the business cycle, from one crises of over-production (recession) to the next one.

Before technological progress and (or) better (more 'rational') labour organisation etc. determines a more than marginal change (in general: decline) in the value of a commodity, and the crisis eliminates less efficient firms, there will be a coexistence of firms with various 'individual values' of a given commodity in a given branch of output, even assuming a single market price. So, in his step-for-step approach towards explaining the immediate phenomena (facts of economic life) like prices and profits, by their essence, Marx introduces at this point of his analysis a new mediating concept, that of market value. The market value of a commodity is the 'individual value' of the firm, or a group of firms, in a given branch of production, around which the market price will fluctuate. That 'market value' is not necessarily the mathematical (weighted) average of labour expenditure of all firms of that branch. It can be below, equal or above that average, for a certain period (generally less than the duration of the business cycle, at least under 'free competition'), according to whether social demand is saturated, just covered or to an important extent not covered by current output plus existing stocks. In these three cases respectively, the more (most) efficient firms, the firms of average efficiency, or even firms with labour productivity below average, will determine the market value of that given commodity.

This implies that the more efficient firms enjoy surplus profits (profits over and above the average profit) in case 2 and 3 and that a certain number of firms work at less than average profit in all three cases, but especially in case 1.

The mobility of capital, i.e. normal capitalist competition, generally eliminates such situations after a certain lapse of time. But when that mobility of capital is impeded for long periods by either unavoidable scarcity (natural conditions that are not renewable or non-substitutable, like land and mineral deposits) or through the operation of institutional obstacles (private property of land and mineral resources forbidding access to available capital, except in exchange for payments over and above average profit), these surplus profits can be frozen and maintained for decades. They thus become rents, of which ground rent and mineral rent are the most obvious examples in Marx's time, extensively analysed in Capital Vol.III.

Marx's theory of rent is the most difficult part of his economic theory, the one which has witnessed fewer comments and developments, by followers and critics alike, than other major parts of his 'system'. But it is not obscure. And in contrast to Ricardo's or Rodbertus's theories of rent, it represents a straightforward application of the labour theory of value. It does not imply any emergence of 'supplementary' value (surplus value, profits) in the market, in the process of circulation of commodities, which is anathema to Marx and to all consistent upholders of the labour theory of value. Nor does it in any way suggest that land or mineral deposits 'create' value. It simply means that in agriculture and mining less productive labour (as in the general case analysed above) determines the market value of food or minerals, and that therefore more efficient farms and mines enjoy surplus profits which Marx calls differential (land and mining) rent. It also means that as long as productivity of labour in agriculture is generally below the average of the economy as a whole (or more correctly: that the organic composition of capital, the expenditure in machinery and raw materials as against wages, is inferior in agriculture to that in industry and transportation), the sum total of surplus-value produced in agriculture will accrue to landowners + capitalist farmers taken together, and will not enter the general process of (re)distribution of profit throughout the economy as a whole.

This creates the basis for a supplementary form of rent, over and above differential rent, rent which Marx calls absolute land rent. This is, incidentally, the basis for a long-term separation of capitalist landowners from entrepreneurs in farming or animal husbandry, distinct from feudal or semi-feudal landowners or great landowners under conditions of predominantly petty commodity production, or in the Asiatic mode of production, with free peasants.

The validity of Marx's theory of land and mining rents has been confirmed by historical evidence, especially in the 20th century. Not only has history substantiated Marx's prediction that, in spite of the obstacle of land and mining rent, mechanisation would end up by penetrating food and raw materials production too, as it has for a long time dominated industry and transportation, thereby causing a growing decline of differential rent (this has occurred increasingly in agriculture in the last 25-50 years, first in North America, and then in Western Europe and even elsewhere). It has also demonstrated that once the structural scarcity of food disappears, the institutional obstacle (private property) loses most of its efficiency as a brake upon the mobility of capital. Therefore the participation of surplus-value produced in agriculture in the general process of profit equalisation throughout the economy cannot be prevented any more. Thereby absolute rent tends to wither away and, with it, the separation of land ownership from entrepreneurial farming and animal husbandry. It is true that farmers can then fall under the sway of the banks, but they do so as private owners of their land which becomes mortgaged, not as share-croppers or entrepreneurs renting land from separate owners.

On the other hand, the reappearance of structural scarcity in the realm of energy enabled the OPEC countries to multiply the price of oil by ten in the 1970s, i.e. to have it determined by the oilfields where production costs are the highest, thereby assuring the owners of the cheapest oil wells in Arabia, Iran, Libya, etc. huge differential minerals rents.

Marx's theory of land and mineral rent can be easily extended into a general theory of rent, applicable to all fields of production where formidable difficulties of entry limit mobility of capital for extended periods of time. It thereby becomes the basis of a marxist theory of monopoly and monopoly surplus profits, i.e. in the form of cartel rents (Hilferding, 1910) or of technological rent (Mandel, 1972). Lenin's and Bukharin's theories of surplus profit are based upon analogous but not identical reasoning (Bukharin, 1914, 1926; Lenin, 1917).

But in all these cases of general application of the marxist theory of rent, the same caution should apply as Marx applied to his theory of land rent. By its very nature, capitalism, based upon private property, i.e. 'many capitals'-that is competition-cannot tolerate any 'eternal' monopoly, a 'permanent' surplus profit deducted from the sum total of profits which is divided among the capitalist class as a whole. Technological innovations, substitution of new products for old ones including the fields of raw materials and of food, will in the long run reduce or eliminate all monopoly situations, especially if the profit differential is large enough to justify huge research and investment outlays.

MARX'S THEORY OF MONEY

In the same way as his theory of rent, Marx's theory of money is a straightforward application of the labour theory of value. As value is but the embodiment of socially necessary labour, commodities exchange with each other in proportion to the labour quanta they contain. This is true for the exchange of iron against wheat, as it is true for the exchange of iron against gold or silver. Marx's theory of money is therefore in the first place a commodity theory of money. A given commodity can play the role of universal medium of exchange, as well as fulfil all the other functions of money, precisely because it is a commodity, i.e. because it is itself the product of socially necessary labour. This applies to the precious metals in the same way it applies to all the various commodities which, throughout history, have played the role of money.

It follows that strong upheavals in the 'intrinsic' value of the money-commodity will cause strong upheavals in the general price level. In Marx's theory of money, (market) prices are nothing but the expression of the value of commodities in the value of the money commodity chosen as a monetary standard. If £1 sterling = 1/10 ounce of gold, the formula 'the price of 10 quarters of wheat is 1 means that 10 quarters of wheat have been produced in the same socially necessary labour times as 1/10 ounce of gold. A strong decrease in the average productivity of labour in gold mining (as a result for example of a depletion of the richer gold veins) will lead to a general depression of the average price level, all other things remaining equal. Likewise, a sudden and radical increase in the average productivity of labour in gold mining, through the discovery of new rich gold fields or through the application of new revolutionary technology, will lead to a general increase in the price level of all other commodities.

Leaving aside short-term oscillations, the general price level will move in medium and long-term periods according to the relation between the fluctuations of the productivity of labour in agriculture and industry on the one hand, and the fluctuations of the productivity of labour in gold mining (if gold is the money-commodity), on the other. Basing himself on that commodity theory of money, Marx therefore criticized as inconsistent Ricardo's quantity theory. But for exactly the same reason of a consistent application of the labour theory of value, the quantity of money in circulation enters Marx's economic analysis when he deals with the phenomenon of paper money.

As gold has an intrinsic value, like all other commodities, there can be no 'gold inflation ', as little as there can be a 'steel inflation'. An abstraction made of short-term price fluctuations caused by fluctuations between supply and demand, a persistent decline of the value of gold (exactly as for all other commodities) can only be the result of a persistent increase in the average productivity of labour in gold mining and not of an 'excess' of circulation in gold. If the demand for gold falls consistently, this can only indirectly trigger a decline in the value of gold through causing the closure of the least productive old mines. But in the case of the money-commodity, such overproduction can hardly occur, given the special function of gold of serving as a universal reserve fund, nationally and internationally. It will always therefore find a buyer, be it not, of course, always at the same 'prices' (in Marx's economic theory, the concept of the 'price of gold' is meaningless. As the price of a commodity is precisely its expression in the value of gold, the 'price of gold' would be the expression of the value of gold in the value of gold).

Paper money, banks notes, are a money sign representing a given quantity of the money-commodity. Starting from the above-mentioned example, a banknote of £1 represents 1/10 ounce of gold. This is an objective 'fact of life', which no government or monetary authority can arbitrarily alter. It follows that any emission of paper money in excess of that given proportion will automatically lead to an increase in the general price level, always other things remaining equal. If £1 suddenly represents only 1/20 ounce of gold, because paper money circulation has doubled without a significant increase in the total labour time spent in the economy, then the price level will tend to double too. The value of 1/10 ounce of gold remains equal to the value of 10 quarters of wheat. But as 1/ 10 ounce of gold is now represented by £2 in paper banknotes instead of being represented by £1, the price of wheat will move from £1 to £2 for 10 quarters (from two shillings to four shillings a quarter before the introduction of the decimal system).

This does not mean that in the case of paper money, Marx himself has become an advocate of a quantity theory of money. While there are obvious analogies between his theory of paper money and the quantity theory, the main difference is the rejection by Marx of any mechanical automatism between the quantity of paper money emitted on the one hand, and the general dynamic of the economy (including on the price level) on the other.

In Marx's explanation of the movement of the capitalist economy in its totality, the formula ceteris paribus is meaningless. Excessive (or insufficient) emission of paper money never occurs in a vacuum. It always occurs at a given stage of the business cycle, and in a given phase of the longer-term historical evolution of capitalism. It is thereby always combined with given ups and downs of the rate of profit, of productivity of labour, of output, of market conditions (overproduction or insufficient production). Only in connection with these other fluctuations can the effect of paper money 'inflation' or 'deflation' be judged, including the effect on the general price level. The key variables are in the field of production. The key synthetic resultant is in the field of profit. Price moments are generally epiphenomena as much as they are signals. To untwine the tangle, more is necessary than a simple analysis of the fluctuations of the quantity of money.

Only in the case of extreme runaway inflation of paper money would this be otherwise; and even in that border case, relative price movements (different degrees of price increases for different commodities) would still confirm that, in the last analysis, the law of values rules, and not the arbitrary decision of the Central Banks or any other authority controlling or emitting paper money.

MARX'S THEORY OF SURPLUS VALUE

Marx himself considered his theory of surplus-value his most important contribution to the progress of economic analysis (Marx, letter to Engels of 24 August 1867). It is through this theory that the wide scope of his sociological and historical thought enables him simultaneously to place the capitalist mode of production in his historical context, and to find the root of its inner economic contradictions and its laws of motion in the specific relations of production on which it is based.

As said before, Marx's theory of classes is based on the recognition that in each class society, part of society (the ruling class) appropriates the social surplus product. But that surplus product can take three essentially different forms (or a combination of them). It can take the form of straightforward unpaid surplus labour, as in the slave mode of production, early feudalism or some sectors of the Asiatic mode of production (unpaid corvée labour for the Empire). It can take the form of goods appropriated by the ruling class in the form of use-values pure and simple (the products of surplus labour), as under feudalism when feudal rent is paid in a certain amount of produce (produce rent) or in its more modern remnants, such as sharecropping. And it can take a money form, like money-rent in the final phases of feudalism, and capitalist profits. Surplus-value is essentially just that: the money form of the social surplus product or, what amounts to the same, the money product of surplus labour. It has therefore a common root with all other forms of surplus product: unpaid labour.

This means that Marx's theory of surplus-value is basically a deduction (or residual) theory of the ruling classes' income. The whole social product (the net national income) is produced in the course of the process of production, exactly as the whole crop is harvested by the peasants. What happens on the market (or through appropriation of the produce) is a distribution (or redistribution) of what already has been created. The surplus product, and therefore also its money form, surplus-value, is the residual of that new (net) social product (income) which remains after the producing classes have received their compensation (under capitalism: their wages). This 'deduction' theory of the ruling classes' income is thus ipso factor an exploitation theory. Not in the ethical sense of the word-although Marx and Engels obviously manifested a lot of understandable moral indignation at the fate of all the exploited throughout history, and especially at the fate of the modern proletariat-but in the economic one. The income of the ruling classes can always be reduced in the final analysis to the product of unpaid labour: that is the heart of Marx's theory of exploitation.

That is also the reason why Marx attached so much importance to treating surplus-value as a general category, over and above profits (themselves subdivided into industrial profits, bank profits, commercial profits etc.), interest and rent, which are all part of the total surplus product produced by wage labour. It is this general category which explains both the existence (the common interest) of the ruling class (all those who live off surplus value), and the origins of the class struggle under capitalism.

Marx likewise laid bare the economic mechanism through which surplus-value originates. At the basis of that economic mechanism is a huge social upheaval which started in Western Europe in the 15th century and slowly spread over the rest of the continent and all other continents (in many so-called underdeveloped countries, it is still going on to this day).

Through many concomitant economic (including technical), social, political and cultural transformations, the mass of the direct producers, essentially peasants and handicraftsmen, are separated from their means of production and cut off from free access to the land. They are therefore unable to produce their livelihood on their own account. In order to keep themselves and their families alive, they have to hire out their arms, their muscles and their brains, to the owners of the means of production (including land). If and when these owners have enough money capital at their disposal to buy raw materials and pay wages, they can start to organise production on a capitalist basis, using wage labour to transform the raw materials which they buy, with the tools they own, into finished products which they then automatically own too.

The capitalist mode of production thus presupposes that the producers' labour power has become a commodity. Like all other commodities, the commodity labour power has an exchange value and a use value. The exchange value of labour power, like the exchange value of all other commodities, is the amount of socially necessary labour embodied in it, i.e. its reproduction costs. This means concretely the value of all the consumer goods and services necessary for a labourer to work day after day, week after week, month after month, at approximately the same level of intensity, and for the members of the labouring classes to remain approximately stable in number and skill (i.e. for a certain number of working-class children to be fed, kept and schooled, so as to replace their parents when they are unable to work any more, or die). But the use value of the commodity labour power is precisely its capacity to create new value, including its potential to create more value than its own reproduction costs. Surplus-value is but that difference between the total new value created by the commodity labour power, and its own value, its own reproduction costs. The whole marxian theory of surplus-value is therefore based upon that subtle distinction between 'labour power' and 'labour' (or value). But there is nothing 'metaphysical' about this distinction. It is simply an explanation (demystification) of a process which occurs daily in millions of cases.

The capitalist does not buy the worker's 'labour'. If he did that there would be obvious theft, for the worker's wage is obviously smaller than the total value he adds to that of the raw materials in the course of the process of production. No: the capitalist buys 'labour power', and often (not always of course) he buys it at its justum pretium, at its real value. So he feels unjustly accused when he is said to have caused a 'dishonest' operation. The worker is victim not of vulgar theft but of a social set-up which condemns him first to transform his productive capacity into a commodity, then to sell that labour power on a specific market (the labour market) characterised by institutional inequality, and finally to content himself with the market price he can get for that commodity, irrespective of whether the new value he creates during the process of production exceeds that market price (his wage) by a small amount, a large amount, or an enormous amount.

The labour power the capitalist has bought 'adds value' to that of the used-up raw materials and tools (machinery, buildings etc.). If, and until that point of time, this added value is inferior or equal to the workers' wages, surplus-value cannot originate. But in that case, the capitalist has obviously no interest in hiring wage labour. He only hires it because that wage labour has the quality (the use value) to add to the raw materials' value more than its own value (i.e. its own wages). This 'additional added value' (the difference between total 'value added' and wages) is precisely surplus-value. Its emergence from the process of production is the precondition for the capitalists' hiring workers, for the existence of the capitalist mode of production.

The institutional inequality existing on the labour market (masked for liberal economists, sociologists and moral philosophers alike by juridical equality) arises from the very fact that the capitalist mode of production is based upon generalised commodity production, generalised market economy. This implies that a propertyless labourer, who owns no capital, who has no reserves of larger sums of money but who has to buy his food and clothes, pay his rent and even elementary public transportation for journeying between home and workplace, in a continuous way in exchange of money, is under the economic compulsion to sell the only commodity he possesses, to wit his labour power, also on a continuous basis. He cannot withdraw from the labour market until the wages go up. He cannot wait.

But the capitalist, who has money reserves, can temporarily withdraw from the labour market. He can lay his workers off, can even close or sell his enterprise and wait a couple of years before starting again in business. The institutional differences makes price determination of the labour market a game with loaded dice, heavily biased against the working class. One just has to imagine a social set-up in which each citizen would be guaranteed an annual minimum income by the community, irrespective of whether he is employed or not, to understand that 'wage determination' under these circumstances would be quite different from what it is under capitalism. In such a set-up the individual would really have the economic choice whether to sell his labour power to another person (or a firm) or not. Under capitalism, he has no choice. His is forced by economic compulsion to go through that sale, practically at any price.

The economic function and importance of trade unions for the wage-earners also clearly arises from that elementary analysis. For it is precisely the workers' 'combination' and their assembling a collective resistance fund (what was called by the first French unions caisses de résistance, 'reserve deposits') which enables them, for example through a strike, to withdraw the supply of labour power temporarily from the market so as to stop a downward trend of wages or induce a wage increase. There is nothing 'unjust' in such a temporary withdrawal of the supply of labour power, as there are constant withdrawals of demand for labour power by the capitalists, sometimes on a huge scale never equalled by strikes. Through the functioning of strong labour unions, the working class tries to correct, albeit partially and modestly, the institutional inequality on the labour market of which it is a victim, without ever being able to neutralise it durably or completely.

It cannot neutralise it durably because in the very way in which capitalism functions there is a powerful built-in corrective in favour of capital: the inevitable emergence of an industrial reserve army of labour. There are three key sources for that reserve army: the mass of precapitalist producers and self-employed (independent peasants, handicraftsmen, trades-people, professional people, small and medium-sized capitalists); the mass of housewives (and to a lesser extent, children); the mass of the wage-earners themselves, who potentially can be thrown out of employment.

The first two sources have to be visualised not only in each capitalist country seen separately but on a world scale, through the operations of international migration. They are still unlimited to a great extent, although the number of wage-earners the world over (including agricultural wage labourers) has already passed the one billion mark. As the third source, while it is obviously not unlimited (if wage labour would disappear altogether, if all wage labourers would be fired, surplus-value production would disappear too; that is why 'total robotism' is impossible under capitalism), its reserves are enormous, precisely in tandem with the enormous growth of the absolute number of wage earners.

The fluctuations of the industrial reserve army are determined both by the business cycle and by long-term trends of capital accumulation. Rapidly increasing capital accumulation attracts wage labour on a massive scale, including through international migration. Likewise, deceleration, stagnation or even decline of capital accumulation inflates the reserve army of labour. There is thus an upper limit to wage increases, when profits (realised profits and expected profits) are 'excessively' reduced in the eyes of the capitalists, which triggers off such decelerated, stagnating or declining capital accumulation, thereby decreasing employment and wages, till a 'reasonable' level of profits is restored. This process does not correspond to any 'natural economic law' (or necessity), nor does it correspond to any 'immanent justice'. It just expresses the inner logic of the capitalist mode of production, which is geared to profit. Other forms of economic organisation could function, have functioned and are functioning on the basis of other logics, which do not lead to periodic massive unemployment. On the contrary, a socialist would say-and Marx certainly thought so-that the capitalist system is an 'unjust', or better stated 'alienating', 'inhuman' social system, precisely because it cannot function without periodically reducing employment and the satisfaction of elementary needs for tens of millions of human beings.

Marx's theory of surplus-value is therefore closely intertwined with a theory of wages which is far away from Malthus's, Ricardo's or the early socialists' (like Ferdinand Lassalle's) 'iron law of wages', in which wages tend to fluctuate around the physiological minimum. That crude theory of 'absolute pauperisation' of the working class under capitalism, attributed to Marx by many authors (Popper, 1945, et a1.), is not Marx's at all, as many contemporary authors have convincingly demonstrated. Such an 'iron law of wages' is essentially a demographic one, in which birth rates and the frequency of marriages determine the fluctuation of employment and unemployment and thereby the level of wages.

The logical and empirical inconsistencies of such a theory are obvious. Let it be sufficient to point out that while fluctuations in the supply of wage-labourers are considered essential, fluctuations in the demand for labour power are left out of the analysis. It is certainly a paradox that the staunch opponent of capitalism, Karl Marx, pointed out as early as in the middle of the 19th century the potential for wage increases under capitalism, even though not unlimited in time and space. Marx also stressed the fact that for each capitalist, wage increases of other capitalists' workers are considered increases of potential purchasing power, not increases in costs.

Marx distinguishes two parts in the workers' wage, two elements of reproduction costs of the commodity labour power. One is purely physiological, and can be expressed in calories and energy quanta; this is the bottom below which the wage cannot fall without destroying slowly rapidly the workers' labour capacity. The second one is historical-moral, as Marx calls it, and consists of those additional goods and services which a shift in the class relationship of forces, such as a victorious class struggle, enables the working class to incorporate into the average wage, the socially necessary (recognised) reproduction costs of the commodity labour power (e.g. holidays after the French general strike of June 1936). This part of the wage is essentially flexible. It will differ from country to country, continent to continent and from epoch to epoch, according to many variables. But it has the upper limit indicated above: the ceiling from which profits threaten to disappear, or to become insufficient in the eyes of the capitalists, who then go on an 'investment strike'. So Marx's theory of wages is essentially an accumulation-of-capital theory of wages which sends us back to what Marx considered the first 'law of motion' of the capitalist mode of production: the compulsion for the capitalists to step up constantly the rate of capital accumulation.

THE LAWS OF MOTION OF THE CAPITALIST MODE OF PRODUCTION

If Marx's theory of surplus-value is his most revolutionary contribution to economic science, his discovery of the basic long-term 'laws of motion' (development trends) of the capitalist mode of production constitutes undoubtedly his most impressive scientific achievement. No other 19th-century author has been able to foresee in such a coherent way how capitalism would function, would develop and would transform the world, as did Karl Marx. Many of the most distinguished contemporary economists, starting with Wassily Leontief (1938), and Joseph Schumpeter (1942) have recognised this.

While some of these 'laws of motion' have obviously created much controversy, we shall nevertheless list them in logical orders rather than according to the degree of consensus they command.

The capitalist's compulsion to accumulate. Capital appears in the form of accumulated money, thrown into circulation in order to increase in value. No owner of money capital will engage in business in order to recuperate exactly the sum initially invested, and nothing more than that. By definition, the search for profit is at the basis of all economic operations by owners of capital.

Profit (surplus-value, accretion of value) can originate outside the sphere of production in a precapitalist society. It represents then essentially a transfer of value (so-called primitive accumulation of capital); but under the capitalist mode of production, in which capital has penetrated the sphere of production and dominates it, surplus-value is currently produced by wage labour. It represents a constant increase in value.

Capital can only appear in the form of many capitals, given its very historical-social origin in private property (appropriation) of the means of production. 'Many capitals' imply unavoidable competition. Competition in a capitalist mode of production is competition for selling commodities in an anonymous market. While surplus-value is produced in the process of production, it is realised in the process of circulation, i.e. through the sale of the commodities. The capitalist wants to sell at maximum profit. In practice, he will be satisfied if he gets the average profit, which is a percentage really existing in his consciousness (e.g. Mr Charles Wilson, the then head of the US automobile firm General Motors, stated before a Congressional enquiry: we used to fix the expected sales price of our cars by adding 15% to production costs). But he can never be sure of this. He cannot even be sure that all the commodities produced will and a buyer.

Given these uncertainties, he has to strive constantly to get the better of his competitors. This can only occur through operating with more capital. This means that at least part of the surplus-value produced will not be unproductively consumed by the capitalists and their hangers-on through luxury consumption, but will be accumulated, added to the previously existing capital.

The inner logic of capitalism is therefore not only to 'work for profit', but also to 'work for capital accumulation'. 'Accumulate, accumulate; that is Moses and the Prophets', states Marx in Capital, Vol. I. Capitalists are compelled to act in that way as a result of competition. It is competition which basically fuels this terrifying snowball logic: initial value of capital-> accretion of value (surplus-value)-> accretion of capital-> more accretion of surplus-value-> more accretion of capital etc. Without competition, the fire of growth would burn out.

The tendency towards constant technological revolutions. In the capitalist mode of production, accumulation of capital is in the first place accumulation of productive capital, or capital invested to produce more and more commodities. Competition is therefore above all competition between productive capitals, i.e. 'many capitals' engaged in mining, manufacturing, transportation, agriculture, telecommunications. The main weapon in competition between capitalist firms is cutting production costs. More advanced production techniques and more 'rational' labour organisation are the main means to achieve that purpose. The basic trend of capital accumulation in the capitalist mode of production is therefore a trend towards more and more sophisticated machinery. Capital growth takes the dual form of higher and higher value of capital and of constant revolutions in the techniques of production, of constant technological progress.

The capitalists' unquenchable thirst for surplus-value extraction. The compulsion for capital to grow, the irresistible urge for capital accumulation, realises itself above all through a constant drive for the increase of the production of surplus-value. Capital accumulation is nothing but surplus-value capitalisation, the transformation of part of the new surplus-value into additional capital. There is no other source of additional capital than additional surplus-value produced in the process of production.

Marx distinguishes two different forms of additional surplus-value production. Absolute surplus-value accretion occurs essentially through the extension of the work day. If the worker reproduces the equivalent of his wages in 4 hours a day, an extension of the work day from 10 to 12 hours will increase surplus-value from 6 to 8 hours. Relative surplus-value accretion occurs through an increase of the productivity of labour in the wage-goods sector of the economy. Such an increase in productivity implies that the equivalent of the value of an identical basket of goods and services consumed by the worker could be produced in 2 hours instead of 4 hours of labour. If the work day remains stable at 10 hours and real wages remain stable too, surplus-value will then increase from 6 to 8 hours.

While both processes occur throughout the history of the capitalist mode of production (viz. the contemporary pressure of employers in favour of overtime!), the first one was prevalent first, the second one became prevalent since the second half of the 19th century, first in Britain, France and Belgium, then in the USA and Germany, later in the other industrialized capitalist countries, and later still in the semi-industrialised ones. Marx calls this process the real subsumption (subordination) of labour under capital, for it represents not only an economic but also a physical subordination of the wage-earner under the machine. This physical subordination can only be realized through social control. The history of the capitalist mode of production is therefore also the history of successive forms of-tighter and tighter-control of capital over the workers inside the factories (Braverman, 1974); and of attempts at realising that tightening of control in society as a whole.

The increase in the production of relative surplus-value is the goal for which capitalism tends to periodically substitute machinery for labour, i.e. to expand the industrial reserve army of labour. Likewise, it is the main tool for maintaining a modicum of social equilibrium, for when productivity of labour strongly increases, above all in the wage-good producing sectors of the economy, real wages and profits (surplus-value) can both expand simultaneously. What were previously luxury goods can even become mass-produced wage-goods.

The tendency towards growing concentration and centralisation of capital. The growth of the value of capital means that each successful capitalist firm will be operating with more and more capital. Marx calls this the tendency towards growing concentration of capital. But in the competitive process, there are victors and vanquished. The victors grow. The vanquished go bankrupt or are absorbed by the victors. This process Marx calls the centralisation of capital. It results in a declining number of firms which survive in each of the key fields of production. Many small and medium-sized capitalists disappear as independent business men and women. They become in turn salary earners, employed by successful capitalism firms. Capitalism itself is the big 'expropriating' force, suppressing private property of the means of production for many, in favour of private property for few.

The tendency for the 'organic composition of capital' to increase. Productive capital has a double form. It appears in the form of constant capital: buildings, machinery, raw materials, energy, It appears in the form of variable capital: capital spent on wages of productive workers. Marx calls the part of capital used in buying labour power variable, because only that part produces additional value. In the process of production, the value of constant capital is simply maintained (transferred in toto or in part into the value of the finished product). Variable capital on the contrary is the unique source of 'added value'. Marx postulates that the basic historic trend of capital accumulation is to increase investment in constant capital at a quicker pace than investment in variable capital; the relation between the two he calls the 'organic composition of capital'. This is both a technical/physical relation (a given production technique implies the use of a given number of productive wage earners even if not in an absolutely mechanical way) and a value relation. The trend towards an increase in the 'organic composition of capital' is therefore a historical trend towards basically labour-saving technological progress.

This tendency has often been challenged by critics of Marx. Living in the age of semi-automation and 'robotism', it is hard to understand that challenge. The conceptual confusion on which this challenge is most based is an operation with the 'national wage bill', i.e. a confusion between wages in general and variable capital, which is only the wage bill of productive labour. A more correct index would be the part of the labour costs in total production costs in the manufacturing (and mining) sector. It is hard to deny that this proportion shows a downward secular trend.

The tendency of the rate of profit to decline. For the workers, the basic relation they are concerned with is the rate of surplus-value, i.e. the division of 'value added' between wages and surplus-value. When this goes up, their exploitation (the unpaid labour they produce) obviously goes up.

For the capitalists, however, this relationship is not meaningful. They are concerned with the relation between surplus-value and the totality of capital invested, never mind whether in the form of machinery and raw materials or in the form of wages. This relation is the rate of profit. It is a function of two variables, the organic composition of capital and the rate of surplus-value. If the value of constant capital is represented by c, the value of variable capital (wages of productive workers) by v and surplus-value by s, the rate of profit will be $s/(c + v)$. This can be rewritten as $[s/v]/[(c+v)/v]$ with the two variables emerging ($(c + v)/v$ obviously reflects c/v).

Marx postulates that the increase in the rate of surplus value has definite limits, while the increase in the organic composition of capital has practically none (automation, robotism). There will be a basic tendency for the rate of profit to decline. This is however absolutely true only on a very long-term, i.e. essentially 'secular', basis. In other time-frameworks, the rate of profit can fluctuate under the influence of countervailing forces. Constant capital can be devalorised, through 'capital saving' technical process, and through economic crises. The rate of surplus-value can be strongly increased in the short or medium terms although each strong increase makes a further increase more difficult; and capital can flow to countries (e.g. 'Third World' ones) or branches (e.g. service sectors) where the organic composition of capital is significantly lower than in the previously industrialised ones, thereby raising the average rate of profit.

Finally, the increase in the mass of surplus-value-especially through the extension of wage labour in general, i.e. the total number of workers-offsets to a large extent the depressing effects of moderate declines of the average rate of profit. Capitalism will not go out of business if the mass of surplus-value produced increases 'only' from £10 to 17 billion, while the total mass of capital has moved from £100 to 200 billion; and capital accumulation will not stop under these circumstances, nor necessarily slow down significantly. It would be sufficient to have the unproductively consumed part of surplus-value pass e.g. from £3 to £2 billion, to obtain a rate of capital accumulation of 15/200, i.e. 7.5%, even higher than the previous one of 7/100, in spite of a decline of the rate of profit from 10 to 8.5%.

The inevitability of class struggle under capitalism. One of the most impressive projections by Marx was that of the inevitability of elementary class struggle under capitalism. Irrespective of the social global framework or of their own historical background, wage-earners will fight everywhere for higher real wages and a shorter work day. They will form elementary organisations for the collective instead of the individual sale of the commodity labour power, i.e., trade unions. While at the moment Marx made that projection there were less than half a million organised workers in at the most half a dozen countries in the world, today trade unions encompass hundreds of millions of wage-earners spread around the globe. There is no country, however, remote it might be, where the introduction of wage labour has not led to the appearance of worker's coalitions.

While elementary class struggle and elementary unionisation of the working class are inevitable under capitalism, higher, especially political forms of class struggle, depend on a multitude of variables which determine the rapidity with which they extend beyond smaller minorities of each 'national' working class and internationally. But there too the basic secular trend is clear. There were in 1900 innumerably more conscious socialists than in 1850, fighting not only for better wages but, to use Marx's words, for the abolition of wage labour and organising working class parties for that purpose. There are today many more than in 1900.

The tendency towards growing social polarisation. From two previously enumerated trends, the trend towards growing centralisation of capital and the trend towards the growth of the mass of surplus-value, flow the trend towards growing social polarisation under capitalism. The proportion of the active population represented by wage-labour in general, i.e. by the modern proletariat (which extends far beyond productive workers in and by themselves), increases. The proportion represented by self-employed (small, medium-sized and big capitalists, as well as independent peasants, handicraftsmen, trades-people and 'free professions' working without wage-labour) decreases. In fact, in several capitalist countries the first category has already passed the 90 per cent mark, while in Marx's time it was below 50 per cent everywhere but in Britain. In most industrialised (imperialist) countries, it has reached 80-85 per cent.

This does not mean that the petty entrepreneurs have tended to disappear. 10 or 15-20 per cent out of 30 million people, not to say out of 120 million, still represents a significant social layer. While many small businesses disappear, especially in times of economic depression, as a result of severe competition, they also are constantly created, especially in the interstices between big firms, and in new sectors where they play an exploratory role. Also, the overall social results of growing proletarisation are not simultaneous with the economic process in and by itself. From the point of view of class consciousness, culture, political attitude, there can exist significant time-lags between the transformation of an independent farmer, grocer or doctor into a wage-earner, and his acceptance of socialism as an overall social solution for his own and society's ills. But again, the secular trend is towards growing homogeneity, less and less heterogeneity, of the mass of the wage-earning class, and not the other way around. It is sufficient to compare the differences in consumer patterns, attitudes towards unionisation or voting habits between manual workers, bank employees and government functionaries in say 1900 and today, to note that they have decreased and not increased.

The tendency towards growing objective socialisation of labour. Capitalism starts in the form of private production on a medium-sized scale for a limited number of largely unknown customers, on an uncontrollably wide market, i.e. under conditions of near complete fragmentation of social labour and anarchy of the economic process. But as a result of growing technological progress, tremendously increased concentration of capital, the conquest of wider and wider markets throughout the world, and the very nature of the labour organisation inside large and even medium-sized capitalist factories, a powerful process of objective socialisation of labour is simultaneously set in motion. This process constantly extends the sphere of economy in which not blind market laws but conscious decisions and even large-scale co-operation prevail.

This is true especially inside mammoth firms (inside multinational corporations, such 'planning' prevails far beyond the boundaries of nation-states, even the most powerful ones!) and inside large-scale factories; but it is also increasingly true for buyer/seller relations, in the first place on an inter-firm basis, between public authorities and firms, and more often than one thinks between traders and consumers too. In all these instances, the rule of the law of value becomes more and more remote, indirect and discontinuous. Planning prevails on a short and even medium-term basis.

Certainly, the economy still remains capitalist. The rule of the law of value imposes itself brutally through the outburst of economic crises. Wars and social crises are increasingly added to these economic crises to remind society that, under capitalism, this growing objective socialisation of labour and production is indissolubly linked to private appropriation, i.e. to the profit motive as motor of economic growth. That linkage makes the system more and more crisis-ridden; but at the same time the growing socialisation of labour and production creates the objective basis for a general socialisation of the economy, i.e. represents the basis of the coming socialist order created by capitalism itself, within the framework of its own system.

The inevitability of economic crises under capitalism. This is another of Marx's projections which has been strikingly confirmed by history. Marx ascertained that periodic crises of overproduction were unavoidable under capitalism. In fact, since the crisis of 1825, the first one occurring on the world market for industrial goods, to use Marx's own formula, there have been twenty-one business cycles ending (or beginning, according to the method of analysis and measurement used) with twenty-one crises of overproduction. A twenty-second is appearing on the horizon as we are writing.

Capitalist economic crises are always crises of overproduction of commodities (exchange values), as opposed to pre-and post-capitalist economic crises, which are essentially crises of underproduction of use-values. Under capitalist crises, expanded reproduction-economic growth-is brutally interrupted, not because too few commodities have been produced but, on the contrary, because a mountain of produced commodities finds no buyers.

This unleashes a spiral movement of collapse of firms, firing of workers, contraction of sales (or orders) for raw materials and machinery, new redundancies, new contraction of sales of consumer goods etc. Through this contracted reproduction, prices (gold prices) collapse, production and income is reduced, capital loses value. At the end of the declining spiral, output (and stocks) has been reduced more than purchasing power. Then production can pick up again; and as the crisis has both increased the rate of surplus-value (through a decline of wages and a more 'rational' labour organisation) and decreased the value of capital, the average rate of profit increases. This stimulates investment. Employment increases, value production and national income expand, and we enter a new cycle of economic revival, prosperity, overheating and the next crisis.

No amount of capitalists' (essentially large combines' and monopolies') 'self-regulation', no amount of government intervention, has been able to suppress this cyclical movement of capitalist production. Nor can they succeed in achieving that result.

This cyclical movement is inextricably linked to production for profit and private property (competition), which imply periodic over-shooting (too little or too much investment and output), precisely because each firm's attempt at maximising profit unavoidably leads to a lower rate of profit for the system as a whole. It is likewise linked to the separation of value production and value realisation.

The only way to avoid crises of overproduction is to eliminate all basic sources of disequilibrium in the economy, including the disequilibrium between productive capacity and purchasing power of the 'final consumers'. This calls for elimination of generalised commodity production, of private property and of class exploitation, i.e. for the elimination of capitalism.

MARX'S THEORY OF CRISES

Marx did not write a systematic treatise on capitalist crises. His major comments on the subject are spread around his major economic writings, as well as his articles for the New York Daily Tribune. The longest treatment of the subject is in his Theorien über den Mehrwert, subpart on Ricardo. Starting from these profound but unsystematic remarks, many interpretations of the 'marxist theory of crises' have been offered by economists who consider themselves marxists. 'Monocausal' ones generally centre around 'disproportionality' (Bukharin, Hilferding, Otto Bauer)-anarchy of production as the key cause of crises-or 'underconsumption'-lack of purchasing power of the 'final consumers' as the cause of crises (Rosa Luxemburg, Sweezy). 'Non-monocausal' ones try to elaborate Marx's own dictum according to which all basic contradictions of the capitalist mode of production come into play in the process leading to a capitalist crises (Grossman, Mandel).

The question of determining whether according to Marx, a crisis of overproduction is first of all a crisis of overproduction of commodities or a crisis of overproduction of capital is really meaningless in the framework of Marx's economic analysis. The mass of commodities is but one specific form of capital, commodity capital. Under capitalism, which is generalised commodity production, no overproduction is possible which is not simultaneously overproduction of commodities and overproduction of capital (overaccumulation).

Likewise, the question to know whether the crisis 'centres' on the sphere of production or the sphere of circulation is largely meaningless. The crisis is a disturbance (interruption) of the process of enlarged reproduction; and according to Marx, the process of reproduction is precisely a (contradictory) unity of production and circulation.

For capitalists, both individually (as separate firms) and as the sum total of firms it is irrelevant whether more surplus-value has actually been produced in the process of production, if that surplus-value cannot be totally realised in the process of circulation. Contrary to many economists, academic and marxist alike, Marx explicitly rejected any Say-like illusion that production more or less automatically finds is own market. It is correct that in the last analysis, capitalist crises of overproduction result from a downslide of the average rate of profit. But this does not represent a variant of the 'monocausal' explanation of crises. It means that, under capitalism, the fluctuations of the average rate of profit are in a sense the seismograph of what happens in the system as a whole. So that formula just refers back to the sum-total of partially independent variables, whose interplay causes the fluctuations of the average rate of profit.

Capitalist growth is always disproportionate growth, i.e. growth with increasing disequilibrium, both between different departments of output (Marx basically distinguishes department I, producing means of production, and department II, producing means of consumption; other authors add a department III producing non-reproductive goods-luxury goods and arms-to that list), between different branches and between production and final consumption. In fact, 'equilibrium' under capitalism is but a conceptual hypothesis practically never attained in real life, except as a border case. The above mentioned tendency of 'overshooting' is only an illustration of that more general phenomenon. So 'average' capital accumulation leads to an over-accumulation which leads to the crisis and to a prolonged phenomenon of 'underinvestment' during the depression. Output is then consistently inferior to current demand, which spurs on capital accumulation, all the more so as each successive phase of economic revival starts with new machinery of a higher technological level (leading to a higher average productivity of labour), and to a bigger and bigger mountain of produced commodities. Indeed, the very duration of the business cycle (in average 7.5 years for the last 160 years) seemed for Marx determined by the 'moral' life-time of fixed capital, i.e. the duration of the reproduction cycle (in value terms, not in possible physical survival) of machinery.

The ups and downs of the rate of profit during the business cycle do not reflect only the gyrations of the output/disposable income relation; or of the 'organic composition of capital'. They also express the varying correlation of forces between the major contending classes of bourgeois society, in the first place the short-term fluctuations of the rate of surplus-value reflecting major victories or defeats of the working class in trying to uplift or defend its standard of living and its working conditions. Technological progress and labour organisation 'rationalisations' are capital's weapons for neutralizing the effects of these fluctuations on the average rate of profit and on the rate of capital accumulation. In general, Marx rejected any idea that the working class (or the unions) 'cause' the crisis by 'excessive wage demands'. He would recognise that under conditions of overheating and 'full employment', real wages generally increase, but the rate of surplus-value can simultaneously increase too. It can, however, not increase in the same proportion as the organic composition of capital. Hence the decline of the average rate of profit. Hence the crisis.

But if real wages do not increase in times of boom, and as they unavoidably decrease in times of depression, the average level of wages during the cycle in its totality would be such as to cause even larger overproduction of wage goods, which would induce an even stronger collapse of investment at the height of the cycle, and in no way help to avoid the crisis.

Marx energetically rejected any idea that capitalist production, while it appears as 'production for production's sake', can really emancipate itself from dependence on 'final consumption' (as alleged e.g. by Tugan-Baranowski). While capitalist technology implies indeed a more and more 'roundabout-way-of-production', and a relative shift of resources from department II to department I (that is what the 'growing organic composition of capital' really means, after all), it can never develop the productive capacity of department I without developing in the medium and long-term the productive capacity of department II too, admittedly at a slower pace and in a lesser proportion. So any medium or long-term contraction of final consumption, or final consumers' purchasing power, increases instead of eliminates the causes of the crisis. Marx visualised the business cycle as intimately intertwined with a credit cycle, which can acquire a relative autonomy in relation to what occurs in production properly speaking. An (over) expansion of credit can enable the capitalist system to sell temporarily more goods that the sum of real incomes created in current production plus past savings could buy. Likewise, credit (over) expansion can enable them to invest temporarily more capital than really accumulated surplus-value (plus depreciation allowances and recovered value of raw materials) would have enabled them to invest (the first part of the formula refers to net investments; the second to gross investment). But all this is only true temporarily. In the longer run, debts must be paid; and they are not automatically paid through the results of expanded output and income made possible by credit expansion. Hence the risk of a Krach, of a credit or banking crisis, adding fuel to the mass of explosives which cause the crisis of overproduction.

Does Marx's theory of crisis imply a theory of an inevitable final collapse of capitalism through purely economic mechanisms? A controversy has raged around this issue, called the 'collapse' or 'breakdown' controversy. Marx's own remarks on the matter are supposed to be enigmatic. 'The expropriators are expropriated'. But the relevant paragraphs of that chapter describe in a clearly non-enigmatic way, an interplay of 'objective' and 'subjective' transformations to bring about a downfall of capitalism, and not a purely economic process. They list among the causes of the overthrow of capitalism not only economic crisis and growing centralisation of capital, but Also the growth of exploitation of the workers and their indignation and revolt in the face of that exploitation, as well as the growing level of skill, organisation and unity of the working class. Beyond these general remarks, Marx, however, does not go.

MARX AND ENGELS ON THE ECONOMY OF POST-CAPITALIST SOCIETIES

Marx was disinclined to comment at length about how a socialist or communist economy would operate. He thought such comments to be essentially speculative. Nevertheless, in his major works, especially the Grundrisse and Das Kapital, there are some sparse comments on the subject. Marx returns to them at greater length in two works he was to write in the final part of his life, his comments on the Gotha Programme of united German social-democracy, and the chapters on economics and socialism he wrote or collaborated with for Engels' Anti-Dühring (1878). Generally his comments, limited and sketchy as they are, can be summarised in the following points.

Socialism is an economic system based upon conscious planning of production by associated producers (nowhere does Marx say: by the state), made possible by the abolition of private property of the means of production. As soon as that private property is completely abolished, goods produced cease to be commodities. Value and exchange value disappear. Production becomes production for use, for the satisfaction of needs, determined by conscious choice (ex ante decisions) of the mass of the associated producers themselves. But overall economic organisation in a postcapitalist society will pass through two stages.

In the first stage, generally called 'socialism', there will be relative scarcity of a number of consumer goods (and services), making it necessary to measure exactly distribution based on the actual labour inputs of each individual (Marx nowhere refers to different quantities and qualities of labour; Engels explicitly rejects the idea that an architect, because he has more skill, should consume more than a manual labourer). Likewise, there will still be the need to use incentives for getting people to work in general. This will be based upon strict equality of access for all trades and professions to consumption. But as human needs are unequal, that formal equality masks the survival of real inequality. In a second phase, generally called 'communism', there will be plenty, i.e. output will reach a saturation point of needs covered by material goods. Under these circumstances, any form of precise measurement of consumption (distribution) will wither away. The principle of full needs satisfaction covering all different needs of different individuals will prevail. No incentive will be needed any more to induce people to work. 'Labour' will have transformed itself into meaningful many-fold activity, making possible all-round development of each individual's human personality. The division of labour between manual and intellectual labour, the separation of town and countryside, will wither away. Humankind will be organised into a free federation of producers' and consumers' communes.

13

Marx's Theory of Alienation

We live in a world where technological achievements unimaginable in previous societies are within our grasp: this is the age of space travel, of the internet, of genetic engineering. Yet never before have we felt so helpless in the face of the forces we ourselves have created. Never before have the fruits of our labour threatened our very existence: this is also the age of nuclear disasters, global warming, and the arms race. For the first time in history we can produce enough to satisfy the needs of everyone on the planet. Yet millions of lives are stunted by poverty and destroyed by disease. Despite our power to control the natural world, our society is dominated by insecurity, as economic recession and military conflict devastate lives with the apparently irresistible power of natural disasters. The more densely populated our cities become, the more our lives are characterised by feelings of isolation and loneliness. To Karl Marx these contradictions were apparent when the system was still young. He noted that:

On the one hand, there have started into life industrial and scientific forces, which no epoch of the former human history had ever suspected. On the other hand, there exist symptoms of decay, far surpassing the horrors of the Roman Empire. In our days everything seems pregnant with its contrary. Machinery, gifted with the wonderful power of shortening and fructifying human labour, we behold starving and overworking it. The new-fangled sources of wealth, by some strange weird spell, are turned into sources of want. The victories of art seem bought by loss of character.

Marx developed his theory of alienation to reveal the human activity that lies behind the seemingly impersonal forces dominating society. He showed how, although aspects of the society we live in appear natural and independent of us, they are the results of past human actions. For Hungarian Marxist Georg Lukács Marx's theory 'dissolves the rigid, unhistorical, natural appearance of social institutions; it reveals their historical origins and shows therefore that they are subject to history in every respect including historical decline'. Marx showed not only that human action in the past created the modern world, but also that human action could shape a future world free from the contradictions of capitalism. Marx developed a materialist theory of how human beings were shaped by the society they lived in, but also how they could act to change that society, how people are both 'world determined' and 'world producing'. For Marx, alienation was not rooted in the mind or in religion, as it was for his predessesors Hegel and Feuerbach. Instead Marx understood alienation as something rooted in the material world. Alienation meant loss of control, specifically the loss of control over labour. To understand why labour played such a central role in Marx's theory of alienation, we have to look first at Marx's ideas about human nature.

What is Human Nature?

Marx opposed the common sense idea that humans have a fixed nature which exists independently of the society they live in. He demonstrated that many of the features attributed to unchanging human nature in fact vary enormously in different societies. However, Marx did not reject the idea of human nature itself. He argued that the need to labour on nature to satisfy human needs was the only consistent feature of all human societies, the 'ever lasting nature-imposed condition of human existence'. Human beings, like all other animals, must work on nature to survive. The labour of humans, however, was distinguished from that of animals because human beings developed consciousness. Marx gave a famous description of this at the beginning of Capital:

A spider conducts operations that resemble those of a weaver, and a bee puts to shame many an architect in the construction of her cells. But what distinguishes the worst architect from the best of bees is this, that the architect raises his structure in imagination before he erects it in reality. At the end of every labour-process, we get a result that already existed in the imagination of the labourer at its commencement.

In a useful introduction to Marx's ideas, How to Read Karl Marx, Ernst Fischer also described what is unique about human labour. He explained how, because we act on nature consciously, we build on our successes and develop new ways of producing the things we need. This means that we have a history, whereas animals do not: 'The species-nature of animal is an eternal repetition, that of man is transformation, development and change'.

Working on nature alters not only the natural world, but also the labourer himself. Marx frequently reinforced this idea, as in the following quote from Capital: 'By thus acting on the external world and changing it, he at the same time changes his own nature. He develops his slumbering powers and compels them to act in obedience to his sway.' Thus labour is a dynamic process through which the labourer shapes and moulds the world he lives in and stimulates himself to create and innovate. Marx called our capacity for conscious labour our 'species being'.

Our species being is also a social being, as Marx explained in the Economic and Philosophical Manuscripts (1844): 'The individual is the social being.' People have to enter into relationships with each other regardless of their personal preferences because they need to work together to get what they need to live. In the Grundrisse, Marx emphasised the point: 'Society does not consist of individuals; it expresses the sum of connections and relationships in which individuals find themselves.' Humanity relates to the physical world through labour; through labour humanity itself develops and labour is the source of human beings' relationships with each other. What happens to the process of work, therefore, has a decisive influence on the whole of society.

Our ability to work, to improve how we work and build on our successes, has tended to result in the cumulative development of the productive forces. One such development gave rise to class society. When society became capable of producing a surplus, it also became possible for a class to emerge which was liberated from the need to directly produce and could live from its control over the labour of others. This process was necessary in order to develop and direct the productive forces, but it also meant that the majority of society, the producers, lost control of their labour. Thus, the alienation of labour arose with class society, and Ernst Fischer has given a brilliant description of how it reversed the limitless potential of labour:

The first tool contains within it all the potential future ones. The first recognition of the fact that the world can be changed by conscious activity contains all future, as yet unknown, but inevitable change. A living being which has once begun to make nature his own through the work of his hands, his intellect, and his imagination, will never stop. Every achievement opens the door to unconquered territory... But when labour is destructive, not creative, when it is undertaken under coercion and not as the free play of forces, when it means the withering, not the flowering, of man's physical and intellectual potential, then labour is a denial of its own principle and therefore of the principle of man.

The emergence of class divisions in which one class had control over the means of producing what society needed, led to a further division between individuals and the society to which they belonged. Certain forms of social life 'drive a wedge between the two dimensions of the self, the individual and the communal', producing a separation between individuals' interests and those of society as a whole. However, alienation is not an unalterable human condition which exists unchanged in every class society.

Four Aspects of Alienation

The development of capitalism proved irresistible and it brought alienation on a scale previously unimaginable. In his Economic and Philosophical Manuscripts (also known as the 1844, or Paris Manuscripts) Marx identified four specific ways in which alienation pervades capitalist society.

The product of labour: The worker is alienated from the object he produces because it is owned and disposed of by another, the capitalist. In all societies people use their creative abilities to produce objects which they use, exchange or sell.

Under capitalism, however, this becomes an alienated activity because 'the worker cannot use the things he produces to keep alive or to engage in further productive activity... The worker's needs, no matter how desperate, do not give him a licence to lay hands on what these same hands have produced, for all his products are the property of another'. Thus workers produce cash crops for the market when they are malnourished, build houses in which they will never live, make cars they can never buy, produce shoes they cannot afford to wear, and so on. Marx argued that the alienation of the worker from what he produces is intensified because the products of labour actually begin to dominate the labourer. In his brilliant Essays on Marx's Theory of Value, I I Rubin outlines a quantitative and a qualitative aspect to the production of commodities. Firstly, the worker is paid less than the value he creates. A proportion of what he produces is appropriated by his boss; the worker is, therefore, exploited. Qualitatively, he also puts creative labour into the object he produces, but he cannot be given creative labour to replace it. As Rubin explains, 'In exchange for his creative power the worker receives a wage or a salary, namely a sum of money, and in exchange for this money he can purchase products of labour, but he cannot purchase creative power. In exchange for his creative power, the worker gets things'. This creativity is lost to the worker forever, which is why under capitalism work does not stimulate or invigorate us and 'open the door to unconquered territory', but rather burns up our energies and leaves us feeling exhausted.

This domination of dead labour over living labour lies behind Marx's assertion in the Manuscripts that 'the alienation of the worker means not only that his labour becomes an object, an external existence, but that it exists outside him, independently of him and alien to him, and begins to confront him as an autonomous power; that the life which he has bestowed on the object confronts him as hostile and alien'. For Marx this state of affairs was unique to capitalism. In previous societies those who work harder could usually be expected to have more to consume. Under capitalism, those who work harder increase the power of a hostile system over them. They themselves, and their inner worlds, become poorer. 'The worker becomes an ever cheaper commodity the more goods he creates. The devaluation of the human world increases in direct relation with the increase in value of the world of things'.

The labour process: The second element of alienation Marx identified is a lack of control over the process of production. We have no say over the conditions in which we work and how our work is organised, and how it affects us physically and mentally. This lack of control over the work process transforms our capacity to work creatively into its opposite, so the worker experiences 'activity as passivity, power as impotence, procreation as emasculation, the worker's own physical and mental energy, his personal life-for what is life but activity?- as an activity directed against himself, which is independent of him and does not belong to him'. The process of work is not only beyond the control of the workers, it is in the control of forces hostile to them because capitalists and their managers are driven to make us work harder, faster and for longer stints. In addition, as Harry Braverman points out, 'in a society based upon the purchase and sale of labour power, dividing the craft cheapens its individual parts', so the bosses also have an interest in breaking down the labour process into smaller and smaller parts. The resulting rigidly repetitive process buries the individual talents or skills of the worker, as Marx described:

Factory work exhausts the nervous system to the uttermost, it does away with the many-sided play of the muscles, and confiscates every atom of freedom, both in bodily and intellectual activity... The special skill of each individual insignificant factory operative vanishes as an infinitesimal quantity before the science, the gigantic physical forces, and mass of labour that are embodied in the factory mechanism and, together, with that mechanism, constitute the power of the master.

Modern methods of production have increased the fragmentation of the labour process since Marx's day. The organisation of modern production is still based on the methods of the assembly line. Scientific research is used to break the production process down into its component parts. This has led, firstly, to the deskilling of white collar jobs and to a situation where managers have a monopoly of control over the production process: 'The unity of thought and action, conception and execution, hand and mind, which capitalism threatened from it beginnings, is now attacked by a systematic dissolution employing all the resources of science and the various engineering disciplines based upon it'. Conditions of work, from the length of the working day to the space we occupy, are predetermined: 'The entire work operation, down to it smallest motion, is conceptualised by the management and engineering staff, laid out, measured, fitted with training and performance standards-all entirely in advance'. Workers are treated as machines, with the aim of transforming the subjective element of labour into objective, measurable, controlled processes. In some brilliant passages in History and Class Consciousness, Lukács describes how the increasingly rationalised and mechanised process of work affects our consciousness. As the following extract shows, his analysis was prophetic and gives a strikingly accurate picture of today's white collar work:

In consequence of the rationalisation of the work-process the human qualities and idiosyncrasies of the worker appear increasingly as mere sources of error when contrasted with these abstract special laws functioning according to rational predictions. Neither objectively nor in his relation to his work does man appear as the authentic master of this process; on the contrary, he is a mechanical part incorporated into a mechanical system. He finds it already pre-existing and self-sufficient, it functions independently of him and he has to conform to its laws whether he likes it or not.

Our fellow human beings: Thirdly, we are alienated from our fellow human beings. This alienation arises in part because of the antagonisms which inevitably arise from the class structure of society. We are alienated from those who exploit our labour and control the things we produce. As Marx put it:

If his activity is a torment for him, it must provide pleasure and enjoyment for someone else... If therefore he regards the product of his labour, his objectified labour, as an alien, hostile and powerful object which is independent of him, then his relationship to that object is such that another man-alien, hostile, powerful and independent of him-is its master. If he relates to his own activity an unfree activity, then he relates to it as activity in the service, under the rule, coercion and yoke of another man.

In addition, we are connected to others through the buying and selling of the commodities we produce. Our lives are touched by thousands of people every day, people whose labour has made our clothes, food, home, etc. But we only know them through the objects we buy and consume. Ernst Fischer pointed out that because of this we do not see each other 'as fellow-men having equal rights, but as superiors or subordinates, as holders of a rank, as a small or large unit of power'. We are related to each other not as individuals but as representatives of different relations of production, the personification of capital, or land or labour. As Bertell Ollman wrote, 'We do not know each other as individuals, but as extensions of capitalism: "In bourgeois society capital is independent and has individuality, while the living person is dependent and has no individuality".' The commodities of each individual producer appear in depersonalised form, regardless of who produced them, where, or in what specific conditions. Commodity production means that everyone 'appropriates the produce of others, by alienating that of their own labour'.

Marx described how mass commodity production continually seeks to create new needs, not to develop our human powers but to exploit them for profit: Each attempts to establish over the other an alien power, in the hope of thereby achieving satisfaction of his own selfish needs...becomes the inventive and ever calculating slave of inhuman, refined, unnatural and imaginary appetites. He places himself at the disposal of his neighbour's most depraved fancies, panders to his needs, excites unhealthy appetites in him, and pounces on every weakness, so that he can then demand the money for his labour of love. We see other people through the lens of profit and loss. Our abilities and needs are converted into means of making money and so we consider other human beings as competitors, as inferiors or superiors.

Our human nature: The fourth element is our alienation from what Marx called our species being. What makes us human is our ability to consciously shape the world around us. However, under capitalism our labour is coerced, forced labour. Work bears no relationship to our personal inclinations or our collective interests. The capitalist division of labour massively increased our ability to produce, but those who create the wealth are deprived of its benefits. Marx's descriptions of this process in the Manuscripts are extremely powerful indictments of the system: It is true that labour produces marvels for the rich, but it produces privation for the worker. It produces palaces, but hovels for the worker. It procures beauty, but deformity for the worker. It replaces labour by machines, but it casts some of the workers back into barbarous forms of labour and turns others into machines. It produces intelligence, but it produces idiocy and cretinism for the worker.

Human beings are social beings. We have the ability to act collectively to further our interests. However, under capitalism that ability is submerged under private ownership and the class divisions it produces. We have the ability to consciously plan our production, to match what we produce with the developing needs of society. But under capitalism that ability is reversed by the anarchic drive for profits. Thus, rather than consciously shaping nature, we cannot control, or even foresee, the consequences of our actions. For example, new, cheaper techniques of production may, when repeated across industry, produce acid rain or gases which destroy the ozone layer.

Similarly, when one capitalist improves production in his factory, he is unwittingly contributing to the slowing up of the rate of profits for his class as a whole by lowering the rate of profit. One firm can produce to fulfil a particularly sharp demand, only to find when the goods hit the market that other firms got there first. Instead of simply meeting demand, there is a glut in the market. This means that we produce more but what we produce is unwanted. All previous societies suffered from shortages, famines and the failure of crops. Under capitalism recessions mean that workers 'consume less because they produce too much. And they consume less, not because their labour is inadequately productive, but because their labour is too productive'. There is nothing natural about the economic crises we face: it is our social organisation which prevents us enjoying the potential of our ability to produce.

What is Commodity Fetishism?

The domination of commodities in our society is so pervasive that it seems to be an inevitable, natural state of affairs. All our achievements, everything we produce, appear as commodities, as Marx noted: 'The wealth of societies in which the capitalist mode of production prevails appears as an immense collection of commodities'. Capitalism is the first system of generalised commodity production, in which the commodity has become 'a universal category of society as a whole'. The dominance of commodity production has implications for how we experience the world we have created.

The mysterious commodity: In every society human beings have laboured to created objects which help them fulfil their needs. So Marx began his analysis of commodities under capitalism by asserting that 'a commodity is an external object, a thing which through its qualities satisfies human needs of whatever kind', regardless of whether that need comes from stomach or the imagination. Commodities must have a use value, but they also have an exchange value. In capitalist society our many different human needs can only be met through the purchase of commodities: to eat we have to buy food in a shop, to travel we have to buy a car or a bus ticket, to have access to knowledge we have to buy books, TVs or computers. Yet the usefulness of all these commodities is overwhelmed by their exchange value and the satisfaction of human needs becomes inseparable from the workings of the market.

The circulation of commodities on the market is even more cloaked in mystery than the process of their production, where workers have some direct relationship with the commodity they produce. This relationship is lost when commodities are sent to market and exchanged for money, which, in turn, is exchanged for other commodities. As Marx wrote, 'The actual process of production, as a unity of the direct production process and the circulation process, gives rise to new formations, in which the vein of internal connections is increasingly lost, the production relations are rendered independent of one another, and the component values become ossified into forms independent of one another'. Marx explained how the circulation of commodities transforms relationships between individual producers into relationships between the commodities they produce. They are divided from each other, yet utterly dependent on each other's commodities:

The owners of commodities find out that the division of labour which turns them into independent private producers also makes the social process of production and the relations of the individual producers to each other within that process independent of the producers themselves; they also find out that the independence of the individuals from each other has its counterpart and supplement a system of all-round material dependence.

In the capitalist system individuals have to possess certain things-labour power, or materials of production, for example-in order to enter into productive relationships with each other. As a consequence, 'it seems as if the thing itself possesses the ability, the virtue, to establish production relations', rather than the individuals themselves. Commodities acquire social characteristics because individuals enter the productive process only as the owners of commodities. Marx described this process: 'To the producers, therefore, the social relations between their private labours...do not appear as direct social relations between persons in their work, but rather as material relations between persons and social relations between things'. Thus it appears as if the market itself causes the rise and fall of prices, and pushes workers into one branch of production or out of another, independent of human agency. 'The impact of society on the individual is carried out through the social form of things'. This adds another dimension to alienated relationships because, as Marx argued, 'the characters who appear on the economic stage are merely personifications of economic relations; it is as the bearers of these economic relations that they come into contact with each other'.

Marx described the whole process of the reification of human relationships, the attribution of human powers to inanimate objects, and the way in which social organisation appears as independent of human will as commodity fetishism. Commodity fetishism has increased with the growth of capitalism, in which 'the capitalist mode of production takes over the totality of individual, family, and social needs and, in subordinating them to the market, also reshapes them to serve the needs of capital'. Today there is a market for everything, for sex and art, for labour itself, as well as for TVs and cars. As Ernst Fischer wrote, 'We have become so accustomed to living in a world of commodities, where nature is perhaps only a poster for a holiday resort and man only an advertisement for a new product, we exist in such a turmoil of alienated objects offered cheaply for sale, that we hardly ask ourselves any longer what it is that magically transforms objects of necessity (or fashion) into commodities, and what is the true nature of the witches' Sabbath, ablaze with neon moons and synthetic constellations, that has become our day to day reality'.

Money: the 'universal pimp': The creation of exchange values and the circulation of commodities requires a commodity which can represent all other commodities, through which all other commodities can be compared. Marx described how the development of capitalism brought with it the problem of how to evaluate different commodities and simultaneously created the solution in the form of money, the universal commodity. Physical objects, gold or silver become the 'direct incarnation of all human labour'. With the development of money people's relationship to their production assumes a material shape which is independent of their control and their conscious action: 'This situation is manifested first by the fact that the products of men's labour universally take on the form of commodities. The riddle of the money fetish is therefore the riddle of the commodity fetish, now become visible and dazzling to our eyes'.

Marx called money the 'universal pimp', mediating between men and their desires. The value of money, the metals in which it was originally embodied, have long since been discarded in favour of intrinsically worthless alloy metal coins or paper money. And yet money can buy everything-it is the most powerful commodity in existence: 'Money is all other commodities divested of their shape, the product of their universal alienation'. The role of money in the circulation of commodities shapes the consciousness of human beings involved in that process. Money takes on the value of the objects it represents, it appears to be the force which can create value itself. As Meszaros explains:

Money is taken to possess these colossal powers as natural attributes. People's attitude toward money is, undoubtedly, the outstanding instance of capitalist fetishism, reaching its height in interest bearing capital. Here, people think they see money creating more money, self-expanding value... workers, machines, raw materials-all the factors of production-are downgraded to mere aids, and money itself is made the producer of wealth.

Thus money acquires great abilities, but on the other side of the coin, all our human desires and abilities contract into what Marx called a sense of having: 'Private property has made us so stupid and one-sided that an object is only ours when we have it, when it exists for us as capital or when we directly possess, eat, drink, wear, inhabit it, etc., in short, when we use it'. Marx also described how this desire for possession is both stimulated and denied: 'The worker is only permitted to have enough for him to live, and he is only permitted to live in order to have'. In a particularly perceptive passage from the Manuscripts, Marx explains how money submerges our personalities. It is a brilliant rejoinder to those who argue that capitalism allows our individuality to flourish:

> That which exists for me through the medium of money, that which I can pay for, ie which money can buy, that am I, the possessor of the money. The stronger the power of my money, the stronger I am. The properties of money are my, the possessors', properties and essential powers. Therefore what I am and what I can do is by no means determined by my individuality. I am ugly, but I can buy the most beautiful women. Which means to say that I am not ugly, for the effect of ugliness, its repelling power, is destroyed by money. As an individual I am lame, but money procures me 24 legs. Consequently, I am not lame. I am a wicked, dishonest, unscrupulous individual, but money is respected, and so also is its owner...through money I can have anything the human heart desires. Do I not therefore possess all human abilities? Does not money therefore transform all my incapacities into their opposite?

Commodity fetishism and class: Alienation and commodity fetishism shape all relationships in society. Those who possess wealth also inhabit a world beyond their control, in which relationships are reified. Their individuality is submerged by the dictates of capitalism-as Marx wrote, the instinct to enrich himself, which 'in a miser is a mere idiosyncrasy, is, in the capitalist, the effect of the social mechanism, of which he is but one of the wheels'. The huge productive forces owned by the ruling class may bring them riches beyond our imaginings, but they cannot control the vast economic forces of the system or even plan any section of it accurately. The capitalists are caught in a contradiction, that 'capital is a social force, but it is privately, rather than collectively, owned so its movements are determined by individual owners necessarily indifferent to all the social implications of their activities'. The capitalist has constantly to compete in order to keep up with his competitors and while his actions may be perfectly sensible for the individual firm, when generalised across society they cause the economic recessions which can destroy many firms. Economic crises are irrefutable proof that the system is more powerful than any individual capitalist. This explains why crises are such a massive blow to the confidence and ideology of the ruling class. The capitalist may like to believe that his daring, entrepreneurial spirit creates his wealth, but in reality he 'rides a wave another has created'. The class struggle, which he cannot prevent, brings home forcibly how dependent he is on the labour of his employees, and, like economic crises, is a wounding blow to the outlook of the ruling class.

In The Holy Family Marx gives a brilliant description of the situation of the ruling class: The possessing class and the class of the proletariat present the same human self-alienation. But the former class feels at home in this self-alienation, it finds confirmation of itself and recognises in alienation its own power; it has in it a semblance of human existence, while the class of the proletariat feels annihilated in its self-alienation; it sees therein its own powerlessness and the reality of an inhuman existence.

Thus, no matter how deeply alienation affects them, the ruling class will always be driven to defend the system that creates their alienation with all the power and brutality at their disposal because of their material position within it. In addition to this, Lukács argued that the ruling class can never rise above the commodity fetishism of capitalism. The bourgeoisie can never recognise the real nature of capitalism without confronting their own role as exploiters and upholders of the system. Therefore the capitalists do not want to recognise the real social relationships which underlie the institutions of capitalist society. They prefer to continue believing that the relations of production are natural and inevitable. In contrast, Lukács argued that workers, though also shaped by commodity fetishism, were not permanently blinded to the reality of capitalism. Rather he argued that the working class is in a unique position to be able to tear the veil of reification from capitalism because its struggle against capitalism reveals its real own role in producing the wealth of society. Class struggle means that workers no longer see themselves as isolated individuals. It means that they can become conscious of the social character of labour. Lukács suggests that when workers glimpse the reality behind commodity fetishism it can help them to realise the need for a revolutionary transformation of society: 'This enables us to understand why it is only in the proletariat that the process by which a man's achievement is split off from his total personality and becomes a commodity leads to a revolutionary consciousness'.

The uses and Abuses of Marx's Theory

The concept of alienation is a central but controversial aspect of Marxism. When Marx's key work on alienation, The Economic and Philosophical Manuscripts, was eventually published in 1932, it had a dramatic impact on the tradition known as 'Western Marxism', which included writers like Herbert Marcuse and John Paul Sartre. However, in the hands of the Western Marxists, the theory of alienation became intermingled with idealist theories, which explained alienation in terms of psychology rather than the organisation of society. The New Left which emerged in the late 1950s reacted against the theory and practice of Stalinism, but some of the writers associated with the New Left threw the Marxist baby out with the Stalinist bathwater.

They abandoned some central aspects of Marxism, such as the central role of the economic structure in shaping the rest of society and the objective class antagonisms at the heart of capitalism. As Perry Anderson wrote, 'The most striking single trait of Western Marxism as a common tradition is thus perhaps the constant presence and influence on it of successive types of European idealism'. Alienation was seized upon to explain the miseries of modern life, and the 'lonely crowd', 'those aggregations of atomised city dwellers who feel crushed and benumbed by the weight of a social system in which they have neither significant purpose nor decision-making power'. Alienation came to refer predominately to a state of mind, rather than an understanding of how social organisation affected human beings.

Typical of the confused ideas about alienation fashionable in some quarters at this time is a book edited by Eric and Mary Josephson, Man Alone: Alienation in Modern Society, first published in 1962 and reprinted eight times before 1968. For the Josephsons, alienation describes 'the untold lives of quiet desperation that mark our age', and the long list of those suffering from alienation includes such diverse group as women, immigrants, sexual deviants, drug addicts, young people and artists. But the editors understand alienation exclusively as a psychological state, 'referring to an extraordinary variety of psycho-social disorders, including loss of field, anxiety states, anomie, despair, depersonalisation, rootlessness, apathy, social disorganisation, loneliness, atomisation, powerlessness, meaninglessness, isolation, pessimism, and the loss of beliefs and values'. If alienation is only a specific psychological problem, then it follows that the solution to alienation must be sought exclusively in the individual consciousness. If alienation is predominantly a state of mind, there is an implication that it can be cured without fundamentally changing the organisation of society. As Eric Fromm suggested, forms of alienation were 'chains of illusion' which can be broken within the context of capitalist society, because they arise from 'stereotyped alternatives of thinking'.

However, Marx's writings on alienation, from the Manuscripts to the Grundrisse and Capital, demonstrate that for him alienation was not merely a state of mind. The roots of the individual psyche were to be located in how society as a whole is organised. As one Marxist described it, 'The life activity of the alienated individual is qualitatively of a kind. His actions in religion, family affairs, politics and so on, are as distorted and brutalised as his productive activity... There is no sphere of human activity that lies outside these prison walls'. Marx's theory offers us an indispensable method of understanding how the production process shapes the whole of society. There are two areas of activity which are particularly controversial in relation to alienation. This first is the place of intellectual, or mental labour, and creativity in alienated production.

The division of labour described in this article leads to a sharp division between work and creativity. Work is regimented, broken down into separate tasks. The creative elements in each process are dispersed into a million fragments. Labour itself is a commodity and its value is determined by the labour time which went into its creation, for example, the amount spent on training or educating a worker. A highly skilled technician or engineer will therefore be paid more than an unskilled labourer. As Braverman wrote, 'In this way, a structure is given to all labour process that at its extremes polarises those whose time is infinitely valuable and those whose time is worth almost nothing'. However, this does not mean that the intellectual whose time is valuable escapes from the general pattern of alienation. On the contrary, one of the features of modern capitalism is the commercialisation of knowledge. The design of a microchip or computer software is just as much the property of the capitalist as a tin of beans or a car. Capitalists enrich themselves through the appropriation of mental labour in the same way as they do through material labour.

The social division of labour undermines the potential of intellectuals to discover new truths about society. As Franz Jakubowski wrote, The social division of labour creates a series of sub-spheres, not only in the economy but in the whole of social life and thought. These develop their own autonomous sets of laws. As a result of specialisation, each individual sphere develops according to the logic of its own specific object.

Intellectual activity takes place within these limitations, in isolation from society as a whole. In the end, the individual sciences 'cannot understand either the method of the principle of even their own concrete substratum of reality'. All the potential we have to develop new techniques and methods is subordinated to competition. The very structure of capitalist society condemns our intellectual developments to the chase of facts in blind isolation from the real movements of society. This does not mean that nothing useful can be developed, rather that research takes place within a framework which constrains and limits its development.

The same processes are at work in the production and consumption of art in capitalist society. As Eugene Lunn explained in his excellent book Marxism and Modernism, bourgeois society offers artistic freedom on one hand and snatches it back with the other: 'Bourgeois society-with all its progressive advance over "feudal" constrictions-is also inimical to many forms of art, for example because of division of labour, the mechanisation of many forms of human activity, and the predominance of quantitative over qualitative concerns'. Marx argued that artists, like scientists and intellectuals, could not escape from the general conversion of all human creativity into commodities. Firstly this is because artists, like all other workers, are dependent on their ability to make money: 'The bourgeoisie has stripped of its halo every occupation hitherto honoured and looked up to with reverent awe. It has converted the physician, the lawyers, the priest, the poet, the man of science, into its paid wage labourers'. Secondly, Lunn points out how commodity production shapes art. The fact that works of art are sold on the market shapes every level of their conception and production. Marx gave one example of this in his critique of the novels of Eugene Sue, in which he 'stresses the influence upon the author of the ethical and political assumptions of its intended bourgeois public'. Neither can art escape commodity fetishism: 'If one form of spiritualising mystification has been eroded by expansion of commerce-the romantic apotheosis of the arts as soaring above material reality-a new fetishism has replaced it: the fetishism of commodities'. This also points to how new, challenging cultural developments are rapidly incorporated into the system as mere commodities.

This does not mean that works of art can be reduced to exactly the same status as a tin of beans. Art stimulates our imagination and emotions. It enriches our understanding of society and can reveal something of the contradictions behind reified appearances: 'It can pierce through the ideological clouds which enshroud social realities.' Some artists devote their energies to attempting to reach beyond capitalism, while others choose to celebrate the system as it exists, but even then the art they produce can penetrate the reified appearance of capitalism. As Lunn wrote: We cannot reduce art to exchange rates reflecting the pervasive alienation. Even with its halo removed, art was capable of diagnosing, and pointing beyond alienating social and economic conditions... All art has the capacity to create a need for aesthetic enjoyment and education which capitalism cannot satisfy. Although coming increasingly under the influence of the marketplace, art is produced and consumed in relative autonomy and is not identical to factory work or to a pure commodity.

The second controversial application of Marx's theory of alienation is in the formulation of an analysis of other activities outside the sphere of work, which we undertake through choice rather than necessity. The more the world of work confronts us as hostile, exhausting and miserable, the more people pour their energies into their lives outside work. As the system develops new markets are constantly being carved out of our needs and wishes. For example, consider the multimillion pound industries which have developed around commodities which are said to make us look thin or young, our desire to play games, to experience nature or enjoy art. The very fact that we have the 'leisure industry' and the 'entertainment industry' points to the fact that the separation of work from leisure has left a void in our free hours: 'Thus filling time away from the job also becomes dependent upon the market, which develops to an enormous degree those passive amusements, entertainments, and spectacles that suit the restricted circumstances of the city and are offered as substitutes for life itself'.

The retreat into the privatised world of the individual and the family is a pronounced feature of life in the 1990s. Adopting particular lifestyles seems to offer the only real chance of personal fulfilment. Hence the increasing fascination for TV programmes and magazines about fashion, cooking, holidays and gardening and the boom in the Do-It-Yourself market. The family and the home have become leisure activities in and of themselves; they have also become subject to the priorities of the market. All the commodities which could increase our free time simply reinforce the family as a unit of consumption not an emotional haven: 'As the advances of modern household and service industries lighten the family labour, they increase the futility of family life; as they remove the burden of personal relations, they strip away its affections; as they create an intricate social life, they rob it of every vestige of community and leave in its place the cash nexus'.

In addition, Meszaros describes how the retreat into private life simply increases the power of capitalism over us: 'The cult of privacy and of individual autonomy thus fulfils the dual function of objectively protecting the established order against challenge by the rabble, and subjectively providing a spurious fulfilment in an escapist withdrawal to the isolated and powerless individual who is mystified by the mechanisms of capitalist society which manipulate him'. Meszaros also makes the point that alienation has deprived us of our ability to have genuinely human relationships. We are forced to seek compensation for the loss of our humanity in the limited area of our privatised personal lives, yet this merely reinforces our alienation from each other: 'To seek the remedy in autonomy is to be on the wrong track. Our troubles are not due to a lack of autonomy but, on the contrary, to a social structure-a mode of production-that forces on men a cult of it, isolating them from each other'.

Our attempts to express the creativity of which capitalism has deprived us cannot negate the totality of alienation. The eradication of alienation depends on the transformation of society as a whole. However we organise our personal lives and leisure time, we cannot individually fulfil our collective ability to shape the natural world we live in. Lifestyles and leisure activities cannot liberate us from alienation, or even create little islands of freedom in an ocean of alienation. As alienation is rooted in capitalist society, only the collective struggle against that society carries the potential to eradicate alienation, to bring our vast, developing powers under our conscious control and reinstitute work as the central aspect of life. As Marx wrote in Capital, 'The veil is not removed from the countenance of the social life process, ie the process of material production, until it becomes production by freely associated men and stands under their conscious and planned control'.

KARL MARX AND HIS THEORY OF ALIENATION

The reality of alienation in the modern world is prevalent and can be seen everywhere. Alienation simply stated means separation from that which is desired or desirable. It floods the news channels and is seen in day to day life in our interactions with others. But Karl Marx's slant on the idea comes from his understanding in the context of capitalist modes of production for profit. It is this focus that allows us to see the source of alienation in its true context in society and how all other forms of alienation are rooted in this prime cause. Marx identified the process of people finding useful things in nature and then taking them as they were freely available and changing these resources to something of greater use value by working on them to improve their usefulness.

An example that Marx used frequently, is the taking of raw resources like cotton, wool and hemp and turning them into woven cloth. This was then taken and worked on to produce clothing. Other examples are mining for raw ore and then turning this into cutlery, ships, cars and railroads. Wood was cut from trees, converted into chips and lumber to make paper and houses. Plant seeds were sown and mature plants harvested for food and animals kept and raised for the same purpose. Some animals were trained to help in the production process. As long as people were in direct contact with nature and created all that was useful directly there from, there was no alienation. Everyone knew exactly where all that was necessary and useful for life came from. They had to work well with each other in order to survive. There was as a result, an awe and respect for nature and one another that dominated their stories and even their architecture. Alienation has as its roots, the production of surplus value that was over and above basic and immediate need. Surplus value meant wealth and it became a commodity when some realized that it could be used as exchange for something there was a shortage of. As surplus value allowed for the emergence of specialization, succeeding generations lost touch with the way things were done on the solid basis of material nature. Specialization in one direction means that other knowledge and ways of doing things are forgotten over successive generations and the specialist must depend on those who are still in contact with that reality to support them. But they must offer something in value in exchange. No one likes to work for someone else who contributes nothing; there must be some sort of fair exchange as we all have the same basic needs to live.

The production of surplus value meant that some people could now be freed up for other activities, such as defence against marauders, developing of the sciences such as sky watching-astrology-astronomy, alchemy, and the forerunner of modern chemistry, invention, engineering and all other activities that eventually wound up in the contemporary, complex industrial societies in the modern world. These co-exist with societies that are not as developed. The world's societies exist in a condition of combined and unequal development. This leads to alienation between cultures and the possibility exists for the unfolding of permanent revolution in less developed regions and societies. The evolution of society away from subsistence living meant that changes in the structure of society was inevitable. Marx was aware of this and described it in great detail. He was also aware of how the toiler became alienated from nature and the very thing he now works to produce. This has a lot to do with how the idea of money evolved to act as a medium of exchange in the form of what he called a universal commodity. The existence of a universal commodity meant the end of strict barter trading and made trade more fluid and dynamic. Barter was often cumbersome and inconvenient, so various items became the medium of the universal commodity. These were items like wampum beads, gold, precious and semi-precious stones, cattle, art objects and the like. As most of these had no real use value in of themselves, they became a tool-medium of exchange to obtain the desired real values that were necessary for life. This is how barter evolved in a qualitative leap. At the same time, one form of alienation crept in as the producer of value was not necessarily the one who consumed or used it.

Another aspect of the theory of alienation is the separation of the means of production froni the ones who produce. This entailed a number of steps that ended in the contemporary world. The principle idea behind this is the acquisition of the means of production by an owner class, such as the aristocracy, a theocracy or the contemporary bourgeois industrialist and bankers. In nature there is no such thing as ownership. If anything is true, nature owns us and not we own nature. Somewhere in history and for some causative reason, some societies decided to act as marauders to other societies and appropriate what they had produced for themselves. Thus a question of ownership developed. The foundation idea is that whatever a person works to create becomes their property. They can then trade with others, or worse, have it taken by theft through force. With the development of states in ancient times, wars of conquest were fought for the means of production, whether land, fishing areas, mines, trees, slaves and so on. The concept of money existed alongside of this and became a focus of attention. As people were for one reason or another, removed from access to the means of production, they became alienated. This alienation continued through history to the present. Alienation became a real problem with the removal of the peasants from the land within the multitude of kingdoms and principalities then existent in the world. Land was expropriated for the purpose of growing cash crops for the landlords, prince, kings and the courts. This burgeoning business of cash crops was assisted by money, managed by emerging banks. Banks made loans with the idea that they would be paid back with interest and/or a service fee for the use of the money to assist in manufacturing expansion.

The landless peasants wound up in growing cities, where trade was done and manufacturing was concentrated and developing. Now lacking everything except their ability to labour, they were forced to work in order to survive and they worked for money, the universal commodity that increasingly became a fetish of adoration due to its seeming magical power to convert into anything else of use. Money of itself cannot be eaten of worn, nor can it keep you sheltered on its own. For the most part, what was produced in the manufacturing centers was a single commodity and the typical landless labourer became alienated from what they produced. As they did not own the means of production as given under royal or banker's entitlement by defined laws, this also served to sever relations between the labourer and what was produced creating deeper alienation. It also severed direct relations between the owner of the means of production from the producer using those means but having no say in their use. Often they could not afford what they produced from the wages they received. Various developments in production beginning with the industrial revolution, assisted by the banks, allowed things like mechanically enhanced production and the assembly line. These developments constantly challenged those who laboured and there have been hundreds of years of cycles between nearly full employment, engineering changes, over-production, economic collapses, unemployment, re-education, employment and more changes and so on in complex repeated cycles. Each round creates further alienation.

Laborers have been encouraged to accept script money as wages and as script money is subject to devaluation and inflation, it becomes what is known as fictitious value, where the real value part decreases and the fictitious part increases over time. Initially script was backed by gold, but this "limitation" was removed. A classic example of expanding fictitious value is the collapse of the Reich mark in pre WWII Germany, where inflation was so intense that everyone had to have wheel barrows full of rapidly devaluing script money to buy a single loaf of bread.

It was so bad toward the end that labour had to be paid every hour and then run out to spend it before it lost even more value. Thus most of what they had was fictitious value as a billion fold more was required to by the same items that cost a tiny fraction of the amount a year earlier. This is one of the realities, triggered both by the Versailles Treaty and depression that assisted Hitler into power. This devaluation was triggered by war reparation payments for war damages to Europe from WWI under the Versailles treaty.

We live in a culture of consumerism where things like planned obsolescence, boring, dirty, dangerous and underpaid work is the norm on a world scale. Our focus has been turned almost totally to the acquisition of money and this no longer backed by traditional value fetishes like gold. We live isolated from and alienated from nature. If we took away the mega-cities, the massive production facilities, our power, transportation, people for the most part would not know how to handle the new environment, which would be what's left of a ruined nature. Pol Pot did something like this with disastrous consequences for his people. He removed the whole population forcibly from the cities for his agrarian reform. People who have been trained virtually from the cradle to function in an industrial mega-city have little or no knowledge of agriculture, nature and skills to deal with these new realities. When the specific job one does disappears, such as going on now in the current cycle of economic collapse, the person who is thus alienated from the now gone job has to retrain or relearn the old ways.

Alienation also exists in the form that many of us have highly specialized functions on the assembly line and none can do the full job. To make a car requires a host of skills that no person is capable of learning them all in a single life time. Further, the amount of collected skills in each finished commodity prices it out of the immediate reach of most labourers. They then turn to the banks who exploit this with loans and credit for houses and cars, charged at interest. When the job is lost, the bank, that holds the legal title, claims the house or car and keeps all the payments made to that point. This forms one of the most prevalent forms of alienation of labour from what they make in modern society. What we see now is lots filled with the over-production of mega-factories that no one can afford to buy due to unemployment. Homes are lost to foreclosure and labourers who struggled so hard to gain title lose the house and all payments to the mortgage held by the bank and end up homeless. The bank then holds the empty houses that bring in no income and become "toxic assets". Governments have to intervene to prevent further disaster, which often is not successful. Whole insurance companies and banks have collapsed due to this. This is modern alienation on a mass scale.

Banks and governments have another trick and that is to nationalize. The government takes ownership until times are good enough again to allow privatization. This cycle goes back and forth in lockstep to the health of the economy. In each round, the weaker businesses are destroyed and the assets are taken over by the survivors. The alienated laborer is left with the struggle for money, continual re-training, consumerism and the distractions aplenty of the modern world. Alienation from nature, the means of production, the product that is manufactured, from employment and by the atomization of the work force by skill and shift work defines the modern state of alienation.

Bibliography

Achermann, R: *The Philosophy of Karl Popper*, Amherst, University of Massachusetts Press, 1976.

Angel, R: *Relativity: The Theory and its Philosophy*, Oxford, Pergamon Press, 1980.

Berlin, Isaiah: *Karl Marx: his Life and Environment,* New York, Oxford University Press, 1963.

Bernard McGinn: *Classics of Western Spirituality,* Paulist Press, New York, 1978.

Bottomore, Tom and Robert Nisbet: *A History of Sociological Analysis,* New York, Basic Books, 1978.

Bottomore, Tom: *A Dictionary of Marxist Thought,* Cambridge, Harvard University Press, 1983.

Cohen, G.A. : *Karl Marx's Theory of History: A Defence*, Althusser, For Marx, Verso, 1999.

Cuff, E. C., W. W.: *Perspectives in Sociology,* London, Routledge, 1992.

David Held: *Classes, Power, and Conflict: Classical and Contemporary Debates,* Berkeley, University of California Press, 1982.

Eisenstein, Zillah: *Capitalist Patriarchy and the Case for Socialist Feminism,* New York, Monthly Review Press, 1979.

Engels, Friedrich: *The Condition of the Working-class in England in 1844,* London, Allen and Unwin, 1952.

Giddens, Anthony: *Capitalism and Modern Social Theory: An Analysis of the Writings of Marx, Durkheim and Max Weber,* Cambridge, Cambridge University Press, 1971.

Grant, G. P.: *Philosophy in the Mass Age*, Copp Clark, Toronto, 1959.

Josephson, Eric and Mary Josephson: *Man Alone: Alienation in Modern Society,* New York, Dell, 1962.

Leo, S.: *Political Philosophy*, The Bobbs Merrill Co., New York, 1975.

Marx, Karl: *Grundrisse: Foundation of the Critique of Political Economy,* New York, Vintage, 1973.

Mittal, Kewal Krishan: *Materialism in Indian Thought,* Munshiram Manoharlal Publishers, New Delhi, 1974.

Morgan, Lewis Henry: *Ancient Society,* Cambridge, Belknap Press, 1964.

Rattansi, Ali: *Marx and the Division of Labour,* London, Macmillan, 1982.

Reyna, Ruth: *Dictionary of Oriental Philosophy,* Munshiram Manoharlal, New Delhi, 1984.

Ritzer, George: *Sociological Theory*, New York, McGraw-Hill, 1992.

Seidman, Steven: *Liberalism and the Origins of European Social Theory,* Berkeley, University of California Press, 1983.

Spengler, Oswald: *Man and Technics: A Contribution to Philosophy of Life*, MacMillan, New York, 1932.

Sydie, R. A.: *Natural Women Cultured Men: A Feminist Perspective on Sociological Theory,* Toronto, Methuen, 1987.

Tong, Rosemarie: *Feminist Thought: A Comprehensive Introduction,* Boulder, Westview Press, 1989.

Turner, Jonathan H.: *The Structure of Sociological Theory*, Belmont, Ca., Wadsworth, 1991.

Zeitlin, Irving M.: *Ideology and the Development of Sociological Theory*, Englewood Cliffs, Prentice Hall, 1990.

Index

A

C

D

E

G

I

L

M

P

□□□